*Acquired Taste*

# LE CVISINIER FRANÇOIS,

ENSEIGNANT LA MANIERE de bien apprester & assaisonner toutes sortes de Viandes grasses & maigres, Legumes, Patisseries, & autres mets qui se seruent tant sur les Tables des Grands que des particuliers.

*Par le Sieur de* LA VARENNE *Escuyer de Cuisine de Monsieur le Marquis d'*VXELLES.

A PARIS,
Chez PIERRE DAVID, au Palais, à l'entrée de la Gallerie des Prisonniers.

M. DC. LI.
*Auec Priuilege du Roy.*

Title page of *Le Cuisinier françois*, by François Pierre de La Varenne (1651). Courtesy of the Bibliothèque Nationale, Paris.

# Acquired Taste

## The French Origins
## of Modern Cooking

# T. Sarah Peterson

Cornell University Press
*Ithaca and London*

First published 1994 by Cornell University Press.

Printed in the United States of America

♾ The paper in this book meets the minimum requirements of the American National Standard for Information Sciences—Permanence of Paper for Printed Library Materials, ANSI Z39.48-1984.

Library of Congress Cataloging-in-Publication Data

Peterson, T. Sarah.
    Acquired taste : the French origins of modern cooking / T. Sarah Peterson.
      p.    cm.
    Includes bibliographical references and index.
    ISBN 0-8014-3053-4
    1. Gastronomy—History.   2. Food—History.
3. Cookery—France—History.   4. France—Social life and customs.  I. Title.
TX637.P48  1994
641.3′0944—dc20                      94-19133

*For Bill, Mitzi, and the students
at Martin Luther King Jr. High School
in Manhattan*

# Acknowledgments

I am grateful to Anthony Grafton for his support, Kathryn Argetsinger for going over the Latin translations, and all the numerous people in the United States, Europe, and the Middle East who kindly responded to my questions. John G. Ackerman and Barbara Salazar at Cornell University Press continued to ask intelligent questions which in the end made my ideas more accessible. The huge chore of bringing the text together with the illustrations has been handled by an excellent staff. Most of all I am beholden to my husband, Willard Peterson, for providing me with the time and space to finish this work, which has taken many more years than I ever conceived it would.

T. SARAH PETERSON

*Princeton, New Jersey*

# Contents

# Appetizer

To what do we owe the awesome and enduring reputation of French cuisine? How did the French become the supreme arbiters of Western cooking? This book explores one of the most dramatic and stubbornly influential cultural changes in the history of food: the appearance in the mid–seventeenth century of modern French cuisine. The basic characteristics of the new French cooking were first manifested in *Le Cuisinier françois,* a cookery book printed in Paris in 1651 and attributed to the otherwise unknown cook François Pierre de La Varenne. To us the recipes in *Le Cuisinier françois* do not on the whole seem strange, but to contemporaries, who had been accustomed to dining on sweetly fragrant dishes, the salt-acid taste characteristic of most of these new dishes must have come as a shock. Indeed, sugar, saffron, and spices, the trio essential to cookbooks since the medieval era, were strikingly absent.

Why did food change so drastically in seventeenth-century Europe? Why was saffron, once central to the European diet, suddenly relegated to obscurity even as sugar was restricted to dessert dishes? In the eighteenth century, the *Encyclopédie* claimed that French cooking was the glorious climax to a linear process begun by the ancients and taken up again by the Renaissance Italians. The Italians, the *Encyclopédie* tells us, inherited the "debris" of cookery from the ancients and passed them on to the French, who, grasping the essentials, brought this kind of cooking to its inevitable culmination. The "debris" to which the

*Encyclopédie* referred were such ingredients as asparagus, artichokes, foie gras, sweetbreads, salty-acidulous foods, and other wanton delicacies that the Italians had resurrected from antiquity. But was seventeenth-century French food inevitable? Was it just the obvious result of what the Italians had unearthed? Strong evidence argues that it was not. What the *Encyclopédie* said nothing about was the kind of cooking that had held sway in France and across Europe before the powerful proponents of the new cuisine brandished La Varenne's book before first Paris and then all of Europe.

From at least the fourteenth century, Europeans had dined on an aromatic, sweet, golden food, which revealed the strong influence of the Arabic world. These fragrant, jewel-like dishes were thought to be connected to celestial substance through their luster, odor, and color, and so to have divine healing powers. Indeed, medieval and Renaissance cooking, with its links to cordial, alchemical, and astrological medicine, was part of the occult culture that, by the seventeenth century, was thought to threaten the stability of the existing social and political order. This book claims that the invention and rapid spread of the new French cooking were part of a larger cultural shift that marked the break between the Renaissance and the modern world. France's enduring authority in food dates from this historical moment, and that authority rests on the expulsion from the dining hall of the magus with his spices and saffron.

In retrospect, *Le Cuisinier françois* was much more than a cookbook; it was the programmatic statement of a whole new way of thinking about food, and as such it reflected many of the most important political and philosophical notions of its day. The new cuisine that it championed traveled quickly across Europe, and its basic assumptions about ingredients, their preparation, and the design of the meal remain with us still.

*Acquired  Taste*

# PART I  Middle Eastern Influence on European Cooking

The people [of Damascus] are as delectable as
their place. They have as many delicacies and
varieties of food as a human mind can conceive,
and even more.

        The pilgrim Thietmar in a bazaar (1217)

The *third Chapter* for the love of One,
Shall trewly disclose the Matters of our Stone;
Which the *Arabies* doon *Elixir* call,
Whereof it is, there understonde you shall.

        Thomas Norton, *The Ordinall of Alchimy*
                (fifteenth century)

Replacement

Checkin Receipt

Fullerton Public Library
(714) 738-6334
DATE RETURNED: Nov 17, 2014  05:11PM

PATRON: MASSEY, BRIAN J

The battle of the Labyrinth /
CALL NO: R
ITEM: 31440010863950

# CHAPTER 1 "Eat and Drink with Relish"
## *An Islamic Anticipation of Paradise*

We catch the last good view of the food of Roman antiquity in a fourth-century cookery work familiarly known as Apicius, after its presumed author.[1] When next we see cookbooks in Europe, in the thirteenth century, the recipes have changed dramatically. The use of spices and coloring agents, especially saffron, has soared, and honey, the principal sweetener of ancient Greece and Rome, has declined in favor of sugar. A golden-hued food, suffused with scent and often sprinkled with white crystals, has arisen. Dishes are now studded with pomegranate seeds or infused with citrus juice, rose water, or almond milk, as were preparations in Middle Eastern cookery. The new style had been brought to Europe by way of traders, military forays, and territory newly conquered for Islam, especially Sicily, the Iberian Peninsula, and parts of the eastern Mediterranean.

In 652 the Arabs crushed the Byzantine navy at Alexandria; in 837 Naples enlisted their military support, and in 841 they took Bari on the Adriatic, which became their principal stronghold over the next thirty years. From that base the Arabs moved into the center of the Italian peninsula and may have made their way into Switzerland. Toward the end of the century they won Sicily, and their influence persisted even after the Normans captured the island two centuries later. Sicily's Norman kings lived in a style "more reminiscent of a Muslim sultan than of a medieval Christian prince." Roger II wore ceremonial robes embroidered with Christian texts in Arabic lettering, spoke and read Arabic, and kept a harem. "The Christian women of the island," one Arab traveler noted, "followed the fashions of Muslim women."[2]

Arabic influences moved on to Normandy and England, and in the thirteenth century they spread out through Frederick II's Holy Roman Empire. Frederick himself lived like a sultan, as the Norman kings had done, surrounded by Muslim teachers, courtiers, officers, and ministers, who accompanied him in his travels across Italy. In 710 Arabs started to create a province for the caliph of Damascus in Spain. By the next century, a Spanish scholar tells us, the Mozarabs (Arabicized Christians) of Cordova had adopted the Islamic customs of circumcision and harems. In the tenth century European monks and soldiers who had absorbed Arabic learning were rewarded with positions at the Christian court of León. In the eleventh century the Christian Alfonso VI, who had reconquered Toledo, married the daughter of the Moorish king of Seville. "The Christians dressed in Moorish style, and the rising Romance language of Castile was enriched by a large number of Arabic words," the Spanish scholar relates. "In commerce, in the arts, in trades, in municipal organization as well as in agricultural pursuits, the influence of the Mudejars [Muslim subjects] was predominant."[3]

From the eleventh to the fourteenth centuries, Europeans descended upon the Middle East, when pilgrims, merchants, and travelers joined the crusading conquerors in exploring the newly acquired lands. Politic rulers often encouraged them to mingle with easterners, and European and Arab nobility were graciously received at each other's courts, even when hostilities were intense. In the heyday of commercial activity and social contact European residents tried to interfere with plans for the Fifth Crusade. The bishop of Acre (part of the Christian possessions in the Holy Land) complained bitterly that European settlers in his domain had become "completely Oriental," the knights having adopted the silk burnous and turban, the women the long underrobe and short tunic embroidered in gold. Their quarters shimmered with damask, faience, carpets, and gold and silver dinner services.[4]

Arabic styles in food pervaded the cooking customs of Europe. European cookery texts of the High Middle Ages and of the Renaissance resembled those of the medieval Arabic world.[5] From the fourth-century Roman Apicius to the medieval cookbooks, the use of sugar, spice, and saffron changed remarkably. The Greeks and Romans used honey and were probably ignorant of sugar; if it was available at all, it was rare. The eponymous Apicius never mentions it, though he constantly calls for honey. He seldom uses any spices other than pepper, and saffron appears only three times—with no mention of its potential as a coloring agent. It was not yet thought important to impart a golden color to food.

## THE COMING OF SUGAR

After the Arabs captured Persia in the seventh century, sugar cane and the sugar industry spread westward into North Africa, and from there into Cyprus, Sicily, and Spain as Arabs conquered those areas. By the first years of the seventeenth century sugar was being produced in India, all of North Africa, Valencia, the Canary Islands, and Madeira, and on the islands of the Mediterranean.[6]

Sugar became available in Europe in both loaf and granulated form. The mistress of a fifteenth-century manor in Norfolk was always on the lookout for ways to obtain sugar loaves from a dealer in London. "I pray you that you will vouchsafe to send me another sugar loaf, for my old [one] is done." White sugar is specified in a fourteenth-century French recipe for *brouet blanc* and in a fifteenth-century English recipe for creme boylede.

LE MÉNAGIER DE PARIS (FOURTEENTH CENTURY)
Take capons or chickens killed the appropriate length of time before, either whole or cut in half or in quarters, and some pieces of veal and cook them in pork fat [*lart*] with water and wine. When they are through cooking take them out. Take almonds, peel and pound them and add some of the cooking stock from the chicken. The stock should be clear and not murky. Strain the almond stock mixture. Then take pared or peeled white ginger and grains of paradise moistened as above, and put the mixture through a fine strainer. Mix with the almond milk. And if it is not thick enough, add starch or boiled rice. Add a little verjuice and put in a great deal of white sugar. When you want to serve it, powder on top a spice that one calls vermilion coriander with pomegranate seeds, candies, and fried almonds around the edge of each bowl.

*Source: Ménagier de Paris*, p. 217.

"Eat and Drink with Relish"

Very occasionally dark-brown sugar (blake sugre) is called for in English cooking manuscripts of the fifteenth century, but highly refined sugar was the most desirable of all—the whiter the better. Here again the Arabic taste is copied. A medieval Arabic poem on food in a tenth-century history of the world called *Meadows of Gold* speaks of the delight of sugar that is refined to the purest degree. The most refined was reserved for the sultan's use. The *Thrésor de santé*, published in Lyon in 1607, notes that although the loaves of sugar from North Africa are big, they are rather blackish; the best is the white sugar from the Canary Islands. An intensely white sugar was imported from Madeira.[7]

Sugar eclipsed honey in Europe's recipes; it became the principal sweetener in meat, fish, vegetable, and poultry dishes, and in cakes and fruit preparations. Even in France, where sugar had not made a strong showing at the beginning of the fourteenth century, it came to be highly prized by the century's end. Italy had taken to sugar earlier. In 1475 Bartolomeo Platina lamented the ancients' ignorance of sugar and insisted that sugar could spoil no dish. About five decades later the Italian Ermolao Barbaro concurred with this opinion. Toward the end of the sixteenth century an Italian physician was reporting that sugar appeared in most dishes and that honey was now eaten only with fruit or other sour foods. In 1560 the physician to the late French king Henry II wrote: "Sugar is used instead of honey. . . . It hardly needs to be pointed out how many condiments and foods to which it is added. . . . There is hardly anything today prepared for the stomach without sugar. Sugar is added to baked goods, sugar is mixed with wines, water with sugar is tastier and healthier, meat is sprinkled with sugar, as are fish and eggs. We use salt in no more places than sugar." Honey, loved by the ancients, no longer appeared on luxurious tables, he observed.[8]

Middle Eastern Influence on European Cooking

Toward the end of the sixteenth century William Harrison described the meals provided by merchants, including gelatins, tarts, cakes, conserves, fowl, venison, and "sundry outlandish confections," as "altogether seasoned with sugar." The English physician Thomas Moffett averred that "it were infinite to reherse the necessary use of [sugar] in making of good gellies, cullises . . . white broths." In 1599 Henry Buttes observed that "no kind of meat refuseth Sugar for his condiment, but only the inwards of beasts, as tripes: which if you condite with it, they grow most unsavoury." At the beginning of the seventeenth century Olivier de Serres also saw sugar as a sign of status. Preserves made with honey "are opportunely used when people of moderate standing call. . . . Preserves made with sugar, which involve more expense and skill to prepare, are reserved for the most honorable people."9

Sugar was to be added during the cooking, so that it would be melted by the heat and liquids in the dish, or sometimes sprinkled on just before the dish was served. A late-sixteenth-century Spanish cookbook instructs the cook to grate "white sugar on top [of a dish of pigs' feet] before serving it to the master." These were also the patterns among Arabic cooks. "A Baghdad Cookery Book" calls for sugar to be sprinkled on meat or dissolved in the liquid in the cooking vessel.10

Measurements for sugar are lacking in the French fourteenth-century *Ménagier de Paris*, but the authors used a great deal ("du succre largement"; "du sucre blanc grant foison"; "foison succre"). A fourteenth-century Italian cookery manuscript called for a pound and a half of sugar in a dish of four hens, as did a *bramagere* (blancmange) for twelve. In a fifteenth-century French cookbook a dish of one suckling pig takes a pound of sugar; in 1570 Bartolomeo Scappi required two pounds of sugar for a recipe calling for ten pounds of meat. An increasing number of French recipes in the sixteenth century called for large amounts of sugar, but they had a hefty precedent in a thirteenth-century Hispanic-Moorish recipe that called for three pounds of sugar in a dish made with one hen.11

PERFUME IN FOOD

Before the thirteenth century we find few references to fragrance or perfume—that is, to spices—in food. Pliny reported that perfumes were abundantly used in Persia, and we may surmise that the Persians emphasized fragrance in food. When Alexander the Great, Aristotle's pupil, conquered Persia in the fourth century B.C., he was transformed by the customs of the people he had crushed. It is likely that the Persian influence stimulated the use of spices in Greece—a development that some Greeks deplored. Aristotle tells us that Euripedes had already been admonished for adding perfume to lentil soup. The fragrance of flowers was pleasant, he observed, but it failed to provoke the appetite. It was thus superfluous to put perfumes in food and drink; the enjoyment of scented food was a pleasure derived only from custom, a taste that one had to make an effort to acquire.[12] Theophrastus, who, like Alexander, had been Aristotle's pupil, admitted that "perfume and other fragrant things" add "a pleasant taste to wine," but that was all: "[In] all cases [spices] spoil food, whether it be cooked or not." Pliny the elder, in first-century Rome, seldom mentions the use of fragrance in food, though he does observe that bdellium is rolled into cakes. (Pepper has become the rage, he says, but pepper does not have a sweet scent.) Having been introduced to aromatic wines, an innovation in Rome, he exclaims with astonishment, "Nowadays some people actually put scent in their drinks, and it is worth the bitter flavor for their body to enjoy the lavish scent both inside and outside." Plutarch, writing in Greece only a few decades later, reports wryly that spices are now being inserted into food, as if to preserve the dead: "We need 'supplements' for the flesh itself, mixing oil, wine, honey, fish paste, vinegar, with Syrian and Arabian spices, as though we were really embalming a corpse for burial."[13]

In the fourth century pepper appears in almost all of Apicius's recipes and ginger in some. From Apicius to a small, possibly sixth-century set of recipes referred to as the "Apician *Excerpta*" there is almost no change except for a single reference to the use of saffron "for coloring." Pepper still appears, in fact, in most recipes. Ginger is used only once, as is cardamom. Sometime later a list (undated) included, under "Condimenta," saffron, pepper, ginger, clove, and cardamom.[14] A ninth-century recipe of the monks of St. Gall in Switzerland shows pepper, cinnamon, and clove going into a fish dish.[15]

In fact, a multitude of aromatics were available, and it is significant that when cookbooks once again emerged in Europe, the spices they called for were strikingly similar to those named in the Arabic cookery texts: pepper, ginger, cinnamon, clove, cardamom, mace, nutmeg, betel, and musk. These spices, by and large the ones found both in the Hispanic-Moorish text and in "A Baghdad Cookery Book," overlap with the list of spices at the end of the fourteenth-century *Viandier de Guillaume Tirel*. Its last lines read, "Spices that belong to the present cook are first ginger, cinnamon, clove, grains of paradise [probably cardamom], long pepper, mace, spice powder, . . . saffron, galingale, [and] nutmeg." Its fifteenth-century edition has a few additions, including sugar: "Spices belonging to this present cook: ginger, cinnamon, clove, grains of paradise, pepper, mastic, galingale, nutmeg, saffron, sugar, anis, and fine [spice] powder."[16]

The thirteenth-century Hispanic-Moorish cookery text places its heaviest emphasis on spices: "Know that the knowledgeable use of spices is the principal base of prepared dishes, because it is the cement of cooking, and upon it cooking is built." So essential were spices thought to be that a family of middling means in the Middle East would spend almost as much on them as on meat. Western texts also stress spices by instructing that the dishes be "powerful with spice" or "heavy with spice," and by insisting that the cook add them to the mixture as late as possible, "so as not to lose their flavor."[17]

Although most recipes say nothing about measurements, those that do give them provide a clear idea of the leading role played by spices. Two fourteenth-century Italian recipes, each to serve twelve, call for a base of one-half pound of spice. Even the lesser quantities of spice still seem quite high to a post-seventeenth-century palate: a dish for twelve people in the same text calls for two ounces of spice (about half an ounce more than the amount in the typical powdered spice container one buys in the supermarket). To prepare for a wedding feast for twenty and a supper for ten, one marketing list directs the purchase of a pound and a quarter of ginger, a half pound of cinnamon, an ounce of saffron, a quarter pound of cloves mixed with grains of paradise, and an eighth of a pound each of long pepper and mace. The grander the occasion and the more one wished to impress, the more spice. In 1549 Cristoforo di Messisbugo wrote, "Take notice that all the above tortes are very appropriate for every great prince, and at banquets, and other [such occasions]. But for ordinary use a little more than half the spices will do, and will be judged good."[18]

Two Arab cookery texts use lesser quantities of spices than some European books, but my sample of Arabic recipes is small in comparison with my European sample. In one meat dish, for which the quantity of meat is not specified, the author of "A Baghdad Cookery Book" calls for "two dirhams of coriander, cummin, mastic, and cinnamon" (whether for two dirhams of each spice or of all four combined is unclear; one dirham is said to be equal to 0.13 ounce). The dish is sprinkled with more cinnamon before it is served. Another recipe, again with the quantity of meat unspecified, calls for "finely ground cummin, coriander, cinnamon, and mastic, about 2½ dirhams in all"; that is, about one-third ounce of spice. The Hispanic-Moorish text sometimes calls for somewhat larger quantities: for a roast bird, three dirhams each of coriander, cinnamon, ginger, and cumin; for a dish of one hen, four dirhams of pepper and four dirhams of cinnamon.[19] Each of these recipes uses more than an ounce of spice.

The availability of all these spices depended on uninterrupted trade between the Arabic world and Europe. Thus, throughout the Middle Ages ships and caravans traveled back and forth to satisfy tastes acquired from the Levant.

## SAFFRON

Saffron, too, became indispensable as the Arabic style of food spread throughout Europe. The Italian physician Andrea Mattioli wrote in 1550:

> The crocus is truly known to everybody and is called saffron throughout Italy and especially in Tuscany, even though it is an Arabic word. . . . The best, even better than the Aquiline saffron, is found in all parts of Germany, in Austria, in its territory of Vienna, principal city of that province. But of this very little comes into Italy, since the Hungarians and Germans, because of the great use they make of spices, do not willingly allow it to leave their country. In some places in Tuscany and especially in Siena the choicest saffron grows, which is able to compare with all these.[20]

Jean-Baptiste Bruyerin, the French royal physician, observed in 1560 that "no revenue is greater today for many important men in Narbonne than that from the crocus." In France, said Olivier de Serres, saffron was grown in gardens between the fruit trees; in some places whole areas were devoted to it. Among the Albigensians of southern France "the crop holds the rank of

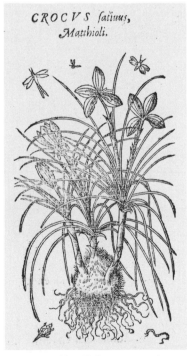

1. "Saffron," from *Historia generalis plantarum*, by Jacques Dalechamps (Lyon, 1532), 2:1532. Courtesy of the History of Science Collections, Cornell University Library.

Middle Eastern Influence on European Cooking

being among the most famous revenues of the region." An eighteenth-century agricultural text said that the Albigensians were the first to grow saffron in France, and that it then migrated to Avignon in Provence, thence north to the Angoumois and Gatinois, and on to Normandy and England. Richard Hakluyt thought a pilgrim had brought it back from Tripoli in the early fourteenth century. It was certainly grown at Saffron Walden, which became the chief English market for saffron by the time of Edward III (1327–1377). Some people considered the saffron grown there the very best in the country and English saffron better than any to be had abroad. The foreign market throughout the Middle East provided another source of saffron, as Francesco Balducci Pegolotti's fourteenth-century manual on trade makes clear.[21]

The European cookery texts call for saffron to add color to countless dishes. Platina observed in 1475 that saffron was a thing apart from the other spices, its taste and color enhancing

---

*EIN BUCH VON GUTER SPEISE* (FOURTEENTH CENTURY)
Take new almonds and soften them. Take millet gruel and boiled eggs and a little nice bread and herbs. Grind these together, so that you make it thick, and put it in a pan. And let it boil until it thickens. Make it yellow with saffron and rich with butter. And let it cool then, and cut it in pieces, and stick it on a spit, and let it roast. Coat it then with eggs and with good herbs. And serve as roasted milk.

*Source: Ein Buch von guter Speise, p. 17.*

---

their qualities. Instructions for a fourteenth-century German dish of almonds, millet gruel, and boiled eggs read, "Make it yellow with saffron." Cooks preparing boiled veal in mid-

---

CRISTOFORO DI MESSISBUGO (1549)
Take a breast of veal, and put it to cook in wine with six slices of ham. And when it has boiled a good length of time, take four large onions and cut in quarters and put them to boil. Then take the soft part of a white bread cut in slices toasted, moisten in verjuice, and push the bread through a strainer with a quarter of ginger, and a little saffron, as much as gives it color, and ten whole cloves. And when it is almost cooked, i.e., the bird or other piece of meat, pour the sauce over and finish the cooking.

*Source: Messisbugo, Banchetti, p. 191.*

---

"Eat and Drink with Relish"

sixteenth-century Italy are advised to use as much saffron "as gives it color."[22]

The manuscripts from the Middle East show a similar emphasis on color. "A Baghdad Cookery Book" frequently instructs the cook to "color with saffron." "Cut [fish] into middling pieces, wash, colour with saffron, and fry in sesame-oil. Add fine-chopped *blattes de Bysance*. Put in a mixture of vinegar and *murri* [a fermented sauce], twice as much *murri* as vinegar." The Hispanic-Moorish text gives the same advice, and in *Meadows of Gold* we find "And saffron well-brayed, for its tinting. . . ."[23]

### Almonds, Citrus, Rose Water, and Pomegranates

Almonds were first brought to Europe by the Romans. Seven of Apicius's recipes call for whole almonds as a garnish. Medieval Arabic cookery often calls for ground almonds, and frequently for almond milk, made by pouring water through ground nuts. A dish for fat meat directs: "Peel sweet almonds and grind, then mix with a little water: flavour to taste with the water and milk of the almond." A 1420 English cookery manuscript uses the "mylke of almaundys," and *Ein buch von guter Speise*, in a recipe for "a baked puree of fish," instructs the cook: "Take a perch steeped in vinegar and throw it then into milk that has been made from almonds." *Le Ménagier de Paris* advises the use of "cow's milk, if it is an ordinary meat or milk day, but if it is during Lent, put in almond milk." Ground almonds were also, but not nearly so frequently, used as a thickener.[24]

Neither rose water nor citrus appears in any of the Greco-Roman recipes compiled by Apicius. The Arabs brought the lemon and orange to Spain perhaps by the ninth century, and to Sicily in the tenth. These fruits were on the Italian mainland by the twelfth century, and probably by this time also in southern France. The Arabs used citrus juices in their cooking, but less frequently than rose water. Rose water was sent to the Maghreb, Spain, Yemen, India, and China from such centers as Shiraz, and Damascus vied for importance as a major distributor by the thirteenth century. It plays a prominent role in "A Baghdad Cookery Book" and in parts of the Hispanic-Moorish text, and appears in texts all over Europe.[25]

In Europe the use of citrus fruit, usually in the form of juice, is for the most part confined to cookery texts of the south. Platina writes that citrus is used all year long on roasted foods.

In *Le Ménagier de Paris* we find one of the rare northern recipes that calls for orange juice. Partridge is to be eaten with a mixture of stock, rose water, and a little wine, or three parts rose water and one part mixed orange juice and wine. Fresh citrus must have been difficult to obtain in the northern countries, although it was in demand.[26]

The bitter or sour orange (now known as the Seville orange) was employed, like vinegar or lemon, as a souring agent. The *Libro di cucina* calls for a dish to be made "sour with orange or lemon."[27]

Apicius does provide instructions on how to keep pomegranates fresh, but he does not indicate how they are to be used in recipes, as Arabic texts do. Pomegranates were so closely associated with the Arabic world in the northern mind that Europeans were convinced, Pisanelli wrote in the sixteenth century, that they were "so called after the Moorish kingdom of Granada." Reexamining the Latin origin, *granata* or *granatum*, he challenged the prevailing etymology—it was the other way around, he said: "Pomegranates received their name from the multitude of seeds they produce, and not from the kingdom of Granada, as some think." The "Kingdom of Granada, which is very rich in these fruits, took from them its name and armory, and took for its particular sign and mark a pomegranate." Whether Granada was named for the fruit or vice versa, the two continued to be associated. *Romania,* the name of a dish that appears in a fourteenth-century Italian cookbook, is derived from *rumman,* Arabic for "pomegranate," and its recipe is very similar to that of a dish called *rummaniya* in "A Baghdad Cookery Book." In Europe the pomegranate was used for both its juice and its seeds. Balducci Pegalotti mentions only the seeds. Perhaps in this case the pomegranate was skinned and set to dry with the seeds still enveloped in their juicy pulp. The seeds, now resembling raisins, could safely be shipped north.[28]

## Sensual Goods Provided by God

In Islam Europeans encountered an ethos that differed radically from the one that had prevailed in the West since late antiquity, when Christians viewed the demands of the body as a hindrance to the soul's quest for God. Not everyone followed Anthony into the desert, where with fasting and vigils he attempted to withdraw from his flesh. Nevertheless, by the fifth century the clergy had firmly coalesced around an ideal of sexual continence, and food was linked to desire. Men and women who denied themselves the pleasures of the world became heroic figures. Those lay devout who continued sexual activity felt guilt when they caught themselves wanting more from sex than procreation for God or more from food than satisfaction of hunger. In curtailing bodily cravings the Christian could look forward to some relief from the agony of denial, for in heaven there was no desire. When Augustine's mother, Monica, lay dying, she and her son contemplated what "the eternal life of the saints would be like." They concluded "that no bodily pleasure, however great it might be and whatever earthly light might shed lustre upon it, was worthy of comparison, or even of mention, beside the happiness of the life of the saints." Two centuries after Monica's illustrious son died in 430, the powerful religious force of Islam began to spread a very different vision of paradise.[29]

A recurring theme in the Koran is the reward of bodily delight to be achieved by the faithful in paradise.

Lo, the pious are in Gardens and delight,
Enjoying what their Lord hath bestowed upon them, and their
　　Lord hath protected them from the punishment of the
　　Hot Place.
Eat and drink with relish, for what ye have been doing.
　　(The Mount 52)

For many Muslims, the joys of this world and the next are corresponding planes of pleasure. The possibility of a sensate heaven on earth found expression throughout Muslim culture. A Moorish garden in Andalusia could be seen as "a reflection or rather an anticipation of Paradise," writes James Dickie; in this "artificial paradise" on earth, voluptuous pleasures were to be enjoyed.[30] Two medieval Arabic cookery manuscripts reflect this sense of continuity between the pleasures of eating in this world and the promised paradise to come. One of the manuscripts draws upon the Koran for authority.

Thanks to the one and only God and Creator, who assures us the means of subsistance. . . . I say he is wrong who has prohibited to worshipers of God a bounty He has given them, and he is wrong who has pointed a finger at one who uses this beneficence. For the

　　Middle Eastern Influence on European Cooking

almighty has said: "Say: Who has forbidden the fair things created by God for his adorers, or the good foods offered by God?—Say: They are for the faithful in this terrestrial life and they are for those alone the day of Ressurection. . . . Moreover, since the greater part of terrestrial and celestial pleasures consists of the consumption of desirable dishes and drinks . . . to enjoy good things reinforces worship in the servant of God. . . . It is for this reason that the mention of these goods of God has been repeated in the precious Book of God, where he has accorded praise and distinction to them. (The Heights 7)

The second conveys a similar message, including food, drink, and scent among the pleasures of this world.[31]

By the mid–twelfth century the Koran was circulating in Latin, thanks to Peter the Venerable, abbot at Cluny, the influential center for more than six hundred monastic establishments throughout western Christendom. In 1142 Peter began to arrange for the study of Islam in Spain. Convinced that the competing religious movement could be defeated only if its theological tenets were laid bare, he arranged to have the Koran and other works translated. The sensate paradise of Islam was revealed to the Christian establishment. Peter's own *Summa totius haeresis Saracenorum* described the Islamic afterworld he abhorred. But even before Peter the venerable Petrus Alfonsi, a Spanish Jewish convert to Christianity, had compiled a collection of "oriental" tales that displayed the seductive pleasures of the Islamic paradise in the very process of trying to discredit them. The book became popular all over Europe.[32]

Islamic ideas of pleasure and paradise also found their way into romantic and fantastic literature. Latin, Spanish, and French versions of the "Book of the Ladder," an account of Muhammad's ascent through the levels of paradise, circulated in manuscript in the twelfth century. It depicts the ultimate garden of paradise as having "all delicacies, that the mind of a man might think of." The faithful imbibe wines "of so many colors and flavors that no man has been able to dream up," and a table set before them "never lacks anything that one might wish to eat or drink." A tree, on request, gives "seventy thousand bowls of food, completely prepared, and the meat and fowl fixed in so many different ways, that the mind of no man could have thought of."[33]

An imitation of the Islamic depiction of the paradise of

"Eat and Drink with Relish"

pleasure circulated in European literature in various forms associated with the notion of a "Land of Cockayne." In the thirteenth century a French poem, and then another in Dutch, celebrated Cockayne as a country with houses made of bass, salmon, and shad, rafters of sturgeon, and lathing of sausage. Food is for the taking. The rivers run with wine. Most scholars have thought these poems to be of Greco-Roman origin, but Dorothee Metlitzki points out that the Land of Cockayne, in the English version of the theme, is "'fur in see, bi west Spayne,'" very possibly the western lands of Islam. The notion of "the land of the cock" appears in the Arabic "Book of the Ladder," where the cock is the guardian of the gate of the seven stages of paradise. The spices referred to in the English version come from a tree that bears ginger, galingale, zedoary, mace, cinnamon, clove, and cubeb—a bounty that points to a Middle Eastern inspiration.[34]

The cookbooks that began to circulate as manuscripts in Europe by the end of the thirteenth century eschewed the severe ascetic ideal of Christendom in favor of a style of cookery that closely resembled the sensual contemporary Arabic cuisine. But late-medieval European food was shaped to fit the Arabic model not only because of the new Western fascination with sensuous experience at table but also because of the association of these foods with medieval concepts of divine medicine. Long before the arrival of medical texts from the Arabic world in the twelfth century, the Arabic theory of the importance of fragrance in medicine was making its way into Europe. New aromatic drugs unknown to antiquity were recorded under their Arabic names. *Cafora*, for example, from the Arabic *kâfoûr* (camphor), is listed in a medical compilation of the early seventh century and again in a ninth-century antidotary, where *ambar*, the Arabic word for ambergris, is also recorded. "Galingale" and "zedoary," the names of other new drugs not in Greek or Roman medical works, are also based on Arabic terms. Word of new drugs to cure the miseries of illness had traveled to Europe along the spice routes. Fragrant, golden food therefore became to medieval Europe both a secular delight and a medical necessity.[35]

# CHAPTER 2  Food as Divine Medicine

Arabic food developed in a culture that associated medical concepts with the divine. The author of the tenth-century history of the world known as *Meadows of Gold* revels in the voluptuous meal that is part of the sensual paradise brought down to earth. Images connect this food to cordial, alchemical, and astral medicine. The tinting of food in hues of rose and gold, the jewel-like quality of the preparations, the emphasis on light coming out of darkness and subtle odors offered to the soul—all point to a cuisine at once sensual and luxurious, medicinal and divine.

The bowls for the meal are scarlet and yellow, and eggs have been dyed red.[1]

> Here capers grace a sauce vermilion
> Whose fragrant odours to the soul are blown
> Like powder'd musk in druggist's fingers strewn.
> Here, too, sweet marjoram's delicious scent
> With breath of choicest cloves is richly blent;
> While cinnamon, of condiments the king,
> Unblemished hue, unrivalled seasoning,
> Like musk in subtle odour rises there,
> Tempting the palate, sweetening the air. (p. 22)

A chicken tinted with saffron is "'delightful to taste.'"

> Like choicest *khaluq* [a yellow or red perfume] it is colored and scented.

The bowl, passed around, spreads its odorous mist,
Its sweetness is sweeter than soul can resist. (p. 29)

Honeyed pastry wafting almond essence "'glitters'" with oil.

Rose-water floats thereon, like flooding sea.
Bubble on bubble swimming fragrantly. . . . (p. 29)

Odor penetrates

Lemons . . . with *nadd* [a mixture of perfumes] besprinkled,
Scented well with ambergris. . . . (p. 23)

*Jūdhāba* glowing within its dish like a heavenly body or precious
stone is ineffably sweet. As its fragrance envelops the diner it
affords the heart escape.

With sugar of Ahwaz complete
In taste 'tis sweeter than the sweet.
Its trembling mass in butter drowned
With scent the eater wraps around;
As smooth and soft as clotted cream,
Its breath like ambergris dothe seem;
And when within the bowl 'tis seen,
A star in darkness shines serene,
Or as cornelian's gold is strung
Upon the throat of virgin young;
It is more sweet than sudden peace
That brings the quaking heart release. (p. 28)

Crystalline sugar of dazzling whiteness

sprinkled upon every side
Flashes and gleams, like light personified. (p. 27)

The sultan himself is partial to fragrant *harisa* of pounded
chicken, for its "charms" make his mental faculties sparkle and
attune him to celestial forces, while his body thrives, his four
humors all in balance.

All, hosts and guests, are eager to attain
This food for which the Sultan's self is fain;
For by its magic mind and brain both shine
And all the bodies humours fall in line. (p. 27)

Middle Eastern Influence on European Cooking

The table bears riches in the likeness of the noble metals.

> Meat that, in slices white and scarlet laid,
> Like gold and silver coin is arrayed. (p. 22)

The cook is portrayed as alchemist.

> Jūdhāba made of choicest rice
> As shining as a lover's eyes;
> How marvelous in hue it stands
> Beneath the cook's accomplished hands!
> As pure as gold without alloy
> Rose-tinted, its Creator's joy. . . . (p. 28)

*Maḍīra* gleaming on an onyx platter delights and cures. This dish

> cannot rivalled be
> To heal the sick man's malady:
> No wonder this our meal we make,
> Since, eating it, no law we break.
> 'Tis as delicious as 'tis good—
> A very miracle of food. (p. 28)

Sugar, spice, and saffron made for more than a sensuous experience at table. Their properties were vital to a system of medicine that offered relief from melancholia and sundry bodily ills and the means to stave off old age. By the fifteenth century, streams of cordial, alchemical, and astral medicine ran together into a broad river of divine medicine. In this system the medicinal properties of fragrance and color did not work directly upon the body, as sweetness did; they worked on the *spiritus*, or the breath—the entity that connected body and soul.

### AVICENNA AND CORDIALS

This divine medicine had Arabic sources. A prominent advocate, known to medieval and Renaissance Europe as the "prince of physicians," was born in 980 near Bukhara, on the eastern edge of the Islamic empire. Avicenna traveled widely, treated the politically powerful, and through his voluminous writings on philosophy and medicine influenced the whole of his society. His *Canon of Medicine* included ideas derived from Galen and from the writings that went under the name of Hippocrates,

Food as Divine Medicine

ideas of Avicenna's predecessors and contemporaries in the Arabic world, and Avicenna's own thoughts. One of his shorter treatises (*Powers of the Heart*), known in Europe as *De viribus cordis*, described a manner of curing melancholia through treatment of the *spiritus*. To this end he prescribed cordials, so called because they were supposed to work upon the heart. The heart in turn was thought to generate food for the *spiritus*.[2]

Avicenna's roll of cordials included spices, rose water, pomegranates, citrus peel, the yolks of eggs, saffron, sandalwood (another yellow dye), wine, and the juices of cut-up meat exuded as it cooked covered over a low flame. Avicenna argued that other physicians were wrong when they said that meat broth—that is, the water in which meat is cooked—was also a cordial. For Avicenna the cordial was pure meat juice, not water with meat juice in it.[3]

Avicenna's roll of cordials also included gold, silver, precious stones, coral, pearls, silk, and sundry other items. He omitted sugar from the list, but he included it in his recipes for cordial medicines for its salutary effect on the body. Avicenna believed spices to be cordial and sugar not, because "the essence of aromaticity lies in its rarefaction; the essence of sweetness lies in its concentration and earthiness"; thus "aromatics are so much better adapted to feed the breath [*spiritus*], while sweet substances are better fitted to nourish the body." When sweetness and fragrance are mixed together, however, they form a more powerful medicament than either alone. Of any two drugs, said Avicenna, the sweeter and more aromatic will be the more "adjuvant"—that is, most likely to help the medicine work.[4]

The aromatic cordial was intended to rarefy the *spiritus*—to make it finer and less matterlike; to make it, that is, into subtle matter. In treating the melancholic with fragrant cordial prescriptions, the physician attempted to attentuate the *spiritus* by forcing it up a ladder of rarefaction. The more rarefied the *spiritus*, the nobler. "The nobler the character possessed by it and the nobler its substance, the more luminous does it become, and the more like celestial substance will it be." In fact, the *spiritus* glows more and more as it "approaches towards the likeness of celestial beings. It is a ray of light." Cordials that "supply the breath with brilliance and luminosity" are pearl and silk. The shinier and more abundant the *spiritus*, the more invigorated the "natural faculties" and the less the darkness of melancholia shadows the mind.[5]

Middle Eastern Influence on European Cooking

A second stream, alchemical medicine, flowed together with cordial medicine to constitute divine medicine in Europe. Early Greco–Middle Eastern alchemy, a marriage of mysticism and technology, at first aimed to create not actual gold but a catalyst. This catalyst, a stone later known in Europe as the philosopher's stone, or *lapis*, was said to be purplish or reddish-gold, of sweet taste, and fragrant.[6] The alchemist claimed that with the stone he could transform matter into a celestial-like or incorruptible substance; he could, for example, turn base metal into gold. The alchemist's aim was to spiritualize the world by restoring it to its former purity. Because the human body was part of the material world, alchemists turned to the magic of the metallic ritual to free themselves of their own corporeal bounds.

The Greco–Middle Eastern alchemist was a dyer. In his attempt to spiritualize base metals and make them into gold, he used tinctures. The tincture might be the color desired to begin with, say yellow, or a substance that, though not itself yellow, would in the chemical process impart the color yellow. The spirit or essence of gold was carried in its tincture. Our earliest clearly alchemical text outside of China, a work from the Hellenistic period, notes that " 'anything which can yellow' is the same as anything which can produce gold or the color of gold." A later European alchemical text based on an Arabic source said that the philosopher's stone was like crushed saffron.[7] Saffron is red, but it dyes other substances a golden yellow.

By the seventh century, technical alchemy seems to have dropped away in Alexandria. The language of the texts is distant from anything that could be followed as a laboratory procedure. The alchemists seem to have ceased their efforts to restore the world, including themselves, to primal purity by chemical means. Their now strictly meditative alchemy aimed, like the procedures of Neoplatonists, Christians, and Gnostics, at ushering them into divine light. The works of these late Alexandrian alchemists present a terrible vision of a constant nightlike, stinking world. Their wails against the dross of darkness and putrescence resemble the cry of melancholics as they flee their shadowy existence. An eighth-century alchemical text mourns the present state and strains toward a future bathed in radiant light: "When the spirit of darkness and of foul odour is rejected, so that no stench and no shadow of darkness appear, then the body is clothed with light and the soul and spirit rejoice, because darkness has fled from the body."[8]

This mystical side of alchemy was all that remained of the Greco–Middle Eastern "art" until the Arabs revitalized its laboratory aspect about the eighth century. Arabic alchemy, however, was not simply a resuscitation of Alexandrian alchemical visionaries. The Arabic alchemist sought an elixir of miraculous medical powers, including the key to longevity. The Chinese had practiced alchemical elixir medicine for centuries before the Arabs took it up, and the Arabs most likely derived the idea of elixir medicine from them, either directly during journeys to China or indirectly through learned communities in Persia, which also traded in East Asia.[9] Whether Chinese and Greco–Middle Eastern alchemy stemmed from a common system we do not know. Alchemy in East Asia and the Hellenistic world did arise at roughly the same time—the first few centuries before the Common Era.

Chinese texts show the alchemist as a person of benevolence, a physician on a holy mission to free the frail human body from the ravages of sickness and melancholy through elixirs, or panaceas. Chinese practitioners prescribed fragrances, gold, and liquid pearl (for its luminous quality) among the materials in their alchemically prepared mixtures to be ingested. Greek pharmacy included no gold or pearl at all to be taken internally; yet both were among Avicenna's cordials. Avicenna is, strictly speaking, not an alchemist in the Greco–Middle Eastern sense (he denied that his peers could transform base metal into gold), but his use of gold and pearl to work upon the *spiritus* does show his connection with Chinese alchemy.[10]

ASTRAL MAGIC: DRAWING ON THE PLANETS

The third principal kind of divine medicine is derived from astral magic. Astrology simply foretold events on the basis of the configuration of the heavenly bodies, but astral magic attempted to interfere with fate by manipulating the environment to ward off evil influences.

The art of controlling planetary influences had been developing since antiquity and perhaps reached its zenith, at least so far as details are concerned, in an Arabic book of magic, the *Picatrix*, in twelfth-century Spain. The theory it embodied was

Middle Eastern Influence on European Cooking

that each planet is associated with certain terrestrial substances, and that a person who wishes benefits from a heavenly body must assemble and use the terrestrial substances that are correlated with that planet. In rites for Saturn, evil-smelling incenses such as castor and asafetida were to be used; for Mars, pepper, long pepper, and ginger; for the sun, musk and amber; for Venus, rose, violet, and green myrtle; for Mercury, a blend of perfumes; for the moon, camphor and rose. General incense fumigations for the planets are said to contain cinnamon, cardamom, and nutmeg. Taste, too, is correlated with the planets. Bad tastes attract Saturn; sweet and mellow ones, Jupiter; the hot, dry, and bitter, Mars; sweet and rich, the sun; all good-tasting sweet things, Venus; all sour things, Mercury; all insipid things, the moon. The planets are also linked with colors, jewels, languages, religion, the arts and crafts, organs of the body, plants, animals, and signs.[11] A prescription for living offered by an astral physician would read something like this: Place yourself in a certain kind of landscape; surround yourself with specific plants and animals; exhibit particular jewels and create gemlike things; eat special foods; and smell certain odors. Do whatever is feasible to adjust to particular configurations of heavenly bodies.

Astral medicine is allied to alchemy. Alchemists, too, claimed to identify a correspondence between those things found in the heavens and those things found on earth.[12] One manifestation of this interpenetration of alchemy and astrology is the alchemists' association of metals with the various planets. They associated Saturn, for instance, with lead and the sun with gold. The sun, the most treasured body of the astral system, is the source of light, so gold and other terrestrial substances that seemed to exhibit any of its characteristics—saffron, for one— were greatly esteemed.

Astrology had primed Europe to be receptive to divine medicine. Astrology and astrological magic had started in Babylonia and with the invasion of the eastern mystery cults had cut deep into Roman society. In the first century of our era an obsession with the powers of the heavenly bodies would keep the emperor Tiberius in seclusion on Capri with his little coterie of star consultants.[13]

In late antiquity Augustine (354–430) and other Christian theologians attempted to align the third-century Platonism of Plotinus with Christian thought. Plotinus, known as the founder of Neoplatonism, conceived of the world (that is, the universe) as possessing a soul that connected all things, thereby creating a sympathy between them. For Plotinus this sympathy between parts of the world accounted for the existence of magic. Humans were able to tap into this sympathy to effect change in the human realm. Magic, however, could not help them with salvation, which was attained through the mystical union of human creatures with God or the Divine Light, for which Plotinus used the image of the sun's golden rays. Only contemplation afforded an opening into the effulgent radiance. Some of Plotinus's early followers, though, were not content with this formula for redemption. In the deepening occult milieu, Porphyry (c. 232–c. 303) thought magic could indeed facilitate salvation. Later Iamblichus and Proclus considered magic essential if one were to be saved.[14]

These Neoplatonists called their special brand of manipulation theurgy, to distinguish it from the common carryings-on of wizards. Augustine would have none of it:

> What a wonderful art is this 'theurgy'! . . . The whole thing is in fact an imposture of malignant spirits. We must beware of it; we must listen to the teaching of salvation. Porphry relates that those who engage in those polluted rites of purification, with their blasphemous ceremonies, have some marvellously beautiful visions, whether of angels or of gods, after the supposed purification. But even if they do in fact see anything of the sort, it is just as the Apostle says: 'Satan transforms himself to look like an angel of light.'[15]

Augustine, in effect, accepted much of Plotinus but rejected the magic of his disciples. Church and emperors now, in the fourth century, sought to stamp out various systems of thought that competed with the soteriological promises and occult ritual of the Christian church. An atmosphere of witch hunting prevailed. Roving gangs of cudgel-bearing monks stamped out paganism in North Africa. In 415 a Christian mob lynched a Neoplatonist teacher, Hypatia, daughter of the mathematician Theon. It was forbidden to consult astrologers, who were ferreted out and slaughtered. The murder of these star readers abated in the fifth century; they were now forced to burn their books in the presence of a bishop. After the emperor Justinian shut down the Platonic academy in Athens in 529, many philos-

Middle Eastern Influence on European Cooking

ophers of theurgical persuasion, together with fringe Christian sects, fled into Persia and Syria, where they were shortly to make their magic and views of the universe available to the Arabs.[16] If the later Christian emperors' war on magic did not snuff out these practices altogether, it certainly checked them. Astrology, like other practices of this nature, entered a relatively quiescent period that lasted until the twelfth century, when Arabic texts on alchemy, astrology, and magic began to circulate widely in Europe in translation. Augustine's acceptance of Plotinus's conception of the world laid the fire, and contact with the Arabs touched it off. A conflagration of magical thinking lit up medieval and Renaissance Europe. As Plotinus's followers had shown, with the proper stimulation it was a few short steps from the cosmological vision of the master to theurgy.

Europeans had also been prepared for divine medicine by a person long erroneously thought to be an Athenian Christian converted by Paul in the first century. The Greek writings of the unknown writer now called Dionysius the Areopagite, often referred to as Pseudo-Dionysius, actually stem from the late fifth or early sixth century.[17] After John of Erigena translated these works into Latin in the ninth century, they became a major influence on Christian mysticism. Pseudo-Dionysius is usually classed only as a Neoplatonic Christian. But a prominent contemplative ritual in his work incorporates the "myron," similar to the chrism of the Eastern and Western churches, which harks back to purification rites and concepts of the Gnostics as described by Christian heresiologists.[18] According to Irenaeus (c. 130–c. 200), Gnostics, for whom matter was evil, were anointed with fragrant oil of balsam to rid them of their earthly qualities. "This oil (*myron*) is said to be a type of the sweet savour which is above all terrestial things."[19]

Hippolytus (c. 170–c. 236) had observed that the universe of the Sethian Gnostics was divided into three layers: a pure layer of light on top, an evil layer of darkness, presumably matter, at the bottom, and a fragrant layer of spirit in the middle. Together the light and the perfume, like "incense burnt in the fire," spread into the darkness to purify it. The Gnostics were influenced by Egyptian magicians, who used perfumes (or incenses) to purge and recreate the body for everlasting life. Perfume, a manifestation of the gods, was thought to spiritualize the flesh. In preparing the body for the next world, an Egyptian priest

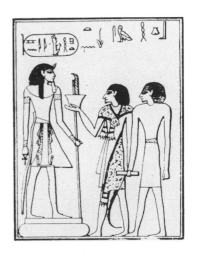

2. "The Sem priest censing the statue," from *The Book of the Opening of the Mouth*, by E. A. W. Budge (London, 1909), 1:93. Courtesy of the Princeton University Library.

Food as Divine Medicine

said, "Thou hast received the perfume which shall make thy members perfect."[20]

In medieval Europe the power of fragrance resumed its earlier importance. Stories circulated in the sixth century that from the flesh of dead saints oozed a sweet smell that could heal the sick. Incense, denied a place during the first few centuries of Christianity, pervaded church ritual after the tenth century in the belief that it could ward off evil spirits.[21] Thus when first a trickle, then a flood of ideas on various medicines from the Arabic world swept over Europe in the late Middle Ages, the notion that sweet fragrance and golden light might cure the ailing human *spiritus* did not seem alien.

## TAKE TWO DRACHMAS EACH OF GOLD AND SILVER . . .

A large number of works dealing entirely or partially with pharmacy began to circulate in Europe by the end of the twelfth century, slightly before the reappearance of cookbooks. Mesuë's thirteenth-century *Antidotarium sive Grabadin medicamentorum compositorum* had almost certainly come in from the Arabic world. The book was so popular that it would go through thirty editions before 1623.[22] Pharmaceutical and alchemical concepts in the works of the Arabic physicians Rhazes and Avicenna were mined together with those in al-Kindi's work on perfumes. Ideas in the influential Arabic *Secretum secretorum* mistakenly attributed to Aristotle and those in the *Picatrix* penetrated deep into European thought.

By the end of the thirteenth century the kind of cordial medical theory that Avicenna's *De viribus cordis* represents had borne fruit in Italian pharmaceutical collections. A prescription concocted by Taddeo Alderotti, who spent his academic career at Bologna, includes as basic components precious stones, pearls, coral, gold, silver, silk, saffron, aromatics, and sugar. The ingredients, which he spelled out in detailed measure, are taken with wine:

> The heart is soothed from the inside and from the outside. To comfort the heart internally take one half drachma each of beryl, emerald, saffire, red jacinth. Also two drachmas each of gold and silver. Also one drachma and a half of both kinds of pearls. Also four drachmas each of bugloss, *doronicum*, and zedoary, white and

Middle Eastern Influence on European Cooking

red ben, cinnamon, clove, aloewood. One drachma each of ground silk, saffron, cubebs, cardamom, amber, camphor, and musk. Also two and a half drachmas of coral, sandal, rose, dross of metals (spodium), *terra sigillata*, coriander. Pulverize everything which must be pulverized. To one ounce of the spices put one pound of sugar. Musk, however, [is not ground] but dissolved with bugloss water. One drachma of this electuary is taken with fragrant wine.[23]

The kind of recipe found in Alderotti appears also in many variations of the cordials in Marsilio Ficino's celebrated late-fifteenth-century *De vita libri tres*. This book exhausted nearly thirty editions as Europeans soaked up its theories and recipes, before it basically dropped out of sight after its 1647 edition. Ficino began his studies in medicine at the University of Florence, but turned more and more to philosophy and especially to Plato. He was in the process of translating Plato's *Dialogues* for his patron, Cosimo de' Medici, when Cosimo put into his hands the *Corpus hermeticum*, which Cosimo had just acquired from a Byzantine source, and asked him to translate it. This mystical and magical collection, thought to be the work of an ancient Egyptian sage known as Hermes Trismegistus, was to influence Ficino's own future work. In the course of his career as head of the Platonic Academy in Florence Ficino became increasingly involved with the concept of a *prisca theologica*, an ancient theology of divine wisdom said to have passed in succession from the Persian Zoroaster to the Egyptian Hermes Trismegistus, then to Moses, to Plato, and finally to the Christian fathers, including Pseudo-Dionysius.[24]

Ficino's fifteenth-century society was in the grip of astrology, which, with the arrival of the new Arabic ideas, had again become a potent force. Royalty and nobility had their personal astrologers to advise them on intimate as well as public matters. An Italian historian has observed that during the Renaissance this system of prognostication became "a philosophy of history, a conception of reality, a fatalistic naturalism and an astral cult."[25]

Saturn, believed to bode evil, was central to these early Renaissance astrological concerns. Saturn was thought to cause melancholy, its principal manifestation an excess of black bile. It was the Arabs who had firmly linked Saturn to this pathological disorder of darkness, but even they conceded that Saturn was not wholly malevolent; melancholy brought benefits along with its disadvantages. Ficino observed that though it was true that Jupiter smiled on those who led ordinary lives, Saturn, "the most powerful of all" to "the Arabic writers," took in the sequestered and intellectual. To them he was "friendly as to his kinfolk." Simply to be born under Saturn got you only bad effects. You were a mere ordinary melancholic. But if you were doubly Saturnian—that is, if you were born under Saturn and were intellectual, as Ficino was—or if you engaged in lofty mental pursuits even though you had been born under another planet, you were a special kind of melancholic and a marvelous path to wisdom was open to you. Not everyone chose this option, for it required an intrepid traveler, an intellectual who did not fear to move by means of contemplative exercises deep into Saturn's shadow. Thus Ficino claimed that gifts awaited persons "who give themselves over with their whole mind to the divine contemplation signified by Saturn himself."[26]

The contemplating melancholic met with God. It was argued in fifteenth-century Italy that by triggering ecstasy (that is, a mystical union with the Father) melancholy made inspiration possible; the mystic was imbued with the creativity of the Divine One. The wish to yield to Saturn coincided with the Neoplatonist's desire to merge through contemplation with the Creator. The undaunted Renaissance Neoplatonist such as Ficino, then, did not flee melancholia, but used it to become wizardlike. By means of melancholia Neoplatonists gained the intelligence of seers and the ability to comprehend the universe. Paradoxically they sought the dark shadow of Saturn in order to emerge into the clearest light. In Albrecht Dürer's *Melencolia* a pensive figure is seized by inspiration as geometry's instruments lie idly round her. Dürer based his engraving on Ficino. Humans are able "to measure and grasp the whole world" not through the conventional tools of ordinary measurement but by means of their *spiritus*.[27]

The physiological basis of the melancholic genius was an alignment of three humors—blood, phlegm, and black bile—so arranged as to resemble the alchemist's instrument of magic, the philosopher's stone; that is, the melancholic's humoral alignment, Ficino explained, was shiny and purplish gold. As a result of this peculiar arrangement of humors, moreover, the melancholic's *spiritus*, his tool for grasping the principles of things, was

Middle Eastern Influence on European Cooking

3. Albrecht Dürer, *Melencolia* (1514). Engraving, 9½″ × 7⅜″. Herbert F. Johnson Museum of Art, Cornell University. Bequest of William P. Chapman, Jr. 57.122.

of such rarefaction or subtlety that it was like the quintessence of wine—that is, distilled alcohol, itself of a nobility akin to celestial matter. "One might ask what it is like—that humoral body composed out of those three humors," Ficino wrote.

> In color [the humoral body] has much the appearance of gold, but somewhat inclining towards purple. And when it is heated, as much by natural heat as by motion of the body or of the mind, it burns and shines much like red-hot gold tinged with purple. . . . One might ask, again, how a humor of this kind conduces to intelligence. Well . . . the spirits born of this humor have the subtlety of that water which is called *aqua vitae* or *vitis* and *aqua ardens,* when this liquor is extracted by the usual process from thicker wine by distillation at the fire. (p. 121)

Food as Divine Medicine

Despite their gifts, intellectual melancholics had as much trouble as ordinary melancholics. Ficino plies all of them with prescriptions to avoid ill effects from Saturn. He drew inspiration and information, he said, from, among others, Mesuë the younger, Rhazes, Avicenna, and the twelfth-century Italian Pietro d'Abano, who had been interested in Neoplatonism and magic. Other medicines Ficino had devised on his own, at least in part. His compounds used many fragrances, raw silk, purple roses, fruit, and the peels of citron and other fruits, all mixed with the "best possible" pure wine. The following pills, he said,

can be called golden or magical, composed partly in imitation of the Magi, and partly through my own invention under the influence of Jupiter and Venus; they draw out phlegm, choler, and black bile without difficulty, strengthen the individual bodily parts, and sharpen and illumine the spirits. They expand the spirits so that they may not, being contracted, engender sadness, but may rejoice in their expansion and light; and in turn they stabilize these spirits so that they do not vanish through being too extended. Take, therefore, twelve grains of gold, especially its leaves if they are pure; one-half dram apiece of frankincense, myrrh, saffron, aloe-wood, cinnamon, citron-peel, melissa, raw scarlet silk, white ben and red; one dram apiece of purple roses, of red sandal, of red coral, and of the three sorts of myrobalans (emblic, chebule, and Indic) [a kind of fragrant fruit also on Avicenna's list of cordials], with an amount of properly washed aloe equal to the weight of all the rest. Make pills with pure wine of the best possible quality. (p. 149)

Besides courting Saturn through contemplation, one could draw down beneficial effects from that and other planets by using specific substances keyed to them—that is, by employing astral magic in a Neoplatonist universe where all things are connected. Ficino's fullest model showing these chains of materials pulling down astral (planetary) influences was actually from the *Picatrix*. He avoided crediting this Arab work directly, as it was an illicit book of magic. Ficino would also have seen some reference to such chains in Proclus, the fifth-century Neoplatonist.[28] In the following recipe, cordial and astral medical systems overlap. Sweet-smelling spices and saffron are prominent in efforts to avail oneself of solar power.

If you want your body and spirit to receive power from some member of the cosmos, say from the Sun, seek the things which

Middle Eastern Influence on European Cooking

above all are most Solar among metal and gems, still more among plants, and more yet among animals, especially human beings; for surely things which are more similar to you confer more of it. These must both be brought to bear externally and, so far as possible, taken internally, especially in the day and the hour of the Sun and while the Sun is dominant in a theme of the heavens. Solar things are: all those gems and flowers which are called heliotrope because they turn towards the Sun, likewise gold, orpiment and golden colors, chrysolite, carbuncle, myrrh, frankincense, musk, amber, balsam, yellow honey, sweet calamus, saffron, spikenard, cinnamon, aloe-wood and the rest of the spices. . . . (pp. 247, 249)

All of these solar-related substances "can be adapted partly to foods, partly to ointments and fumigations, partly to usages and habits (p. 249)." "Wonderful" consequences can be expected if any individual substance has an "elemental" power of its own that "subserves the occult property." Consider saffron: "When saffron seeks the heart, dilates the spirit, and provokes laughter, it is not only the occult power of the Sun which is doing this in a wondrous way; but the very nature of saffron—subtle, diffusible, aromatic, and clear—also conduces to the same end" (p. 303).

In a daring description of a solar rite, Diacetto, one of Ficino's followers, showed how the items in the solar chain could be used in a ceremony that comes dangerously close to sun worship and thus heresy. Donning a priestly solar costume, the magus who would derive powers from the sun to cure disease sets up an altar with an image of the sun, the image wearing a crown and a saffron cloak. The magus anoints himself with fragrances that correspond to the enthroned solar image.[29]

### FRAGRANCE, PRESERVER OF YOUTH AND DEFENSE AGAINST DECAY

Ficino expects cordial medicine to prolong life. His authority is almost certainly Avicenna, who does not say explicitly that a revived *spiritus* will extend longevity but does note that the weak *spiritus* of the melancholic resembles that of the aged.[30]

Odors especially are important to the elderly because they make up for lack of more solid nourishment. Since the *spiritus* is

Food as Divine Medicine

a vapor and odors are also vapors, and since "like is nourished by like," the spirit or life force is readily restored by odors.

> I heartily approve my favorite authority Avicenna saying that the body is nourished by sweetness, the spirit, however, by a certain (to use his term) aromaticity—since the density of the body cannot coalesce without a dense nature such as inheres in sweetness; while the fineness of the spirit cannot be restored otherwise than by a certain smoke and vapor in which that aromaticity flourishes. . . . Accordingly the liver, because it furnishes food to the body through the blood, is much augmented by sweetness; the heart, moreover, because it both creates the spirit and generates food for it, rightly desires spices ["*aromatica*"]. (pp. 221–23)[31]

A fifteenth-century version of the pseudo-Aristotelian *Secretum secretorum* (*Book of Secrets*), which had entered twelfth-century Europe from the Arabic world, urged the use of morning fumigation with incense or other odiferous products for similar reasons. The idea was repeated in later editions of the *Book of Secrets* and still found a place in that of 1702. Perfumes will prevent gray hair, and "the Spirits are refresh'd, with Odours, which are their sweetest Food; and when the Spirits are refreshed, fortified, and delighted the Body will be strengthened, the Heart will rejoice, and the Blood will run briskly in the Veins from the Joy of the heart."[32]

Spices, too, were seen as effective preventive medicine. Ficino offered this prescription "to ward off the decay": "We will season our foods with this powder: one-fourth ounce of emblic myrobalan, one-half ounce of sandal, an ounce of cinnamon, and one-eighth of an ounce of saffron. And so with this powder and with things which are also acrid we shall perhaps be able to ward off the decay which threatens from rotten foods and places" (p. 185). Spices were added to food not to stop it from rotting, as many people have supposed, but to keep the body from the decay induced by bad food and air. (Salt, vinegar, and the drying and storing of foods in fat—not spices—were the principal means of food preservation.)[33]

Sweet fragrance is also prominent in a chapter headed, "On Gold, Foods Made of Gold, and the Revitalization of Old Men." Ficino advised people getting on in years to eat gold because it does not decay. Under the most suitable astrological configurations, he prepared "potable gold" by dissolving bor-

Middle Eastern Influence on European Cooking

age, bugloss, melissa, and the whitest of sugar in rose water and adding gold leaf, or by mixing gold leaves with rose julep (an Arabic syruplike mixture) and the "moisture [ *jus*] dripping from a capon . . . set over a fire," one of Avicenna's own cordials (pp. 195, 197).[34]

"Come, old people, I say, who are taking old age hard," Ficino summoned. Heed the wisdom of the Magi, who once brought gold, frankincense, and myrrh to Christ, "the author of life." It was his conviction that the secrets of the ancients had been handed down to Christians to treasure and use:

> The Magi, observers of the stars, came to Christ, the guide of life, under the guidance of a star; they offered a precious treasury of life—gold, frankincense, and myrrh; they dedicated three gifts representing the lords of the planets to the Lord of the stars. . . . Therefore all you old people, come here to the wise Magi who are bearing gifts for you too—gifts that are going to lengthen your life, gifts with which they are said to have once worshipped the author of life. Come, old people, I say, who are taking old age hard. Come too, you who are just troubled by the fear that old age is quickly approaching. Please receive gladly these gifts: Take two ounces of frankincense, one of myrrh, again one-half dram of gold formed into leaves; grind the three together, mingle them, mix them with a golden wine to form pills, and perform this at the lucky hour when Diana enjoys the favorable aspect of Phoebus or of Jove. (pp. 229, 231)

Those who lacked any of the prescribed precious ingredients were not to despair: "If anyone does not have gold, silver, amber, musk, and precious stones, these confections can be of much help even without them" (p. 157). It was an idea not soon put aside. Oswald Croll drew attention explicitly to it in his 1608 *Basiliea chymica.* "If you have no genuine drinkable gold which is unpolluted by corrosive substances, then you may add instead: twelve drops each of oils of anise, caraway, orange, lemon, nutmeg, clove, cinnamon, and amber."[35] The rationale, Ficino had said (again with Avicenna almost certainly his authority), was that precious substances such as gold medicated the *spiritus* by their powers of illumination, and that the spices did the same with their powers of fragrance (p. 197). Thus aromatics could take the place of the more expensive minerals. Perhaps a combination of shiny and aromatic was best, but either would work alone. An easy way, after all, to whip up an effective cordial, according to Ficino, was to boil a citron with sugar and rose juice and sprinkle on either a mixture of cinnamon and saffron or an "aromatic rose-spice" (p. 157).

## The "Fifth Essence"

Although the cordials were intended to work upon the *spiritus*, some people thought more radical treatments were called for. An English Franciscan, Roger Bacon, influenced by Arabic learning, thought the elixir might be such an approach. He referred to "Aristotle's" words in the *Book of Secrets* (actually, the Arabic pseudo-Aristotelian work) that God had made the medicine and had revealed it to prophets and saints. It was of vital importance, then, to extend life by using God's transforming medicine; that is, the elixir: "For the medicine which would remove all the impurities and corruptions of a baser metal, so that it should become silver and purest gold, is thought by scientists to be able to remove the corruptions of the human body to such an extent that it would prolong life for many ages." Bacon's formula for the elixir overlapped Avicenna's for cordials. The key to its effectiveness, Bacon believed, was the reduction of the medicine's elements "to pure simplicity."[36]

John of Rupescissa, a noted Spanish antipapal preacher and church reformer of the fourteenth century, took Bacon's idea of a medicine of a core purity and developed the concept of medicinal quintessences, or "fifth essences," as a fundamental thesis of pharmacy. Humans, John insisted, could be saved from corruption—that is, from decay—only by treatment with an uncorrupted medicine. One such medicine is alcohol, because it resembles Aristotle's principle or quality later known as the ether, which was of a different order from the four corruptible elements—fire, earth, air, and water. An Arabic manuscript of the eighth century contains an idea, "the fifth nature," similar to that of John's quintessence. John concluded that there was a quintessence in all terrestrial substances. He attempted to take this supposed quintessence from a variety of things, including some on Avicenna's cordial list. These quintessences would be much more potent than Avicenna's cordials themselves, hence their power to transform. John did not believe that the quintessences—that is, his elixirs—could produce immortality, but he did believe that use of them could bring about almost continuous rejuvenation, until the moment of death

Middle Eastern Influence on European Cooking

appointed by God. (A belief in physical immortality would have been heresy.)[37]

Ficino is the great link between the alchemists of the thirteenth and fourteenth centuries, such as John of Rupescissa, and the alchemy of the sixteenth-century Paracelsus, one of the most influential and controversial figures in the history of medicine. In order to get the idea that there was a quintessence in all things, John must have posited that an etherlike strand ran through the terrestrial realm. In Book III of *De vita* Ficino took what John implied and proposed a cosmic *spiritus* made of quintessentia; that is, a layer between the soul of the world and the body of the world. Like the *spiritus* in humans, it occupied a position between body and soul and provided a connection between them. Ficino wrote that "just as the power of our soul is brought to bear on our members [parts of the body] through the spirit, so the force of the World-soul is spread under the World-soul through all things through the quintessence, which is active everywhere, as the spirit inside the World's Body." The best means of getting at this quintessence for human use was to extract it. "This quintessence can be ingested by us more and more if a person knows how best to separate it, mixed in as it is with other elements" (p. 247). Ficino was here acknowledging the approach of John of Rupescissa.[38]

Ficino observed that if one did not use separated quintessences —that is, alchemically derived uncorruptible medicine—the next best things were substances from the terrestrial realm that had a great deal of quintessence in them. For Ficino the fifth essence was unevenly distributed in the body of the world, "instilled especially into those things which have absorbed the most of this kind of spirit"—such things as "choice wine, sugar, balsam, gold, precious stones, myrobalans, and things which smell most sweet and which shine, and especially things which have in a subtle substance a quality hot, moist, and clear; such, besides wine, is the whitest sugar, especially if you add to it gold and the odor of cinnamon and roses" (p. 247). (He included sugar not for its sweetness but for other virtues.) Ficino's list of things highly impregnated with the fifth essence (Book III) never abandons the cordials of Avicenna, which he extols in Book II.[39]

Ficino argued that one absorbs the *spiritus* of the World through one's own *spiritus*, and much more easily if one's own *spiritus* is transformed into a solar *spiritus*, one that is in the "highest degree celestial." Therefore people should flood themselves with sunlight and absorb as much other solar influence as possible (pp. 259, 261). Eat glistening, golden food redolent with spices if you wish to take in more easily the *spiritus* of the world, the layer of quintessence, the uncorrupted medicine that protects against the ravages of life. Thus, even if you prefer drafts of quintessence prepared by a physician to ingesting those items that are naturally most heavily endowed with quintessence, "such as cinnamon and the odor of roses," you still need cinnamon and the other spices to tone your *spiritus* to absorb the prepared drafts of quintessence.

It is clear that Ficino's Book III is aimed at a far wider audience than either Book I, addressed to melancholics, or Book II, addressed to the aged. He invites the man of affairs and government—in fact, his whole society—to stem bodily corruption with uncorrupted medicine. "Hail, intellectual guest!" begins Book III. "Hail to you, too, whosoever you are who approaches our threshold desiring health!"

### Fragrance, the Link between Soul and Body

The cordial and alchemical traditions continued to coalesce after Ficino was gone. Paracelsus, his protégé, did not abandon the idea that fragrance, gold, and the extracted juice of meats are essential for health. Walter Pagel, who elucidated the character of Paracelsus's work and that of other alchemists as well, saw how central odor was in their thought. For Paracelsus fragrance marked life itself; life was, indeed, "astral balsam." Pagel traced alchemy's interest in aromatics to Ficino's *De vita*, which permeated alchemical thinking as well as Renaissance Neoplatonism and Renaissance Gnostic thinking. One passage he cited, from Geronimo Cardano, a sixteenth-century physician and mathematician, is particularly illuminating: "Of all sense-impressions odour alone has direct access to the brain. Hence it can ruin, or recreate, man. It is the divine part in us that is delighted by fragrance, just as incense was burnt to propitiate the gods. Smells form a link connecting soul and body."[40] (Note that here the *spiritus* itself can now be taken as a layer of smells.)

Some of Paracelsus's remedies, like Ficino's, resemble those of the cordial tradition, but Paracelsus insisted that drugs go through a process of purification. He urged people who did not

Middle Eastern Influence on European Cooking

take well to most medicine to try an "odiferous specific." (A "specific" was one of his miraculous cures.) One such "odiferous specific" is a combination of lilies, roses, cardamom, orange juice, ambergris, musk, cinnamon, mace, clove, and civet, which after chemical digestion is added to potable gold. If all else fails, he suggests, use a formula of opium, orange and lemon juice, cinnamon, clove, musk, ambergris, saffron, "juice of corals," "magistery of pearls," and quintessence of gold.[41]

These medicines appear in Paracelsus's *Archidoxies*, printed in 1525. In the same year Philip Ulstad brought out his *Coelum philosophorum*, offering similar recipes for conserving the human body. One for potable gold contains borax, white sugar, camphor, pure gold leaf, amber, musk, and pearl; another potion includes wine, nutmeg, cinnamon, clove, zedoary, galingale, ginger, grains of paradise, and (optional) the *jus* of a capon.[42]

Recipes for these fragrant tonic-elixirs circulated commonly through "books of secrets." The Arabic *Secretum secretorum*, from which Roger Bacon had drawn secrets about God's medicine, gradually took on encyclopedic form, incorporating medical sections with cordial and alchemical recipes. One of these works, known as the *Secreti del reverendo donno Alessio Piemontese*, was first published in Venice in 1555, and shortly thereafter appeared in Latin, French, English, Dutch, and German translations. By 1575 fifty editions had appeared, and by 1700 more than ninety had dazzled Europeans with a fragrant and jewel-strewn path to the fountain of youth. Girolamo Ruscelli, a sixteenth-century humanist, claimed authorship; the book is said to be part of the work of his Accademia Segreta. An English edition opens with a recipe "to conserve a manne's youthe, and to hold backe old age." The secret lies in a "miraculous" distilled liquor made up of spices, saffron, sugar, citrus, minerals, and alcohol to be taken in veal, chicken, or pigeon broth, or white wine.[43]

The fragrant tonic-elixirs were also advocated in works on general health, such as *Via recta ad vitam longam*. Its author, the physician Tobias Venner, thought no one concerned with "health and life" was ever without a distilled mixture made of "one pound of Cinnamon grossly beaten, a pound of white Sugar, a gallon of Sack, and a quart of Rose-water." To Venner cinnamon was the king of spices. In fragrance it "excelleth all other spices: and prevents and corrects putrefaction of humors" and revives the *spiritus*. The elixir saffon is so congruent with the needs of the heart that "it is mixed with all cardiacall medicines," although it must be taken in moderation, for it so relaxes the heart that the *spiritus* begins to dissipate.[44]

Alchemical medicine depended so heavily on fragrances that John Hester, a sixteenth-century English follower of Paracelsus, characterized this type of healing as dependent on two realms, "Mettals and Mineralls" and "Hearbs and Spices." In his allegory *Secrets of Physick and Philosophy* (1633) the alchemist sought the "hidden secretes" in both of these pharmaceutical funds:

> I met in my mind with two such minions, as in my conceit were the only Paragons of the rest: the one gallant and gorgeous garnished with gold and silver bedect with jewels, sole Ladie and Governesse of all the rich Mines and Minerals that are in the bowels of the earth: the other sweet and odoriferous, adorned with flowers and hearbs, beautified with delicat spices, sole Lady and Regent of all pleasant things that grow upon the face of the earth.[45]

Alchemical philosophy and medicine, replete with ideas of the precious virtues of odors and minerals, reached a high point in the seventeenth century, especially in England, where books of secrets such as Hannah Woolley's *Queen-like Closet* went through many editions. Established, highly regarded physicians drew from the theory behind them in their practices. One such physician was Thomas Sydenham, a close friend of Robert Boyle and John Locke; Sydenham called spices the best cordials.[46]

## CHRISTIAN ALCHEMY

Associated with the alchemical pharmaceutical works and books of secrets was an allegorical alchemy assimilated to Christian teachings. This figurative genre, which also reached a high point in the seventeenth century, continuously reinforced alchemy's mystical-religious side. The virtues of color as well as fragrance stood out in these symbolic portrayals. In the thirteenth century the devout physician Arnald of Villanova, translator of Avicenna's *De viribus cordis*, portrayed the cardinal alchemical color transformations—black to white to red—as a mirror of the Passion of Christ.[47] Later Paracelsus wrote that this color change showed the ascension of Jesus, or the production of the philosopher's stone:

Middle Eastern Influence on European Cooking

D.O.M.A

RECVEIL
DES
PLVS CVRIEVX
ET RARES SECRETS
*Tirez des manuscripts de feu M. IOSEPH DV CHESNE S. de la VIOLETTE Con. & Medecin ord.re du Roy.*

HIPOCRATES

HERMES

GALENVS

ARISTOTELES

A PARIS
1648

Avec Privilege du Roy.

Mich. van Lochom

4. Title page of *Recueil des plus curieux et rares secrets tirez des manuscrits de feu M$^{re}$ Ioseph Duchesne* (1648). Courtesy of the Princeton University Library.

After the King has assumed his perfect whiteness, the fire must be continued perseveringly, until the whiteness takes a yellow tint, this being the color which succeeds the white; for so long as any heat acts on the white and dry matter, the longer that action lasts, the more it is tinted with yellow and saffron color, until it arrives at redness, like the color of a ruby. Then at last the fermentation is prepared for gold, and the oriental King is born, sitting in his seat, and powerful above all the princes of this world.[48]

Food as Divine Medicine

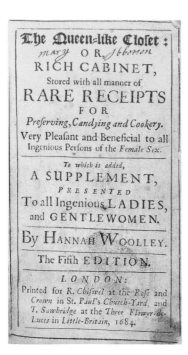

5. Title page of *The Queen-like Closet*, by Hannah Woolley, 5th ed. (London, 1684). Courtesy of the Princeton University Library, Department of Rare Books and Special Collections.

The "oriental King" not only transmutes metals but heals all sickness.

To Robert Fludd (1574–1637), a physician who argued passionately for the Christian alchemical view, Jesus was the true philosopher's stone, as the "oriental King" had been for the Christian Paracelsus. Implicitly Fludd was claiming to have captured the Christ-essence in his laboratory when he said that he had produced a quintessence of such sweet and penetrating fragrance that after touching it only once with his finger, he could perceive its delicious scent for two or three days.[49]

True Christians supposedly had a special understanding and gift for the art of alchemy, a point made in the story of Khalid and Morienus, which appeared in Paris in 1559 and was included in alchemical anthologies for the next two hundred years. It retells an older tale, first recorded by Arabic historians, of an interview between Khalid, king of the Arabs, and Morienus, his counselor, a devout Christian sage. When Morienus told Khalid that the elixir was red and sweet smelling, the king inquired, "How does the blessed water or virgin's milk come to reduce and cleanse things of that foul odor which is like the odor of tombs in which the dead are buried?" Morienus replied, "Fragrance and incense."[50]

Both Christian symbolic alchemical writings and the pursuit of the actual elixir had purification as their aim. Both attracted a wide audience of the devout, Martin Luther among them. He admired alchemy, "the natural philosophy of the ancients," he said, for its distilled potions of metals and herbs, "but also for the sake of allegory and secret signification, which is exceedingly fine, touching the resurrection of the dead at the Last Day."[51]

From the High Middle Ages through the seventeenth century the strong belief persisted that a divinely affiliated pharmacopoeia worked upon the *spiritus* in miraculous ways. It became incumbent on the good Christian to take these medicines.[52] In a dedication to his patron at the beginning of his 1558 English translation of the *Secretes of Alexis of Piemount*, William Warde, a follower of Paracelsus, wrote:

> Let no one say that a sick man must die as that was the wish of God. God has created remedies for disease, which a Christian should not despise. . . . [It is] requisite that medicines, both preservative and curative, be hadde and used among men, which not onelye comforteth the infirme and diseased bodye, but also put-

Middle Eastern Influence on European Cooking

teth the soule in remembrance of Goddes great power and myght, that hath given such vertue unto thinges growing on the earth, for mannes commoditie, preservation, and health.[53]

Whether their ideas of divine medicine derived from the Arabic world or represented an amalgamation of Arabic and recently rediscovered Greek ideas, these physicians and philosophers saw themselves as deliverers of humanity from the ill effects of melancholy and the corruptible realm of the four earthly essences.

## Cookery to Fend Off Harm and Evil

For people who believed in cordial, alchemical, or astral medicines, the experience of eating colored and sweetly fragrant food at table was congruent with taking the tonic-elixirs. Similar ingredients appeared in both. Further, explicit reference in the cookery works to the power of spices to ward off malevolence and their recipes' emphasis on golden preparations and cordial gelatins (seen as jewel-like) reinforce the inference that the philosophical underpinnings of the cooking style and those of divine medicine were one and the same.

The author of the Hispanic-Moorish cookery text refers to the demonifuge properties of aroma; in spices are "benefit and avoidance of harm and evil." A dish is said to appear like gold because of the saffron in it. Diego Granado's *Libro del arte de cocina* (1599) echoes the words of that thirteenth-century text: use saffron specifically "because it has the color of gold." Alchemical texts say that if one colors a base material gold, the properties of gold are imparted to it. By coloring food yellow, one makes the food noble like gold. The diner, then, absorbs food that, like gold, prevents decay. Although saffron dyes food golden more effectively than the other spices, they also were thought of as food dyes. A recipe in the 1420 English cookery manuscript instructs the reader to mix together and then boil wine, almond milk, powdered cinnamon, ginger, and saffron; but if two different colors are desired, make part yellow by using spices and the other white by omitting them. A dish of fish is "colored" with saffron or cinnamon. Two fifteenth-century English texts recommend sandalwood as a red tint. The alchemical texts speak of gold as either yellowish, purplish, or reddish.[54]

6. Frontispiece of *The Queenlike Closet*, by Hannah Woolley, 5th ed. (London, 1684). Note the woman bottling alchemical medicines at center left. Courtesy of the Princeton University Library, Department of Rare Books and Special Collections.

Food as Divine Medicine

Black food, because of its Saturnian connections, is as suspect as golden food is beneficial. Although the *Picatrix* uses the hotness and smell of pepper to court Mars, the harmful blackness of this spice overshadowed Mars's benefits in a Europe stricken with fear of Saturn. The Arabic astrologer Alcabitius, in his list of items linked to the potentially threatening planet, listed black pepper and "everything whatsoever that is black." Ficino also advised the melancholic against anything black. Ginger, by far the most widely used spice in fourteenth-century Italy, France, and England, totally overshadowed pepper in the recipes. When pepper was used, it was mitigated usually by use of a golden spice and presumably by yellowed foods served with the peppered dish. Cooks also avoided pepper by making "yellow pepper" from ginger and saffron.[55]

Golden color was derived from other substances and processes as well. The Hispanic-Moorish text emphasizes decorations of hard-cooked egg yolks. (Recall that the egg yolk was also a cordial for Avicenna.) Dishes were often toasted or roasted, and the Hispanic-Moorish cookbook notes that if a food is toasted and thus takes on color, saffron will not be needed. The process was included in the cookery texts that followed in the West. Cooks made food "golden" by painting it with egg yolk, as the Hispanic-Moorish text prescribed. The fourteenth-century *Libro di cucina* advised the reader to make the dish yellow by adding orange or lemon juice.[56]

Gelatin recipes called for a base of fish or meat stock, not Avicenna's cordial derived from the *jus* of meat but a broth obtained by the boiling of meat or poaching of fish. Some of Avicenna's contemporaries did call such a broth a cordial. For the gelatins cooks usually added saffron to the stock for color, and occasionally other tints to produce red, green, blue, and pink. Recall that colors were connected to all the planets, not just to the sun and Saturn. Spices were always added to the gelatins, and sugar sometimes. Cooks might clarify the broth by pouring it through doubled linen or adding beaten egg white. But one sixteenth-century Italian cookbook avoids the clarifying process, labeling the result a cloudy gelatin for its translucent, not transparent, appearance. The liquids, clarified or not, were put to cool, and thus to set, to be served simply as a gelatin or as a covering poured over meat or fish to create the equivalent of today's chicken or fish in aspic.[57]

The contrast between the solid fish or meat and its translucent or transparent jewel coating of gelatin was seen as a symbol of the contrast between the body and the spirit of the meat. In the light of candles, oil, or sunshine these colored cordials appeared like luminescent jewels. If the sweet cherry is made into a jelly and is looked at "in the brightness of the Sun or by the lamp, you will find it is beautiful as a ruby." So observed the physician Michel de Nostredame in 1556. The color of quince jelly is so diaphanous that it resembles "an oriental ruby."[58] To swallow these jewel-like jellies in which the essence or juice had been extracted from the flesh of the fruit was akin to swallowing *jus*, an extract of meat or fish.

This jewel-like food was linked to drugs endowed with divine power. When the Plotinian world fell from favor in the seventeenth century, the idea of a heavenly connected pharmacy fell with it. Food, in consequence, changed dramatically. The French led the way, drawing on the motifs the Italians had culled from the texts of Greek and Roman antiquity. It was France, not Italy, that first jettisoned fragrant golden food with its magical implications. All Europe came to recognize the new French cooking as the required taste.

# PART 2     The Delights of Antiquity

. . . this tireless gluttony, which is ever
wandering about and seeking for flavours,
and this eager quest of dainties from all
quarters . . .

   Aulus Gellius, *The Attic Nights* (second century)

# CHAPTER 3   The Search for a Greco-Roman Food Tradition

Many people were alarmed by the inroads the Arabic world had made into the cultural fabric of Europe, and perhaps none more so than Petrarch, though he was seduced in a variety of ways by what he struggled to resist. He lived in a world where the serving of highly aromatic, yellow, sugared food had become imperative, where architecture was now characterized by the pointed arch of the Arabic world, where light poured through jewel-like stained-glass church windows to bathe the worshipers in color. Petrarch, the great fomenter of humanism, set himself against the growing appeal of logic, against the pervasive resort to astrology, and against studies of the natural world and especially of medicine. He wrote to his doctor and friend: "You know what kind of physicians the Arabs are. I know what kind of poets they are. Nobody has such winning ways." Beware, he cautioned: "No . . . good can come from Arabia."[1]

By the fifteenth century the military threat from the Arab East had become increasingly menacing. The Turkish advance was of vital concern. In 1453 Constantinople fell to the Ottoman Empire; soon the fleet was at war with Venice. In 1480 a Turkish force occupied Otranto, in southern Italy, and was stayed from moving forward only by the death of Muhammad II. Some Europeans ventured to hope that it would be less onerous to live under Islam than under the papacy, and considered not resisting the Turks. In these dark and troubled times the search for "true" roots, untainted by an "alien" heritage, took hold. In 1460 the humanist pope Aeneas Silvius, Pius II, wrote an exhortatory letter to Muhammad II, conqueror of the Byzantine empire, inviting him to convert to Christianity and thus to rule Constantinople by right. The strength of the West, Pius insisted, stemmed from Greece and Rome as well as from Christianity. Eugenio Garin has observed that "the Greek divinities returned to Florence at the very moment when the Christian world was trying to reunite itself in the face of the threat from the Turks." George Sarton, too, saw that the humanists' "love of Greece and Rome was nourished by their hatred of Islam." Even so, he observed, the Arabic medical tradition would continue in full force through the sixteenth century.[2]

To counter the culture of the Arabic world, the revival of antiquity was carried forth on many fronts. In an attempt to appropriate the world of the ancients, Renaissance men embraced a wide spectrum of thought and participated in a broad range of activities that they associated with Greece and Rome. They were aware that they followed the ancients in lofty as well as low pursuits. A peculiar feature of the Renaissance is a mix of moral revival with a slavish catering to base sensual tastes.[3] A famous precedent for this polarity in antiquity was Lucius Licinius Lucullus (c. 114 B.C.–57 B.C.), in whom two extremes of temperament met. Lucullus spent his vast wealth on a great collection of books, which he shared with philosophically oriented Greeks residing in Rome, and on a lavish table of much renown, where he gave himself up to sensual abandonment. He maintained numerous dining rooms, each with a special allowance for meals. When he told his servants that he wished guests to be entertained in the Apollo hall, for example, the cooks knew that the dinner was to cost 50,000 drachmas. "The daily repasts of Lucullus were such as the newly rich affect," Plutarch tells us. "Not only with his dyed coverlets, and beakers set with precious stones, and choruses and dramatic recitations, but also with his arrays of all sorts of meats and daintily prepared dishes, did he make himself the envy of the vulgar."[4]

One of the ways in which the Renaissance recreated the sensuality of the Greco-Roman world was by bringing back both the idea of the male connoisseur of eating—that is, by encouraging new Luculluses—and by reintroducing or giving status to various foods of antiquity, especially those that ancient commentators had given a certain notoriety.

The Delights of Antiquity

Plato had made it quite clear that fine dining was part of base sensuality and that titillation of the palate, no less than titillation of the sexual appetite, prevented humans from focusing on the higher things that set them apart from animals; "bent upon the earth and heads bowed down over their tables they feast like cattle, grazing and copulating, ever greedy for more of these delights." Aristotle clung firmly to this moral stance, as did the Spartans, the Stoics, and even the moderate Solon of Athens. In late antiquity the philosopher Macrobius epitomized this position: "Now these two pleasures, the pleasure of taste and the pleasure of touch, that is to say, indulgence in food and drink and indulgence in sexual intercourse, are the only pleasures which we find common to man and the lower animals, so that whoever is the slave of these animal pleasures is regarded as ranking with the brutes and beasts." Nevertheless, Renaissance men indulged in the bestial life of which the Greek and Roman hedonists had been the paragons.[5]

The texts of the ancients offered numerous derisory descriptions of the voluptuous style, but rather than thwarting the Renaissance development of sensuality, they served as wells of inspiration. The humanists gathered passages illustrating the lengths to which the ancients went to arouse their passions. Thus, for example, they learned that Seneca in the first century had decried the gourmands Nomentanus and Apicius,

> digesting, as they say, the blessings of land and sea, and reviewing the creations of every nation arrayed upon their board! See them, too, upon a heap of roses, gloating over their rich cookery, while their ears are delighted by the sound of music, their eyes by spectacles, their palates by savours; soft and soothing stuffs caress with their warmth the length of their bodies, and, that the nostrils may not meanwhile be idle, the room itself, where sacrifice is being made to Luxury, reeks with varied perfumes.[6]

Seneca had also portrayed the enormous wealth thrown about to garner goads to the appetite from all lands:

> They want game that is caught beyond the Phasis to supply their pretentious kitchens, and from the Parthians, from whom Rome has not yet got vengeance, they do not blush to get—birds! From

The Search for a Greco-Roman Food Tradition                    {47} every quarter they gather together every known and unknown thing to tickle a fastidious palate . . . ; . . . they vomit that they may eat, they eat that they may vomit, and they do not deign even to digest the feasts for which they ransack the whole world.[7]

The Roman emperor Vitellius, who also lived in the first century, conducted himself like those against whom Seneca railed. Vitellius sometimes made room for four meals a day by taking emetics to induce regurgitation. But lavish meals did not satisfy his curious palate. As he journeyed through his empire he could not pass up a cookshop for fear of missing out on some goodies. In the midst of sacrifices to the gods, his raging appetite drove him to snatch morsels from the altars.[8]

Two centuries later Rome produced an emperor whose incessant search for ways to prove himself extravagant and stimulate his palate would become the subject of tales in his own day and again in the Renaissance. Garbed as a confectioner or cook, Heliogabulus gave stupendous banquets, serving six hundred ostrich heads so that the brains might be devoured. The palace attendants were invited to be titillated by mullet viscera, huge beardlike barbels taken from the chins of these fish, and various kinds of brains. Not to be left out, his dogs enjoyed goose livers. "For ten successive days, moreover, he served wild sows' udders with the matrices, at the rate of thirty a day, serving, besides, peas with gold-pieces, lentils with onyx, beans with amber, and rice with pearls; and he also sprinkled pearls on fish and truffles in lieu of pepper."[9]

## THE NEW GOURMAND

Renaissance culture revived the image of the male as connoisseur of the table. This is the concept Montaigne satirizes in his ironic portrait of the Italian steward who discourses on food with such astounding earnestness:

I asked him about his job, and he replied with a discourse on the science of guzzling, delivered with magisterial gravity and demeanor as if he had been expounding some great point of theology. He spelled out to me the differences in appetites: the one we have before eating, the one we have after the second and third course; the means now of simply gratifying it, now of arousing and stimu-

The Delights of Antiquity

lating it; the organization of his sauces, first in general, and then particularizing the qualities of the ingredients and their effects; the differences in salads according to the season, which one should be warmed up and which served cold, the way of adorning and embellishing them to make them also pleasant to the sight. After that he entered upon the order of serving, full of beautiful and important considerations.[10]

One might conjecture that Montaigne had sat at more than one table governed by the fastidious taste he mocked.

Attention to culinary detail was coupled with extravagance. The excesses of Petronius's vaingloriously rich parvenu Trimalchio were matched by those of the Renaissance cavalier. At some banquets the lavish outlay for ingredients was matched only by the disregard shown for other expenditures. David Coffin tells us that after each course of one such dinner (it may have been a baptismal celebration) at the Villa Farnesina, near the bank of the Tiber, the servants cleared the table "by ostentatiously tossing the silverplate into the river." The host neglected to mention that nets had been placed in the water to catch it. The 1549 *Banchetti* of Cristoforo di Messisbugo and the *Opera* of Bartolomeo Scappi (head cook to Pius V) show enormous quantities of expensive foods prepared for high-ranking people. Jean-Baptiste Bruyerin cried out in 1560 against his compatriots' gluttony; they were eating more lavishly than the Muslims themselves, he railed. In sixteenth- and seventeenth-century England, the expenses of food and entertainment proved to be crippling at many great establishments.[11]

7. Bartolomeo Scappi, from his *Opera* (Venice, 1750). Courtesy of the Cambridge University Library.

## TRACKING THE DELICACIES OF THE ANCIENTS

In their efforts to revive the sensuality of the ancients, humanist scholars compiled compendia on what the ancients ate. From histories, from comedies, from writings on horticulture and husbandry, the Renaissance humanist was able to glean an array of delights. Passages on depraved gullets and their desires were eagerly ferreted out, even while the same scholars sometimes repeated the condescending platitudes of their ancient authors on sensual excess. They mined Plautus, Horace, Seneca, Juvenal, Martial, Pliny, and the agronomists, among many others. Once on the track, they found no dearth of material.

The Search for a Greco-Roman Food Tradition

Aurispa brought the work of Athenaeus, "a repository of fantasies of the appetites," to Italy from Constantinople in 1423. The text attributed to Apicius (which some Renaissance scholars identify with the first-century Roman gourmand Apicius, although no proof of this connection exists), the only cookbook that had survived from antiquity, was discovered at Fulda and reached humanist circles in 1455.[12]

Rabelais satirizes this craze for learning how and what to eat from ancient authors when he has Gargantua memorize the passages that Rabelais's compatriots and predecessors were working over so thoroughly.

> They began to converse daily together, speaking in the first place of the virtues, properties, efficacy, and nature of whatever was served to them at table: of the bread, the wine, the water, the salt, the meats, fish, fruit, herbs and roots, and of their dressing. From this talk Gargantua learned in a very short time all the relevant passages in Pliny, Athenaeus, Dioscorides, Julius Pollux, Galen, Porphyrius, Oppian, Polybius, Heliodorus, Aristotle, Aelian, and others. As they held these conversations they often had the aforementioned books brought to table, to make sure of their quotations.[13]

Thomas Artus told of the arduous study of the teachings of Epicurus, the Cyrenaics, and the "rules of Apicius . . . for good and happy living."[14]

European culture was held fast in the clutches of antiquity into the eighteenth century, and works exploring the banquets and foods of the ancients continued to appear. The authors of these seventeenth- and eighteenth-century works clearly understood that in foods, as in all other fields, the Renaissance humanists had done the spadework to link the moderns with antiquity. In 1682 the author of the *Traité des festins* acknowledged his debt to earlier scholars who had explored Greek and Roman writings on the subject of food: "I am obliged to them for having furnished me the necessary authorities to support all that I advance." The *Nouveau dictionnaire* (1776) recalled not only the humanist scholarship but sent the reader back to the original sources:

> If one desires to know the manner in which the ancients composed the dishes of their meals, and to have a good idea of their luxury,

one can consult (1) the description that Petronius makes of the feast given by Trimalchio, that is the cruel Nero; (2) Plutarch's *Moralia*, his discourses on the table, etc. where he describes the Spartans; (3) Martial's *Epigrams*; (4) *De convivis* by Jules Cesar Boulenger (1627); (5) *Rerum perditarum [libri II]* of Guido Panciroli with commentary by Salmuth entitled "De cibi capiendi modo veteribus usitato"; (6) the small work that Platina, the famous writer of the lives of the popes, dedicated to the cardinal Rovella, under the title *De honesta voluptate et valetudine.*

The English antiquarian Samuel Pegge pointed the curious reader to Homer, Aristophanes, Aristotle, and especially Athenaeus, and to later commentators.[15]

The authors who put together compendia on food or who annotated works on the subject were men of encyclopedic inclinations, broadly schooled in humanism and natural philosophy. Many of them were physicians, but their writings should not be narrowly construed as medical works. Bruyerin, for example, set the tone of his book with early chapters on luxury. What brings these men together here is their participation in the process of transmitting to their society the culture of food in antiquity. They are the link between the texts of the ancients and the cookbooks, between the dishes of the ancients and the modern table.

Platina was an important figure in humanist circles in both Florence and Rome, where he was in charge of the Vatican library. Among his writings was not only the 1475 *De honesta voluptate*, a work on food repeatedly referred to through the sixteenth century, but a renowned book on the lives of the popes. Porta, a towering figure in sixteenth-century natural philosophy, brought forth *Natural Magick* and *The Villa*, which incorporated the gamut of the ancients' ideas on horticulture (not just the technical ones). He came from a moneyed and titled family, Luigi Cardinal d'Este was his patron, and he advised kings on their health, alchemy, and like concerns. Bruyerin wrote not only one of the most important documents that we have in the history of French food, *De re cibaria*, but also a work on health based on Averroes, and he produced a new edition of *De viribus cordis*. Bruyerin was called to the court of Francis I and became physician to Henry II. He was the nephew of Symphorien Champier, the noted Neoplatonist.

The Search for a Greco-Roman Food Tradition

Konrad Gesner, a Swiss contemporary of Bruyerin and god-son of the Protestant reformer Ulrich Zwingli, traveled to Montpellier, a Protestant stronghold, to work on botanical problems. This physician widened his interests in the natural world with studies in paleontology and zoology, and his learning in ancient languages won him a chair in Greek in Switzerland. Although he did not write a work specifically on food, Gesner described food in antiquity in the course of his lengthy writings on animals and other subjects. With Thomas Moffett we are again moving in the highest intellectual and court circles. He studied at Cambridge, then at Basel, and returned to England in 1582 to take his M.D. Although he was a Paracelsian, his *Healths Improvement* shows his strong sympathies with the humanist tradition. The French physician Louis Nonnius, author of two important works on food published in the early seventeenth century, was interested in natural philosophy and literature, wrote poetry in Latin, and published a social geography of Spain. The seventeenth-century John Evelyn is important from our perspective for his works on horticulture and salads. But he also published on political affairs and natural philosophy, and was involved in the founding of the Royal Society. His interest in the arts was behind his translation from the French of a comparison between ancient and modern architecture and another on the ideal in painting.

These men and others whose acquaintance we will make as we go along participated in an international community of Renaissance learning. They often traveled extensively, buying books as they went or borrowing them from one another. They knew the texts of the ancients well, having been fed on these writings from an early age. Their societies' interest in the foods of antiquity can be traced to their influence.

Beginning in fifteenth-century Italy, and particularly with the publication of Platina's *De honesta voluptate* in 1475, scholars had an enormous impact on what people ate.[16] From this epoch comes the infatuation with fungi; with shellfish, and especially raw oysters; with artichokes, asparagus, and fruit. Here we find the cult of rare and high meats; assorted organs such as fat livers (foie gras), sweetbreads, brains, kidneys; cocks' crests; pâtés and forcemeat. To this period we trace the love of salt-acid foods such as olives, capers, caviar, anchovies, cured meats, and salads dressed with salt, vinegar, and olive oil. Some of these foods, such as artichokes and asparagus, had disappeared until their revival in the fifteenth century. Some, such as oysters and fungi, had lingered on in a limited way, but seem to have lost much of the aura they had in antiquity. Some, such as pork and pork fat, had continued to be basic household staples. In the fifteenth century the status of all these foods began to soar because of their presumed place in the cooking of the ancients.

### The Eclectic Style in Cookbooks and in Still Lifes

The cookery of the High Middle Ages had been characterized by sweetness, golden color, and fragrance—all associated with sensual and luxurious dining in both the Arabic world and Europe. As we have seen, this food was connected to divine medicine. Through the writings of celebrated Arabic physicians, alchemists, astrologers, and other magi, colors and sweet fragrances came to be regarded as powerful medicaments for the *spiritus;* through them the individual drew down benefits from celestial regions. The cooking of the High Middle Ages was thus seen as both spiritually medicinal and sensually provocative. The early humanists failed in their efforts to displace this type of food, just as they proved unable to unseat the authority of the Arab physicians. As a result, food in Italy and elsewhere in Renaissance Europe was eclectic, based as it was on two cultures, the Arabic and the Greco-Roman. By and large, the foods the humanist scholars discovered in the ancients' texts were added to the familiar sweet, golden, fragrant food. This eclectic mix continued until it was challenged by the French in the second half of the seventeenth century.

Like the Renaissance cookery works, the still life paintings of the era reflected this juxtaposition of food cultures. Both the cookbooks and the still lifes spoke to a duality in food theory: food is both spiritually nourishing and enticing to the sensual appetite. The literate, and people advised by the literate, confronted this duality of ingredients constantly—in their libraries, in apothecary shops, in their gardens, on their tables, in their altar paintings, and on their own walls. An exploration of some of these still lifes helps to illuminate this double preoccupation with the revivals of the tastes of the ancients and the view of food as a kind of elixir that promotes spiritual health.

Hugo van der Goes, who suffered severely from melancholy,

made salvation through Christ and divine medicine a prominent theme in his fifteenth-century Portinari altarpiece. Through Christ and elixir medication the melancholic sheds his shadowy, corruptible self and merges with the radiant light of divinity. In the altarpiece Christ appears both as the infant Jesus receiving his tributes and disguised as a sheaf of wheat ready to be threshed and milled into flour to produce the Eucharist wafer, the body of the Lord. The ingestion of the wafer fuses the Christian with the incorruptible Christ. In an analogous fashion the ingestion of elixir medicine transports the Christian into the divine realm. The still life portion of the painting depicts an *albarello* (apothecary jar) and a drinking glass. The apothecary jar contains three flowers, which may be read as representing the prime alchemical color sequence, from black to white to red. (A very dark blue or purple is the closest color in the flower world to black. Hugo's iris has purple outer petals and a large inky center. Below is a pure-white iris, while the bottom stem of the set bears orange-red lilies.) In alchemical literature the colors of the transformation were often compared with the colors of flowers. The drinking glass's parallel motif (it, too, contains flowers) suggests that the glass holds a medicinal mixture derived from plant essences. In the cordial elixirs these essences were used together with jewels, as in the diadem of one of the nearby angels with its coral and pearls sprouting from the gold, and possibly silver. Other paintings in the sixteenth and seventeenth centuries show such medicines as theriac, mithridatium, and distilled alcohol—all thought to work against the devastation of melancholy.[17]

Pieter Aertsen's sixteenth-century *Butcher's Stall* (Figure 8), which juxtaposes a background scene of the flight into Egypt with the still life depiction of a butcher shop, suggests the opposition between spiritual and sensual existences. In the foreground the pig, a favorite food of the Greeks and Romans, is displayed cut into pieces, which the ancients considered titillating. The pig's head, feet, and ribs hang alongside sausages, which were newly esteemed because of their place in the banquets of antiquity. But Aertsen has not allowed the sensuality of food to go unchecked in the butcher's shop: Christian imagery enters this foreground scene as well. Above an ox head lie fish arranged on a plate in the form of a cross, and just below the beast's head are four tarts, two white and two red. In Christian symbolism red is the color of the blood of Christ and those

The Delights of Antiquity

martyred for him; white is the symbol of purity, innocence, and
holiness. In alchemy red and white represent the two stones of
marvelous virtues and the gold (sun) and silver (moon) medicines. In the century before Aertsen's *Butcher's Stall,* in a prefatory
epistle addressed to King Edward IV in his *Compound of Alchymie,*
the alchemist George Ripley wrote that he gave his lordship
"secrets" that he learned on the Continent—secrets of wondrous medicines, "that is to say the great Elixirs both Red and
White."[18]

References to divine medicine are sometimes hidden in the
most common stuffs in the paintings, both inviting viewers to
uncover them and reminding them of the alchemical injunction to seek the philosopher's stone amid the ordinary as well as
the dear. On one level Pieter Claesz's seventeenth-century still
life (Figure 9) depicts worldly pursuits, gaming, drinking, and
smoking, through its playing cards, glass, tobacco spilled on the
table, and dish of embers to light the pipe. Looked at more
closely, the dish reveals its interior meaning. The painter has
endowed the white ash not with the soft, feathery texture of

8. Pieter Aertsen, *The Butcher's
Stall.* Courtesy of the Konst-
vetenskapliga Institutionen,
Uppsala University.

9. Pieter Claesz, *Still Life* (1636). Oil on wood, 50 × 68 cm. Courtesy of the Fondazione Thyssen-Bornemisza, Lugano, Switzerland.

wood ash but with the glisten of crystalline calcite. The red and yellow embers represent respectively realgar, an orange-red mineral (arsenic sulfide), and orpiment, an orange-yellow mineral (arsenic trisulfide), both important components of divine medicine.[19]

A number of seventeenth-century still lifes show small white bumpy objects in a variety of shapes. These are seeds or sticks coated with minerals from a hot spring. The metamorphosis of these objects into "stones" (sometimes opals, depending on the mineral composition of the water) fascinated the alchemical adept. In a work by Lodovico de Susio (Figure 10) these white objects appear on a platter and scattered on the table. A serving dish with a mound of these whitish bits occupies the center of a Georg Flegel painting (Figure 11). To the right is another serving dish of shells or other calcareous materials. In a painting by Osias Beert the Elder, white mineral-coated objects mingle with coral on a plate that sits atop a stack of round wooden boxes. On the table one sees both more calcareous sticks and oysters on the half shell, whose mother-of-pearl lining was used to prepare elixirs. The Arab physician Rhazes had described this

The Delights of Antiquity

lining as a drug substitute for pearls. (Pearls and mother-of-pearl have the same composition, calcium carbonate.) A poor Lazarus in the background of another painting by Beert the Elder begs crumbs from a rich man's table, while the foreground highlights what at first seems a sumptuous spread of oysters on the half shell, a dish of almonds together with white mineral sticks, and cakes inset with pieces of preserved fruit, their colors aglow like the jewels of elixirs. The whitish mineral sticks form a cross at the front of the table, a symbol of Christian alchemical medicine.[20]

In an opulent seventeenth-century still life by the Dutch painter William Kalk, a table is covered by a Middle Eastern rug on which sits a vessel made from a nautilus shell with gold mountings alongside blue-and-white porcelain. A watch, frequently interpreted as a vanity symbol, marks the temporal nature of the precious belongings.[21] But precious stuffs also stand for spiritual materiality in divine medicine. Inside the porcelain bowl is a large mineral setting of calcite and orpiment and a lemon peel, another important element of the cordial and elixir formulas. When the lemon peel appears on a dish of

10. Lodovico de Susio, *Still Life* (1619). Oil on mahogany panel, 35.1 × 46.5 cm. Courtesy of the Saint Louis Art Museum, museum purchase.

The Search for a Greco-Roman Food Tradition

11. Georg Flegel, *Grosses Schauessen.* Engraving, 78 × 67 cm. Courtesy of the Bayerische Staatsgemäldesammlungen, Munich.

oysters, it most likely represents the custom of serving lemon with shellfish, as in Messisbugo's menus.

Sir Kenelm Digby, one of the founding members of the Royal Society, was given to the study of alchemical medicine. A book of recipes that he supposedly collected includes one for an elixir medicine called the Countess of Kent's powder. Among the ingredients of this marvelous drug are "the black ends of the shares of Crabs . . . Crabs-eyes, fine Pearls and Corals . . . the Bones that are found in the hearts of Stags [seen in the elixirs of Roger Bacon and others] . . . juice of Lemons . . . Tincture of Saffron."[22] In seventeenth-century still lifes lobster, crayfish, and crab with bulging eyes are characteristic images. These revivals, along with oysters, read as sensual delight and good cheer. On another level they may also refer to ingredients in divine medicine.

The paintings are strewn with allusions to scent, so central to divine healing. In a painting by Georg Flegel a chicken is

The Delights of Antiquity

12. William van Mieris the
Younger, *The Greengrocer* (1731).
Reproduced by permission of
the Trustees of the Wallace
Collection, London.

punctured with cloves; the same recipe is depicted in a Pieter
Binoit painting, where the bird is accompanied by a cut orange.[23]
Stoskopff pairs nutmeg with citrus. Occasionally the artist
includes a censer. Flowers and fruits are everywhere.

The flower and fruit paintings, together with depictions of
vegetables and fungi, are also paeans to the Renaissance revival
of horticulture in imitation of the ancients' esteem of this art.
The produce of the virtuoso gardener was meant to satisfy the
discriminating palates of both the ancients and their modern
counterparts. The still life paintings often display the bounty
of the garden on tables, suggesting a home, or a market stall,
sometimes fancifully portrayed. The stall we see in Figure 12 is
decorated across the front with a Bacchanalian frieze, in which
some of the putti pluck grapes and others drink wine from jugs.
Occasionally the produce is shown against a landscape, as in

The Search for a Greco-Roman Food Tradition

13. Vincenzo Campi, *La Frutti-vendola.* Courtesy of the Pina-coteca di Brera, Milan.

Figure 13, where a woman holds up a cluster of grapes. Various meanings can be read into the fruit of the vine in these works. Most obviously grapes represent renewed interest in viniculture, a branch of gardening. But the grape also signifies wine, the blood of Christ in the Eucharist, the transforming and purifying sacrament. Wine also leads to a merging with divinity in pagan thought: Bacchanalian (or Dionysiac) ecstasy induced by drunkenness can reveal the mysteries of the universe.[24]

All of these still lifes focus on the pleasures of the table, but mystical meanings are often discernible. In a painting by Frans Snyders (Figure 14) a courtier gazes in Saturnian contemplation, his introspection disconnecting him from the lavish table laden with artichokes, asparagus, boar's head, and an abundance of other game.

Portrayals of individual vegetables, such as the bunch of asparagus by Adrian Coorte (Figure 15), are tributes to this food and the place it had attained on the table. Spears of asparagus, both long, thin ones and short, fat ones, which Pliny tells us are loved by gourmands, and prickly artichokes and cardoons, thought to be the coveted thistles of antiquity, are often found

The Delights of Antiquity

14. Frans Snyders, *Dead Game with Male Figure.* Reproduced by permission of the Trustees of the Wallace Collection, London.

15. Adrian Coorte, *Bunch of Asparagus* (1703). Oil on canvas, 29.3 × 22.8 cm. Courtesy of the Fitzwilliam Museum, Cambridge.

The Search for a Greco-Roman Food Tradition          {61}

among the displays of the garden yield. Seafood, which captivated the Greeks and Romans, is seen in these paintings heaped on the shore, sometimes on a table, sometimes in a shop, like the meats in the *Butcher's Stall*. Salads are represented by olives in a dish and by ham on a platter.

Recipes of the period, as we shall see, lend themselves to being read in much the same way as the iconography of the still lifes. The ingredients revived by the Italian humanists and their followers across Europe allude to specific passages of the ancients as well as to antiquity as a whole.

The Delights of Antiquity

# Chapter 4   Fungi

*T*he risks Renaissance men ran to explore the fungal world illumine the breadth of their identification with antiquity. Little was known about fungi before the great treasure hunt for these possibly poisonous morsels overtook Europe in the fifteenth century. Incurring great danger, collectors searched out fungi with only the scantiest of directions. One slip and the Greek or Roman fungus fancier was dead; a similar slip and his fifteenth-century follower went the way of his ancient hero. The new gatherers sought those varieties the ancients had relished, and experimented in their efforts to become fungus connoisseurs like their models.

The burgeoning interest in fungi cannot be fitted to the claim that the Renaissance turned to antiquity in search of ethical models. Though the ancients esteemed the task of tending their gardens, not a soul among them would have thought it morally uplifting to pick fungal matter off rotting trees or to root around for truffles.

## Held in "Singular Esteem"

What reviews fungi had from the ancient gourmands! Platina, like all humanists who wrote about food, was familiar with these notices. In 1475 he recorded that truffles and boleti were often found on sumptuous tables. Bruyerin, recalling that Suetonius (c. 70–c. 160) discussed a contest to judge whether the boletus, fig pecker, thrush, or oyster was the tastiest morsel, drew a parallel between his own time and that of ancient Rome: "Everyone agrees that truffles were treated with singular esteem at the meals of great men in Rome, and they have firmly kept their position today in great Roman and French houses." He recorded Pliny's sardonic remark that the newest imported stimulant of the appetite was the hog fungus, and Bruyerin observed that these particular fungi were once again to be seen drying in Italy. Many varieties of fungi were devoured. Pope Clement VII loved *spinuli, prunuli,* and *cardeoli* enough to eat them every day. "Certain people judge fresh boleti that they cook over coals, with butter and a little mound of salt thrown on, the highest delicacies," and confectioners had learned "to make pastries with boleti and fungi lest anything be lacking for the pleasure of the stomach and gullet," Bruyerin reported. "Indeed, I think that they who consider that phlegmy excretion among foods as a delicacy are worthy of a fungal life."[1]

In the first century Juvenal had jeered, "Gluttonous males peel truffles and preserve boleti." The humanist and natural philosopher Giambattista della Porta apparently had this line in mind when he wrote in 1592 that fungi are "the only kind of food that exquisites prepare with their own hands, handling sharp knives with amber handles and equipment of silver while already feeding on them in their imagination." Despite his mockery, Porta condescends to give fungus recipes from Apicius and Platina so that the Renaissance "exquisites" could, like the dandies of old, cook these delicacies themselves in their new villas, modeled after those of ancient Rome. Platina was hardly an ancient, but in the eyes of later Renaissance humanists their predecessors took on an aura of the antique. Platina, keeper of the books at the Vatican and author of a history of the popes, became a powerful figure in the revival of the food of antiquity. Although he called his book *De honesta voluptate* (On proper pleasure), he gave many recipes for "suspect" foods—that is, foods that the ancients maligned—taking care to sneer at them from time to time, as other Renaissance food commentators did.[2]

The parallel between the ancients' interest in fungi and that of the moderns continued to be drawn in the seventeenth and eighteenth centuries. In 1650 Giovanni Manelfi wrote that "truffles are thought very highly of in this day, as they formerly were in ancient times." Michel Bicais, a professor of medicine at Aix

The Delights of Antiquity

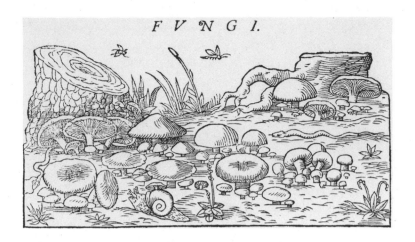

FVNGI.

16. "Fungi," from *Historia generalis plantarum*, by Jacques Dalechamps (Lyon, 1587), 2:1587. Courtesy of the History of Science Collections, Cornell University Library.

and a French contemporary of the Italian Manelfi, observed that "champignons were used at the most refined and magnificent banquets." One simply did not "serve a dish that was not enriched with champignons," and since "truffles, like champignons, tease the appetite, they have the same rank and the same usage." Similarly, a letter printed in the 1693 *Philosophical Transactions* of the Royal Society of London reported: "I need not tell you the Uses to which the Greeks and Romans apply'd these Vegetable Bodies [truffles] nor how they are dress'd and eaten at this day. Pliny, Martial, Plutarch, Athenaeus, Galen, Apicius, &c. may be consulted for the first; Nonnus, Bruyerinus, Ciccarellus, &c. for the last." John Evelyn noted in 1699 that fungi were "exalted indeed . . . to the second Course of the *Caesarian Tables*, with the noble Title . . . a Dainty fit for the *Gods* alone." He bantered about whether the fungus recipes he presented in his *Acetaria: A Discourse of Sallets* had been "*so treated and accommodated for the most Luxurious of the* Caesarean Tables, *when that Monarchy was in its highest Strain of* Epicurism, *and ingross'd this* Haugout [*haut goût*] *for their second Course.*"[3]

The *Encyclopédie* compared the eighteenth-century gluttons' interest in fungi to that of the Roman gourmands: "Our refined sensuality for this food does not at all yield to that of the Romans in the reign of Augustus. If in our time some would-be gourmet in this field would declaim the maxim of Horace's Catius [that is, that] meadow champignons are the best, our least savvy Aufidius would answer that [Horace] understands nothing and that the better tasting champignons are those that are found in the woods or on the heaths or moors."[4]

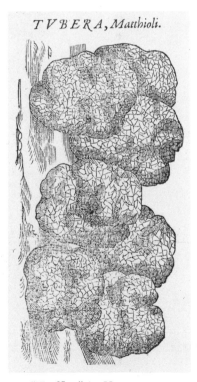

TVBERA, *Matthioli.*

17. "Truffles," in *Historia generalis plantarum*, by Jacques Dalechamps (Lyon, 1587), 2:1585. Courtesy of the History of Science Collections, Cornell University Library.

Fungi        {65}

18. Paolo Porpora, *Natura morta*. Note the serpent in the center. Courtesy of the Museo e Gallerie Nazionali di Capodimonte, Naples.

John Farley, cook at the London Tavern, catered to the fashionable palate and credited the Roman connection in his 1792 cookbooks: "[Fungi] have long been used in sauces, in catchup and other forms of cookery . . . [and] were highly esteemed by the Romans, as they are at present by the French, Italians, and other nations."[5]

## RISKS AND REWARDS

The fungus cult persisted despite the large number of people who died after eating poisonous varieties. At the end of the fifteenth century virtually no written material on the selection of safe wild fungi existed, and human guides proved unreliable. Pliny's two meager passages on boleti and fungi continued to be relied on, supplemented by remarks found in Galen, among others. Only in the eighteenth century was a detailed and illustrated guide for the fungus hunter issued in France.

Staying close to Pliny's text, Bruyerin gave the story of the emperor Claudius's death after eating a dish of boleti in which his wife, Agrippina, had put poison. Bruyerin included material from Suetonius's life of Claudius, and also Juvenal's and Martial's satiric remarks on the poisoning. These texts imply that the poison was not inherent in the boletus that Claudius ate but was added by a human hand. Still, for both Pliny and Bruyerin

The Delights of Antiquity

the boletus was shadowed by the notion that it could be toxic. Of course, that was why it was an extremely useful dish for a would-be murderer to serve, since death could be attributed to the boletus rather than to the killer's poison.

Like Pliny, Bruyerin described poisonous boleti as pale red with a leaden cast, with shallow furrows in their striations and a light rim. Some had small white protuberances on top. Even the nonpoisonous kind could be contaminated by their environment. Boleti that grew close to rusty iron, rotten rags, or snakes could absorb their poisons. But Bruyerin tempered Pliny's warnings by citing Galen, who thought that "only boleti, among fungi, ought to be touched." Such contradictions, of course, only compounded the confusion.[6]

Bruyerin opened his section on fungi with these ominous words:

Nothing ought to deter men more from the eating of fungi than the fact that they are placed among poisonous things by all the renowned writers and also because certain learned men think they are called fungi from bringing death [i.e., from the verb *funero*]. I can but wonder that the gullet of our times rages so, that it does

19. Ambrosiello Faro, *Natura morta*. Courtesy of the Museo e Gallerie Nazionali di Capodimonte, Naples.

Fungi

not wish to draw the line at those substances that are things destructive of life rather than food. For what can we have in common with that phlegmy excretion of trees and with those blemishes of the land among which fungi rank as the greatest evils?

He then turned to a line from Pliny: "For by horrible and almost daily examples, these fungi can be charged with killing households and whole banquets of people." Moreover, Bruyerin continued, Galen and other learned physicians had warned against eating them to excess, maintaining "their nourishment to be phlegmatic and cold and their juice harmful, especially when eaten without measure, which I know many now do." Like Pliny, Bruyerin asked who in the marketplace one could trust to offer fungi that had not been picked from the yew, the oak, or the cypress. Pliny had written that all fungi were of a lead color, said to be a sign of poison, and hence were poisonous, but those whose color more closely resembled the bark of a tree were more poisonous than others. "It is certain," Bruyerin concluded, "that all fungi are most accommodating to poisons." He agreed with Pliny that the hog fungus, popular in Pliny's day and in his own, was well suited to poisoning. But Bruyerin called on other authorities who implied that some fungi were harmless, and this talk of innocuous fungi must certainly have acted as a lure to fungus hunters.[7]

Pliny and Horace live on as guides in, for example, Nicolas de Bonnefons's 1655 cookbook, *Les Délices de la campagne,* and even in the eighteenth century the *Encyclopédie* concluded that "the most able doctors swear that the best champignons taken in great quantity are harmful." But at the end of the century a major field guide on collecting fungi, Jean Jacques Paulet's *Traité des champignons,* offered more detailed advice on how to distinguish between good and bad fungi. Paulet reported that his own motivation for writing the guide was to remove the risk incurred by fungus gatherers, for even fatal accidents would not deter them:

[They] know the passage in Pliny and what was said there; the unhappy end to the emperor Claudius, that of several consular families of Rome; they know those of Pope Clement VII, of the emperor Jovien, of a Borronée of Naples, of the emperor Charles VI, of the widow of the tsar Alexis, all famous victims of their taste for these plants, and yet these fungus lovers do not change their tastes. They know, what is more, the medical observations filled with similar cases; examples of death reigning in the army, similar to epidemics, produced by the same cause; the accident that happened to the late princess of Conti at Fontainebleau in 1751; those that one observes daily in the areas around Paris, Rome, Naples, etc., and nevertheless they have not yet lost the taste. While one is speaking to them of these accidents, they regret not being in the Bearn in order to make use of *oranges, rougillons, coquemalles, poules, savatelles,* etc; in Guyenne, to gather *cèpes;* in Provence, to find the *pinède,* the *baligoule;* in the Piemont, to eat the *truffe-à-l'ail;* in Burgundy, to collect the *mousseron;* in the Bourbonnois, to find *coches;* at Fontainebleau, to eat *barbes-de-chevre;* in Italy, to water the stone that produces fungi—all dishes that they call, with the Roman emperor, the food of the gods.

Even prohibitions had no effect, wrote Paulet. In 1754, when someone died after eating fungi picked in the Bois de Boulogne, a police ordinance banning the gathering of fungi was tacked up on the gates. The prohibition was in vain.[8]

The cultivation of safe fungi was a clear alternative. Knowledge on the subject was extremely limited, and the ancients offered scant help. Writers on horticulture, such as Columella, Cato, Varro, and Palladius, had not mentioned raising fungi. At the end of the sixteenth century in Italy, Porta reported that the first-century Greek physician Dioscorides had testified that if you cut up pieces of poplar bark and sow them in dunged beds, you will have fungi at any time of the year. Porta noted that these procedures were being carried out to cultivate fungi in his own day. Francis Bacon drew on Porta in his *Natural History,* and it was to Bacon, among others, that Evelyn turned for his discussion of fungus cultivation at the end of the seventeenth century.[9]

The story that a stone could produce fungi had circulated for more than two centuries. The stone was of interest to the fabulously wealthy Claude Fabri de Pereisc, who in the early seventeenth century amassed huge collections of fossils, plants, and animals. Pereisc decided that the "stone" was actually a large "toad stool" as hard as stone, which could produce fungi in a moist place. Louis Nonnius, a French physician born in the second half of the sixteenth century, discovered the tale of the stone in the comments of Andrea Mattioli on the first-century herbal of Dioscorides and in the fifteenth-century humanist Ermolao Barbaro's comments on Pliny. With this "stone," Nonnius said, "Italy has given to the world the latest invention whereby anyone may eat fungi all year long."[10]

John Evelyn described a kind of fungus cultivation developed in France and detailed at least as early as the turn of the seventeenth century by Olivier de Serres. Parings of fungi were sown in a bed of "*Asses*-Dung" and moistened with water impregnated with fungi. The process seems to have been of French origin, for the Italian sources (Porta's *Villa* of 1592, for example) fail to mention it. Martin Lister, an English physician, discovered on a trip to Paris in 1698 that fungus cultivation had become an important enterprise there: "The French delight in nothing so much as Mushroomes; of which they have daily, and all the Winter long, store of fresh and new gathered in the Markets. This surprised me; nor could I guess, where they had them, till I found they raised them on hot Beds [dung beds] in their Gardens." He thought that fungi provided as good an income as anything the French planted. By the next century, if not earlier, similar ventures were in place in England. Richard Bradley, a Cambridge botanist and writer on gardening and household affairs, wrote, "I have found that my Observations concerning the Raising of Mushrooms have been so well receiv'd, that there is now hardly a Garden of any Note near London without them, or where there has not been Attempts made to produce them in every Month of the Year." By midcentury the *Encyclopédie* was discussing an abundant fungus culture in both England and France.[11]

Trade developed also in wild varieties of fungi. The natural philosopher John Ray, reporting on his Italian travels in 1673, remarked that the best truffles were from Sicily and sold in Malta for a good deal of money. In the first part of the eighteenth century Nicolas Delamare noted that first-rate truffles seen in Paris markets came up from Limousin, Périgord, Angoumois, Gascogne, and other warm areas. Martin Lister wrote that in the Parisian markets at the "beginning of April, fresh gathered *Moriglios* [morels], the first of that kind of Mushroom, that I remember ever to have seen," were available. "This sort of Mushroom is much esteemed in France."[12]

Soon the "Morille or Morill," as Richard Bradley called it, was sold in England, at Rushton in Northamptonshire, and "very commonly brought to New-market about the Spring Horse Races." Evelyn scorned the idea that England had to send to France for wild fungi, even for truffles. He had gleaned from a letter that appeared in the *Philosophical Transactions* of the Royal Society that truffles had been found on English soil, and

The Delights of Antiquity

a great fungus hunt had sent gatherers scratching and rooting over England for these subterranean "gems." A new cultural imperative had taken hold: one was to eat the delicacies that the ancients had made clear were "fit for the *Gods* alone."[13]

## In the Cookbooks

Apicius's fourth-century Roman cookbook gives fifteen ways to prepare dishes in which truffles and other fungi are the main ingredients and one recipe in which truffles are an auxiliary

---

APICIUS (FOURTH CENTURY)

Ash tree fungi. They are served boiled, hot, drained dry, with peppered *garum*.\*

To put in ash tree fungi. Pepper, *caroenum* [reduced wine], vinegar, and oil.

Another recipe for ash tree fungi. Boiled in water, served with salt, oil, wine, chopped coriander.

Boleti. [Cook in] *caroenum* with a bouquet of fresh coriander. When they have cooked, remove the bouquet and serve.

Another method for boleti. Serve the stalks with *liquamen*\* or sprinkled with salt.

Boleti, another method. Chop the stalks, place in a new shallow pan, having added pepper, lovage, a little honey. Blend with *liquamen*, add a little oil [and let cook].

Truffles. Scrape the truffles, boil, sprinkle with salt, and put them on skewers. Grill lightly, then put in a sauce pan oil, *liquamen*, *caroenum*, wine, pepper, and honey. When this boils, thicken with starch, undo the truffles, and serve [with this sauce].

Marrows with fowl. Peaches, truffles, pepper, caraway, cumin, asafoetida, mixed fresh herbs—mint, celery, coriander, and pennyroyal—*caroenum*, honey, wine, *liquamen*, oil, and vinegar.

*Source:* Apicius, *Roman Cookery Book*, pp. 175–77.

\**Garum* and *liquamen* are the same thing—a fermented fish sauce.

---

Fungi

ingredient. The cookbooks of the Arab world seem to use only truffles; Maxim Rodinson points out the use of Arabic black desert truffles prepared with eggs, meat, and aromatics.[14] The Hispanic-Moorish work employs truffles in two recipes with meat. Fungi do not appear at all in "A Baghdad Cookery Book." Deserts are not, of course, optimum places for fungi, and only the subterranean desert truffle did well. It cannot be said, however, that the Arab world did not pick up the mania for fungi because they were not readily available, for they could have imported dried fungi. The spices of the Arabian peninsula and East Asia, after all, were sold all over the Islamic world. The taste for fungi is cultural, and fungi of all sorts are clearly more esteemed in the Greco-Roman tradition.

European cookbooks seldom refer to fungi until the sixteenth century. The fourteenth-century English *Forme of Cury* does have a recipe with "funges" as the main ingredient and the

---

*LIBRO DI CUCINA* (FOURTEENTH CENTURY)

Fungi. If you wish to prepare fungi, take dry fungi and put them to soften in hot water and wash well. Boil them. Make them good (season them) as you wish and cook them in a brazier. Then take onions and herbs and braise with sweet and strong spice. Put in the fungi and fry everything together. And take unpeeled almonds and pound them and put over the fungi. Others put vinegar on and serve hot.

*Source: Libro di cucina, p. 14.*

---

Italian *Libro di cucina* in the same century has recipes with "*fongi*" as the focus. But no recipes for fungi appear in the French *Traité de cuisine* from the beginning of the fourteenth century, or in the fourteenth- or fifteenth-century *Viandier de Guillaume Tirel*, or in the English cookery manuscripts of 1420 and 1450, or in the English cookery books of 1591 and 1615. With Platina's 1475 text, with its discursive passages on Pliny and other ancients and its grouping of boleti, fungi, and truffles, it becomes clear that interest in fungi is reviving. All the same, fungi do not begin to appear with any frequency in the cookbooks until the sixteenth century. In his 1549 *Banchetti*, Messisbugo clustered his five fungus dishes together, as Apicius had done, and labeled this section "Various Preparations of Fresh and Salted Fungi." When Messisbugo used fungi at all, he used them only as a main ingredient, unlike Bartolomeo Scappi (1570), who used

The Delights of Antiquity

fungi both as principal ingredients and in composite dishes, thus giving them a much greater presence. Like Dioscorides, Scappi used raw truffles, and the sixteenth-century cook served them with salt and pepper (a dual condiment inspired by the ancients, as we shall see).[15] Sixteenth-century French cookbooks still show no strong interest in fungi.

The disjunction between French cookbooks of the period and the observations in sixteenth-century humanist compendia (Bruyerin, for example) on the status of fungi is an important indication of a cultural tension. Platina's book was available in French translation by 1505. Yet the fact that French cookbooks continue in the vein of the High Middle Ages—that is, they incorporate few of the revivals, and put them to much more limited use than the Italians do—reveals that a portion of the French population was not ready to entertain new ideas about food. Perhaps these were the people who were so committed to their spiritual quest that they wanted nothing to do with a food pocked by ancient pagan "debris," as the eighteenth-century *Encyclopédie* was to call the food motifs that the Italians had revived from antiquity. These people with their golden, fragrant food untainted by Roman additions could feel that what they ate was within moral limits and of spiritual value in attracting beneficial celestial forces. They could ignore, or at least not focus on, the luxurious and sensual aspect of spices.

By the mid–seventeenth century, however, fungi were nowhere more important than in Paris. Fungi riddled La Varenne's 1651 *Cuisinier françois* and became a pervasive motif in the French and English cookbooks that followed his. The *Dictionnaire portatif de cuisine*, a century after La Varenne, reported that the champignon was "a necessary ingredient in practically all ragouts." Richard Bradley had a French friend who claimed that the mushroom was "not only a good groundwork for all high sauces, but itself a good Meat to be dress'd after any manner, either to compose a white or brown Fricassee, or fry'd or broil'd, or baked in Pyes with common Seasoning." Bradley, who thought the truffle afforded a "variety of agreeable Dishes," agreed.[16]

In the course of the seventeenth century, then, something had happened to change French taste. The "debris" of the ancients was now, apparently, worth risking one's life for.

# CHAPTER 5 · Fish

*T*he water world provided the Greeks and Romans with the most sensuous morsels to delight the tongue. "I remember," wrote Seneca, "once hearing gossip about a notorious dish into which everything over which epicures love to dally had been heaped together by a cook shop that was fast rushing into bankruptcy; there were two kinds of mussels, and oysters trimmed round at the line where they are edible, set off at intervals by sea-urchins; the whole was flanked by mullets cut up and served without the bones." The sturgeon served at banquets in the time of the emperor Severus, Macrobius wrote, was "brought in by servants crowned with garlands and to the music of the flute, a ceremonial entry which suggested the worship of a god rather than the appearance of a tasty dish at table." In antiquity's hierarchy of luxury foods, fish is always among the top contenders.[1]

Epicurus warned that when he wrote of the quest for pleasure, he was not speaking of "the satisfaction of lusts, nor the enjoyment of fish and other luxuries of the wealthy table." Since fish was thought an extravagance, it is hardly surprising that no Roman who sought to establish himself as a man of proper and moderate pleasures would confess to eating delicacies from the sea. And so Horace claimed that he would welcome a friend or neighbor "not with fish sent for from town, but with a pullet or a kid."[2] Later one of Plutarch's dinner companions argued that fish was the utmost indulgence:

Though there are many delicacies, fish has won the title, either exclusively or pre-eminently, of 'delicacy' [*opson*], because it far excels all others in quality. In fact, we describe as 'eaters of delicacies' and 'lovers of delicacies' not those who enjoy their beef, like Hercules . . . nor any lover of figs like Plato, or of the grape like Arcesilaüs, but those who always show up when fish are sold and who have a keen ear for the bell [which sounds when the fish come in]. Demosthenes, too, by way of an accusation for gluttony and licentiousness, says that Philocrates used money gained by treason to buy harlots and fish.[3]

In the sixteenth century Thomas Moffett advised his readers that "the finest feeders and dainty bellies did not delight in flesh with Hercules, or in fruit with Plato and Arcesilaus, but with Numa and Philocretes in variety of fish." Pierre Duchâtel, a professor of medicine at Antwerp, drew attention not only to Plutarch's passages but to lines in the *Republic* where Plato noted that the army in the *Iliad* did not eat fish. "Plato also brought this in as an example of ancient frugality [that] . . . Homer mentioned no fish at the entertainments of the heroes in the army, although they were on the shore of the Hellespont." Whether Homer meant to imply a modest frugality in the soldiers by having them abstain from fish is open to question; the interesting thing is the later commentators' wish to impute the motive to him. Renaissance writers saw Homer's warriors as heroic consumers of flesh—primarily beef—not as wantons who indulged in fish.[4]

Ponds were created in antiquity to hold and breed fish, for it was important that they be absolutely fresh, still tasting of the sea. Macrobius told of plundering distant seas for the home fish market and cited Pliny's story that Optatus had ships fitted with tanks to bring back huge numbers of wrasse to deposit off the shores of Italy.[5] Seneca mocked people who made a fetish of freshness:

We used to be amazed at the great fastidiousness in those who were unwilling to touch a fish unless it had been captured that very day and tasted, as they say, of the sea itself. So, the fish was carried at a run; a way had to be made for the carriers as they hurried along breathless and shouting. What has pleasure come to? A fish that has been killed by these people is already considered putrid. 'It was caught today? I do not know how to trust you in such an important matter. I should trust only the fish. Bring it here. Let it

The Delights of Antiquity

die in front of me.' The belly of gourmets has reached such daintiness that they cannot taste a fish unless they see it swimming and palpitating in the very dining-room.[6]

The great lengths to which the ancients went to obtain fish were not lost on their Renaissance imitators. In 1518 Leo X, accompanied by fourteen cardinals and several foreign ambassadors, arrived at Agostino Chigi's Villa Farnesina for a meal featuring a sturgeon that was said to have cost 250 ducats. In 1524 Bishop Paolo Giovio published *De romanis piscibis*, drawing for authority on Pliny, Galen, Athenaeus, and other Greeks and Romans, as well as such Renaissance authors as Platina, whom Giovio called not only a historian but a cook. Giovio enriched the text with his own knowledge of banquets and high living, thus conflating the ancient Roman and contemporary Italian experiences. His description of Cardinal Cornaro's lavish hunt party twelve miles from Rome brings to mind the meals that Epicurus and Horace so eloquently spurned. One might think that an inland hunting outing would feature meat—perhaps not the game of the day, for fresh meat had to hang for a time, but some sort of flesh. But Cornaro's table boasted instead "the noblest and finest fishes." Since to these sixteenth-century gourmands the finest fishes were those caught in salt water, the fresh catch must have been carted miles from the port to their encampment in the open countryside.[7]

Montaigne claimed that the ancients were so exacting about the preparation of fish that they themselves instructed their cooks in its preparation.

In summer in their lower rooms they often had clear fresh water run in open channels underneath, in which there were a lot of live fish, which the guest would select and catch in their hands to be prepared to the taste of each. Fish has always had this privilege, as it still does, that the great have pretensions of knowing how to prepare it, and indeed its taste is much more exquisite than that of flesh, at least to me.[8]

Sea fish were more prestigious than freshwater fish to seventeenth-century gourmands, as they had been to the ancients, so it is understandable that when the earl of Bedford sought to improve the pomp of his table, he turned to fresh cod, smelt, flounder, salmon, sole, and oysters from the sea.[9]

Fish

20. Jochim Bueckelaer, *Fischmarkt.* Courtesy of the Bayerische Staatsgemälde-sammlungen, Munich.

The lust for fish was so powerful that it made a mockery of the dietary sacrifices of Lent and of special fast days. A writer in the London *Connoisseur* sneered at the proposed fast called to commemorate the victims of the Lisbon earthquake.

> The very name of a Fast implies a day of abstinence, of mortification and self denial. . . . I could also ask these rigid devotees, who observe this day in all the strictness of the letter, and would be shocked at the sight of a leg of mutton or beef-steak on their table, whether the dining upon salt or other fish may not be considered rather as feasting than fasting, if (as is often the case) it should happen to be a dish they are remarkably fond of.[10]

### THE OYSTER, MOTHER OF THE PEARL

The oyster may well have been tinged by the aura of pearls, which Pliny said "held topmost rank among all things of price." The ancients seem to have held this shellfish in higher esteem than any other sea creature. Seneca singled out oysters and fungi as prodigal pleasures:

The Delights of Antiquity

21. Giuseppe Recco, *Natura morte avec poissons et huitres* (1653). Oil on canvas, 100 × 126 cm. Courtesy of the National-museum, Statens Konstmuseer, Stockholm.

For I had planned my whole life with great resolves. And later, when I returned to the duties of a citizen, I did indeed keep a few of these good resolutions. That is why I have forsaken oysters and mushrooms [boleti] for ever: since they are not really food, but are relishes to bully the sated stomach into further eating, as is the fancy of gourmands and those who stuff themselves beyond their powers of digestion: down with it quickly, and up with it quickly![11]

Their status in antiquity made oysters a royal gift, worthy to be bestowed with truffles on Francis I when he journeyed to the Midi in 1532. A rakish Italian contemporary of Francis I, the writer Pietro Aretino, knew his Seneca, for in playfully expressing gratitude for a gift he described truffles and oysters as "not food, but allurements to the appetite." The physician and humanist Konrad Gesner observed in the mid–sixteenth century, "The palm of tables has long been extended to [oysters], as Pliny wrote." Pliny, Gesner continued, had described oysters

22. Gaspari Traversi, *La Ban-carella del pesce.* Courtesy of the Civici Musei di Storia ed Arte, Trieste.

from various waters and shown certain ones to be the gourmand's choice. Echoing the mocking tone of his Roman model, Gesner scoffed that "so in our age lovers of delicacies fastidiously choose between types of oysters." In Italy Baldassare Pisanelli noted that the oyster, formerly such a delicacy of the ancients, was in demand now on princes' tables. In England Thomas Moffett reported that everybody was eating these shellfish; oysters "justly deserve a full treatise, being so common," and loved by "almost every man." In the early eighteenth century Nicolas Delamare claimed: "The oyster surpasses all other shellfish in goodness, and according to Pliny it is the most delicate morsel of the sea."[12]

Indeed, "there are those who devour fifty and those who eat a hundred oysters at the first course. There are those who eat more," gasped Bruyerin. Saint-Evremond wrote to Ninon de Lanclos in 1698, "At eighty years of age, I eat Oysters every morning." The *Encyclopédie* reported that "every day, in the evening and in the morning, one sees people eating a rather large quantity." In fact, "it is not rare to find people who have

The Delights of Antiquity

swallowed a hundred or even a hundred and fifty oysters . . . which is only the prelude to a very copious dinner."[13]

Many of those oysters were being consumed raw, as the ancients ate them, though warnings by Galen and Athenaeus were often cited. How early this custom of eating raw oysters became stylish is not clear. Platina did not mention it in 1475. An early-sixteenth-century French expanded edition of his work, however, notes that some people eat oysters raw. One finds no indication that the Italians ever shared the French and English passion for this raw food of the ancients. Some people spoke of being brought oysters at a table laid at the shore and of swallowing them as soon as they were opened. Moffett avowed that "onely oisters of all fish are good raw (yet he was no Coward that first ventured on them) being called of Athenaeus the Prologue of the feast, because ever (as we use them) they were eaten foremost." The author of the 1607 *Thrésor de santé* said that oysters were eaten raw "with their liquid in the manner of the ancients." By the mid–eighteenth century Menon would write that oysters "were eaten ordinarily raw."

23. Jacques Linard, *Still Life with Flowers and Oysters* (ca. 1638–42). Oil on canvas, 19⅛″ × 25⅜″. Copyright © Indianapolis Museum of Art, 1986. James E. Roberts Fund and Gift of Dr. and Mrs. G. H. A. Clowes.

Fish                    {83}

24. "Twelve Pence a Peck Oysters," from *The Cryes of the City of London Drawne after the Life*, by Pierce Tempest (London, 1711). Print Collection, Miriam and Ira D. Wallach Division of Art, Prints, and Photographs, The New York Public Library, Astor, Lenox, and Tilden Foundations.

Observations such as this from Delamare had been reinforcing the pattern for two hundred years: "The Romans began their banquets with oysters. The party was complete when plenty of the best kinds were served. . . . The Greeks before the Romans knew the goodness in oysters. They served them raw at all their most important meals, and principally at supper at the beginning of the meal."[14]

ANCIENT LESSONS ON OYSTER CULTIVATION

Pliny was Platina's source for the report that Cicero ironically called some important men "the Fishermen" because they cultivated oysters as a lucrative hobby. The ancients' methods of

The Delights of Antiquity

oyster cultivation were followed into the eighteenth century. Giving his authorities as Pliny, Varro, Columella, Petronius, and Martial, Delamare observed that oysters profited from being moved from one body of water to another, especially to a shallow, sunny spot. "It is, thus, on this basic idea that fishermen still today work the shallowest areas off the coast, and where the sea's waters are able to be channeled in, they build reservoirs or parks, which they fill with oysters to grow large and fat, and of which the best are brought to Paris."[15]

Like other commentators before him, Delamare cited Athenaeus in describing places that yielded the best noncultivated oysters, and he spoke of an oyster merchant who had a fleet of five or six ships to bring in the shellfish from the sea. In 1598 a foreigner traveling near "Queenborough" in Britain observed "the fishing of oysters out of the sea which are no where in greater plenty or perfection." Though the oysters taken in the waters off Italy perhaps did not have the same reputation for quality, Scappi reported a sizable oyster business at Chiozza and Ancona as early as 1570.[16]

Coveting fish beyond all delicacies, heads of households dispatched their servants early to market to get first chance at the fresh catch. Great men, sometimes preparing the catch with their own hands, avowed their esteem for these delicacies. Swallowing raw oysters one after another and devouring an array of saltwater fish on fast days, the new gourmands evaded the church's prescription that bodily pleasures be denied.

## In the Cookbooks

Apicius offers six recipes that call for oysters. The Arabic cookery works, in contrast, do not mention them at all. Though some European cookbooks of the fourteenth century include oysters in a few recipes, they accord them no special

APICIUS (FOURTH CENTURY)
Patina with milk. Soak pine-kernels and let them dry. Have ready fresh, unprepared sea-urchins. Take a shallow pan and arrange in it the following ingredients: hearts of mallows and beets; fully grown leeks; celery sticks; vegetable puree; boiled greens; pieces of chicken cooked in broth; boiled brains; Lucanian sausages; hard-boiled eggs cut in halves; pork sausages stuffed with Terentian sauce cooked and chopped; chicken liver;

fried fillets of hake; jellyfish; oysters without their shells; fresh cheese. Arrange all this in layers. Add the pine-kernels and peppercorns on top and pour over the following sauce: pepper, lovage, celery-seed, asafoetida. Cook. When it is done strain milk into which you mix raw eggs to a smooth mixture. Pour it over the dish. When it is set garnish with the fresh sea-urchins, sprinkle with pepper, and serve.

Embractum Baianum. Put in a saucepan minced oysters, mussels, sea-urchins, chopped toasted pine-kernels, rue, celery, pepper, coriander, cumin, *passum* [reduced wine], *liquamen*, Jericho date, oil.

Source: Apicius, *Roman Cookery Book*, pp. 101, 217.

TWO ENGLISH COOKERY BOOKS (C. 1420)
Oysters in gravy. Take good almond milk, and combine with wine and good fish broth. Set it on the fire and let boil. Throw in cloves, mace, sugar, and powdered ginger, and a few minced parboiled onions. Then take fair oysters and parboil them in fair water, and then cast them together [with the first mixture] and let boil.

Source: *Two Fifteenth-Century Cookery-Books*, 1:13.

CRISTOFORO DI MESSISBUGO (1549)
Make a round pastry, in the same way as you have made for fruit, either small or large according to what you want.

Then take twelve or fifteen oysters, and open them, and take out the good with the water that is inside. Put them into a tin saucepan and fry with fragrant herbs cut small, a little good oil, a little mixed spice, the juice of four oranges or a little verjuice, a very little bit of raisins picked clean of stems, and two egg yolks.

And when everything is done frying, put into a little pot and put on the lid. Cook in an oven that is not too hot.

And if you want to put in two or three slices of lemon, it will not be unsuitable.

Source: Messisbugo, *Banchetti*, p. 130.

status. The Italian *Libro di cucina* contains no recipe that calls for oysters. A century later, however, Platina drew attention to their importance and said they were usually baked in the coals and then might be removed from their shells and fried in oil with spices and verjuice (the juice of unripe fruit, usually grapes) sprinkled on top. Although in 1549 Messisbugo evinced no real

The Delights of Antiquity

interest in oyster cookery—he gave only one recipe—his menus show great platters of oysters scattered throughout. Twenty years later Scappi gave but a handful of recipes for this shellfish, but again platters of oysters appear in the menus. Whether these oysters were raw or cooked he does not say.

As in the case of fungi, the sixteenth-century French cookbooks show no great interest in oysters, again revealing a cultural split between what the humanists were reporting and what

### FRANÇOIS PIERRE DE LA VARENNE (1651)

Fry the fish until they are almost done, and open them along the backbone and take it out. Take roe, oysters, capers, champignons, and truffles, and sauté everything together in a pan with parsley and whole green onions. Stuff your soles with this mixture, and put them to simmer with a little stock, fresh butter, lemon, orange, or verjuice. Simmer bread with any fish stock that you have and like, and garnish it with your soles together with champignons, truffles, roe, and *jus* of champignons. Place lemon slices all around.

*Source:* La Varenne, *Cuisinier français,* p. 152.

### PIERRE DE LUNE (1656)

Fresh molue as a ragout. Scale the fresh molue, and cook it in water and vinegar with a bouquet, green lemon, bay leaf, salt, and pepper, and make your sauce by melting butter until it is brown, adding flour, and then capers, anchovies, oysters, slices of green lemon; add the juice of a lemon and white pepper when serving.

*Source:* Lune, *Cuisinier,* p. 134.

### ROBERT MAY (1660)

Take the greatest oysters you can get, being opened parboil them in their own liquor, save the liquor, and wash the oysters in some water, wipe them dry, and being cold, lard them with eight or ten lardons through each oyster, the lard being first seasoned with cloves, pepper, and nutmeg beaten very small; being larded, spit them on two wooden scuets [skewers], binde them to an iron spit and roast them, baste them with anchove sauce made of some of the oyster liquor, let them drop in it, and being enough, bread them with the crust of a roul [roll] grated, then dish them, blow the fat off the gravy, put it to the oysters, and wring on the juyce of a lemon.

*Source:* May, *Accomplisht Cook,* p. 376.

FRANÇOIS MASSIALOT (1691)

Stuffed oysters. Open and blanch your oysters. Now chop well with parsley, green onion, thyme, salt, pepper, anchovy, and good butter. Moisten a little bit of bread crumbs, and mix in with nutmeg and other sweet spices, and two or three egg yolks. Pound all together. Stuff your oyster shells, and having painted them with egg yolks or sprinkled bread crumbs on the top, put them to cook in the oven on a grill, and serve with no sauce or with lemon juice.

*Source:* Massialot, *Cuisinier roial et bourgeois*, p. 275.

VINCENT LA CHAPELLE (1736)

A young Turkey with Oysters. Pick your Turkey, draw it and singe it neatly, cut the Liver into bits, and put it in a Stew-pan, together with a dozen of Oysters and a bit of Butter, season'd with Salt, Pepper, sweet Herbs, all Spice, Mushrooms, Parsley, Chibbol; let it be a moment over the fire; then stuff your Turkey with these ingredients, and let it be blanch'd a little as before, then spit it, and tie over it bards of Bacon and Paper; meanwhile have a Ragout ready for your Turkey, make it thus: Take three dozen of Oysters and blanch them in boiling water, drain them, take out your Bards, then put in a Stew-pan some Essence of Ham, set it a boiling; skim off the Fat, taste it, and put this with your Oysters into another Pan; When your Turkey is roasted, dish it up, and put your Ragout over it, with the Juice of a Lemon; let it be relishing, and serve it up hot for a Course.

*Source:* La Chapelle, *Modern Cook*, p. 131.

HANNAH GLASSE (1747)

Oyster sauce. Take half a pint of Oysters, put them into a Saucepan with their own Liquor, two or three blades of Mace; let them simmer till they are plump, then with a Fork take out the Oysters, strain the Liquor to them, put them into the Sauce-pan again, with a Gill of White Wine hot, a Pound of Butter rolled in a little Flour, shake the Sauce-pan often, and when the Butter is melted, give it a boil up.

*Source:* Glasse, *Art of Cookery*, p. 188.

the cookbooks specify. The great oyster vogue began in France in the seventeenth century. Now a legion of oysters troop through the cookery works in sauces, ragouts, and stuffings. Oysters are even larded into roasts. The use of oysters reaches its zenith in eighteenth-century England, where they become one of the most important tastes in fashionable food.

# Chapter 6    Flesh

A slab of grilled beef would hardly merit a second glance from Lucullus or any of his fancy friends. And few creatures that flew held the interest of these belly gods in the way a nice, fat fish straight out of the salty sea did. No four-footed beast could compare to a good-looking fungus freshly sprung from the forest floor—that is to say, no beast save one. The common pig, so fecund that it was anything but rare, reeled in the compliments. The ancients considered all pork tasty, though they relished some parts of the pig more than others. Certain morsels were so coveted that sumptuary laws were passed to ban the killing of a beast so that a diner might feast on the jowls or glands alone. In fact, the wealthy ancient would gladly eat the tender organs and cartilaginous and bony parts of many beasts and fling the rest of the carcass away. One might make a good organ even better, this ancient voluptuary thought, by making the small effort to fatten the animal, so that its liver, for example, might melt in the mouth.

## Pork

Hoisting the pig to new heights of culinary status, Renaissance gourmands turned their favor to a meat exalted by the ancients but prohibited by the Muslim world. In 1475 Platina observed that "pork titillates the palate," and Bruyerin remarked that the Greeks and Romans lusted after pigs, which were plentiful among them. Drawing on Cicero and Pliny, he wrote that "pigs are nothing beyond food, and are bestowed by nature only for feasting, as is related by the most ancient and wise philosophers." What else were pigs for but food, since they could neither pull a cart nor carry a pack or a man? One witty ancient sage commented, "The soul was actually given to the pig as salt to preserve the flesh, and because this beast was so suitable for the feeding of man, nature made it the most prolific of her offspring."[1]

Bruyerin, who had traveled in the highest social circles as physician to Henry II, wrote that Frenchmen prized suckling pigs, much as the Romans had loved these tender creatures fed on milk alone. "In our age," he noted, "the tables of the great are enriched with boars. Our nobility put themselves in mortal danger as they zealously hunt them. But the insanity of the gullet rages so, that many judge it better to die than go without this food." Bruyerin felt no less disdain for the ancients' lavish and foolhardy ways. Siding with the saner element of old Rome, he wrote, "Not a few have testified that the Romans used to consume whole boars daily. . . . The satirist Juvenal cries out against customs of this kind." And, continued the sixteenth-century physician, Pliny had observed that wild boar were "a popular luxury" as far back as Cato the Censor, who lived into the second century B.C. A chorus of other humanist voices joined Bruyerin's in reporting the pig as antiquity's favorite quadruped, and a favorite again on Renaissance boards. In late-sixteenth-century England, Moffett characterized pork as "sweet, luscious, and pleasant to wantons," and in the early seventeenth century the French physician Nonnius wrote: "I see that pork is preferred in our age to other meats [for chopped-meat preparations]. When [the chopped pork is] enclosed in an intestine casing with fat and condiments, the [resulting] sausages are considered delicacies." In eighteenth-century France, Delamare observed that the pig "was in such high reputation among the Greeks, that the Historian of their meals and high seasoned dishes, Athenaeus, does not talk about any other so often or in terms so laudatory."[2]

By quoting Pliny's assertion that no other meat was so prevalent in cookshops and that pork had fifty flavors, Bruyerin left his peers with the idea that the possibilities for pork dishes might be almost limitless. He underscored the point in retelling Plutarch's tale about a remarkable experience of the consul

The Delights of Antiquity

Titus Quintius Flaminius. While dining with a friend, the consul expressed amazement at the lavish array of meat his host had provided. The friend confessed that all the meats were really but one—pork, seasoned and prepared in various ways.[3]

Pork, including the fat, came to be so highly esteemed in Renaissance Europe that it was used to season other meat. "In our cities," wrote Bruyerin, "the millers of grain fatten pigs . . . so that . . . they can hardly move. . . . These animals are, in fact, not suitable for food [that is, meat], but they provide the most suitable condiment for other foods." According to Thomas Moffett, Pope Leo X "loved pork so exceedingly" that he would mix "Pork's flesh" with the brawn of peacocks to make his sausages tastier. In the early seventeenth century an Italian writer on household management observed that cooks in the kitchens of society's leaders used pork fat copiously. But by this time, according to Fynes Moryson, the French outdid all others in larding all meats with pork fat; they used so much of it that they took "away all variety of taste, making all meates savor of Porke." Renaissance cooks were moved by the desire to introduce the taste of the pig into the flesh of animals they considered otherwise uninteresting.[4] Today most of us believe that we lard meats only to moisten them, but when we do so we are introducing a characteristic taste of the cooking the French made famous in the seventeenth century.

## TOOTHSOME ORGANS AND OTHER TIDBITS

Because the ancients were wild about entrails and cartilaginous and bony bits such as ears and feet, Renaissance Europe applauded these morsels.[5] Sweetbreads, like truffles, were rediscovered after centuries of neglect. Other items, such as feet, had been in continuous use, as had fungi, although they had not been held in particular cultural esteem.

Renaissance readers relished Athenaeus's descriptions of platters brimming over with crunchy extremities and tender innards. These serving dishes contained "many kinds of meat prepared with water—feet, hands, ears, jawbones . . . guts, tripe and tongue, in accordance with the custom in shops at Alexandria called 'boiled meat shops.'" The diners fed on these luscious bits as they racked their brains to recall who had written of them. Someone thought of Aristophanes for his pertinent passage in the *Masters of the Frying Pan:* "Bring me a piece of liver or a

Flesh

glandule from a young boar, or failing that, a rib or a tongue or a spleen: or fetch me the paunch of a suckling-pig killed in the autumn, with some hot rolls."[6]

At productions of the Roman playwright Plautus's *Captives*, Renaissance audiences could guffaw at the moocher named Ergasibus, who ransacks the kitchen for delicacies the moment his host is called away. What a guest! "In he came and tugged down the meat, rack and all—grabbed a knife and cut out glands [the throat sweetbreads] from three necks of pork."[7]

Whole birds were raised so that the gourmands could nibble on itty-bitty parts. Pliny commented on the decadent folly (which was to become important in France) of Messalinus Cotta, son of the orator Messala, who grilled the soles of the feet of geese and invented dishes that mingled them with cock crests. To ensure that grain would not be wasted in raising animals only to enable gourmands to feed upon the choicest pieces, the Romans had written sumptuary laws against eating, for example, hog's sweetbreads, paunches, testicles, matrix, and cheeks at banquets. Much good these edicts must have done against the voracious desires of a Roman spendthrift, unless, of course, they were enforced by the men Julius Caesar stationed in the markets to seize unauthorized "dainties" or ordered into dining halls to snatch contraband delicacies off the serving dishes set upon the tables.[8]

Plutarch had observed in the first century that somewhere along the way the attitude toward eating brains must have changed, because in his day people enjoyed them, whereas "they say that the ancients did not even eat brains, which is why Homer said, 'I care for him no more than brains,' speaking of brains in this way because they found them revolting and so rejected and discarded them." The Roman emperor Vitellius, a contemporary of Plutarch's renowned for his appetite, created an enormous platter of pheasants' and peacocks' brains mixed with pike livers, flamingo tongues, and lamprey milt, which he had brought together from the corners of the empire.[9]

The second-century physician Galen said that the glands of the tongue, the neck or throat, the breast, the testicles, and the kidneys all "have something in common, and that is they seem to be pleasant and easily chewable." When the mammary glands are filled with milk, they "bring with them something of the sweetness of the milk." The testes of younger animals are more

The Delights of Antiquity

succulent than those of older animals, but the testicles of the fattened cock are the sweetest of all.[10]

These and other ancient passages on delectable morsels of flesh were quoted throughout the Renaissance and early modern literature on food, and helped to change tastes in imitation of antiquity. In 1475 Platina wrote that the feet and crests of birds make "an outstanding dish." Bruyerin claimed that while everything in the pig was eatable, the ancients especially "celebrated the belly, sweetbreads, testicles, womb, liver, and cheeks." Other parts—"hams, ears, feet, ribs, the snout, the backbone, and lastly the blood and intestine [tripe] itself"—had become so popular "within our memory" that "the ears and feet of pigs are seen among us, indeed, as cold foods in the highest honor." Once seated at table, one might find oneself staring into an animal's face. "Calves' heads decorate the splendid tables in great houses . . . ," Bruyerin observed, "and the heads of wethers are tasty both to the attendants of kings and to rustics and commoners." Not only the calf's head but the boar's head "today is the most celebrated of foods." Galen the physician had discussed breasts and testicles in a nonjudgmental manner, saying simply that they were pleasant and succulent, but the moralist in the humanist Bruyerin bridled at his society's delight in such wanton delicacies. Food was not entertainment. Bruyerin scoffed at tony people who patronized the "right" food shops. "I have seen breasts filled with milk offered among the distinguished foods of today's cookshop. The taste setters set high value especially on sow and cow teats." He was disgusted by people who defied medical advice to chase the latest fashion at table. "I have seen today at the most elegant of banquets the brain of certain animals being served: the brain of the goat, calf, and hare, and in fact of many birds and fish even though the most famous physicians have condemned it." Further, "I know the kidneys of calves and other young animals are looked upon favorably as food by some." No doubt that is why Bruyerin provided seventeen chapters on cartilage, tongue, sweetbreads, testicles, kidneys, fat, bone marrow, spine marrow, brain, liver, spleen, lung, heart, stomach, intestines, womb, and blood. To birds in particular he devoted eleven chapters: the neck, the wings, the crest, the stomach, the liver, the brain, the tongue, the stones (testicles), the intestines, and the feet.[11]

Like Bruyerin, Henri Estienne recalled the time in France

when "calves' and mutton feet, the ears and the skin of a suckling pig, capon livers, and the feet, etc. [*abatis*] of geese were thrown away." Bernard Palissy noted that in the past people had shied away from the feet, the head, and the stomach of a sheep, which now were the most esteemed of foods.[12]

At prodigal banquets on the parodic Isle des Hermaphrodites, crests and tongues were in demand. In a wry account of the latest English pleasures in carnal joy, William Harrison told of "Delicate dames" who delighted in serving "stones" (testicles) for "the provocation of fleshly lust." The Scot Fynes Moryson, traveling in Italy at the beginning of the seventeenth century, observed that "the inner parts of Goates (vulgarly Animale) [sweetbreads], and the stones of Rammes and Regles (vulgarly Granella) [testicles], are esteemed great dainties, especially in Toscany, which we cast away, being very good meate fried." Twenty years later, Nonnius reported that sweetbreads were a sought-after delicacy in northern Europe. According to the *Encyclopédie*, cooks made great use of the "*abatis*," which it defined as "the head, the feet, the wings, the liver, and a part of the viscera of a goose, turkey, capon, or other birds." Nevertheless, Delamare said, his own French society could not match the ancients in love of entrails. He acknowledged "that beef palate, all the entrails and intestines of veal, tongues, and sometimes even sheep's foot can be found on the best and the most refined tables for entrées or for ragouts"; but the rest of this sort of thing, he sniffed, was for people who could not afford the best.[13]

## FOIE GRAS

The Renaissance love of foie gras was also linked to the ancients' texts. Porta and Nonnius alluded to passages on fattened liver in Horace, Pliny, Martial, Juvenal, Galen, and Palladius. Observing that fattened pig livers were elegant fare for the Greeks and the Romans, Bruyerin noted that Pliny thought the cramming of sows and geese with figs to enlarge their livers was an invention of Marcus Apicius. Pliny had also explained, continued Bruyerin, that once the liver had been removed from the animal, it was soaked in milk and honey to increase its size still further, a procedure said to have been invented by Scipio, Metellus, or Marcus Seius. Porta offered detailed instructions from Palladius on how to enlarge goose livers, and Francis

The Delights of Antiquity

Bacon, quoting Porta's work, reminds his readers that artificially fattened goose liver was a Roman delicacy. In France, Bruyerin claimed, the fatted cock's or hen's liver was more highly thought of than the liver of a crammed goose, though fifty years later the *Thrésor de santé* called goose liver "a royal dish, of which the Romans also had made much, as reported by Pollux and Athenaeus."[14]

In 1570 Bartolomeo Scappi credited the Jews with creating a business out of the interest in foie gras. Some of the livers they sold, he reported, weighed as much as three pounds. In the late eighteenth century Pierre Le Grand d'Aussy wrote that "the Jews of Metz and of Strasbourg possess the same secret [as did the ancients], though their precise methods we do not know. And the secret is one of the branches of commerce that made them rich. As is well known, Strasbourg makes these livers into pâtés whose reputation is renowned."[15]

## Well Done, Medium, or Rare

In 1560 Bruyerin avowed that he had "more than once" seen "half-cooked meats devoured so that blood almost flowed from the mouths of those who were eating. The leading lights like beef well cooked, though some of them nevertheless devour it bloody after the fashion of the Cyclops. They commend the wether almost raw, but pork cooked until it almost melts [that is, until it falls apart]. And indeed, among winged creatures they eat with pleasure wood pigeons still running with blood and scarcely touched by fire." Bruyerin advocated the middle way, warning that there would be a penalty to pay for eating either half-raw or "melting" meat.[16]

When today we ask for our steak well done, medium, or rare, we are repeating a choice that the Renaissance writers revived from Hippocratic writings. In 1626 Pierre Duchâtel noted the physical reactions to be expected from meat prepared in each of the three ways: "(1) . . . well-boiled meat is suitable to the digestion. Well-roasted meats are more sluggish. (2) . . . those meats that have been medium boiled or medium roasted add moderately to vigor and digestion. (3) . . . rawer meats are conducive to vigor but in fact are rather poor for digestion."[17] Because bloody meat was thought to increase one's vitality and zest, eating half-raw meat became intertwined with the goal of arousing the body at table.

Flesh

25. Alexandre François Desportes, *Volaille, gibier, légumes et
fruits dans une cuisine.* The
Louvre, Paris. Photo by
Musées Nationaux.

## HIGH OR GAMY MEAT

Things were changing fast at the Renaissance table. Fashion
setters crunched on ears; blood from meat nearly oozed from
the mouth; livers silken with fat melted on the tongue; and the
taste for pronouncedly high meat, decomposed to the fine
point just this side of maggoty, so that a smell of he-goat
wafted from it, as Apicius says, was cultivated in France. "The
French alone," Fynes Moryson observed, "delight in mortified
meates." By at least the eighteenth century the stylish English
were more than partial to them, too. Although he considered
himself to be in the new French fashion, Richard Bradley, the
Cambridge botanist, was aghast at the high meat he was now
served. "In many places I have sat down to a Dinner which has
sent me out of the Room by the very smell of it."[18] An article
that appeared in the English journal *Common Sense* and shortly
afterward in the French journal *Pour et contre* ridiculed English-
men who snatched at any change in fashion the Parisians
adopted:

The Delights of Antiquity

My Lord having sagaciously smelt at the Breech of a Rabbit, wiped his Nose, gave a Shrug of some Dissatisfaction, and then informed the Company, that it was not absolutely a bad One, but that he heartily wish'd it had been kept a Day longer; ay, said Sir *Thomas*, with an Emphasis, *a Rabbit must be kept,*—and with the Guts in too, added the Colonel, *or the Devil would not eat it.* Here the Maître D'Hôtel again interposed, and said, that they eat their Rabbits much sooner now, than they used to do at *Paris.*—Are you sure of that, said my Lord, with some Vivacity? Yes, replied the Maître D'Hôtel, the Cook had a Letter about it last Night. I am not sorry for that rejoin'd my Lord, for to tell you the Truth, I naturally love to eat my Meat before it stinks. The rest of the Company, and even the Colonel himself, confess'd the same.[19]

## Chopped Meats

In the sixteenth century the traveler to the Isle des Hermaphrodites satirically noted that "the meats of the first course were so cut, chopped up, and disguised, they were not recogniz-

26. Frans Snyders, *Kochin mit Esswaren.* Wallraf-Richartz-Museum, Cologne. Photo courtesy of the Rheinisches Bildarchiv, Cologne.

Flesh

able."[20] Finely pounded and chopped meat and fish mixtures—sausages, forcemeat balls, stuffings, and other concoctions of that nature—rocketed to new fame because of the interest in the ancients' *insicia, lucanica, farcimina, tomacla,* and other such preparations.

It fell upon the humanists both to discover the delights of antiquity and to attempt to find the defining characteristics of the delicacies, so that they could either reproduce them for contemporary tables or pair them with an existing food. Once a contemporary food had been labeled as one that had also existed in antiquity, it took on new meaning. In 1475 Platina was raising the status of the sausage known as *mortadella* when he called it the *insicia* of the ancients. Another commentator thought that the Italian vernacular for sausage, *salsiccia,* showed that the ancients must have eaten sausages, for it was obvious to him that the Italian word had come from the Latin *salsum* (salty) and *insicium* (chopped meat). In 1548 Francesco Alunno described two kinds of Roman chopped-meat preparations: *lucanica* (which he translated simply as *salsiccia*) and *tomacula* or *tomacla* (which he translated into the vernacular as *tomacella*), made with meat or liver. Moffett called the sausages that Pope Leo X loved his *insicia.*[21]

Under the rubric "Pig" in Konrad Gesner's monumental work on quadrupeds we see the humanist wielding his skills to revive the ancients' tastes. For all of their moral stance and snide remarks about the dainties of the Roman world, the humanists sometimes relaxed their guard and betrayed their fascination with sensual cookery. Gesner's interest in the food of the ancients is palpable. He obviously had tried Platina's recipe for *lucanica* himself, and he urged his readers to try it too, providing them with the recipe. He exhorted them not to miss out on Apicius's Lucanian sausage recipe, either. If by chance a fellow humanist had not yet handled a copy of Platina, he would stumble across the recipes in works where today we would hardly think to look for cooking instructions. In writing what today is seen as an attempt to categorize animals, Gesner became thoroughly engrossed in sorting out the chopped-meat mixtures of antiquity. Moving in and out of passages of the ancients and reviewing Renaissance commentaries on Apicius, he compared descriptions of what he had read with what he found on his own table and in shops in Switzerland. He concluded, "Grammarians explain *Lucanica* as a kind of chopped-

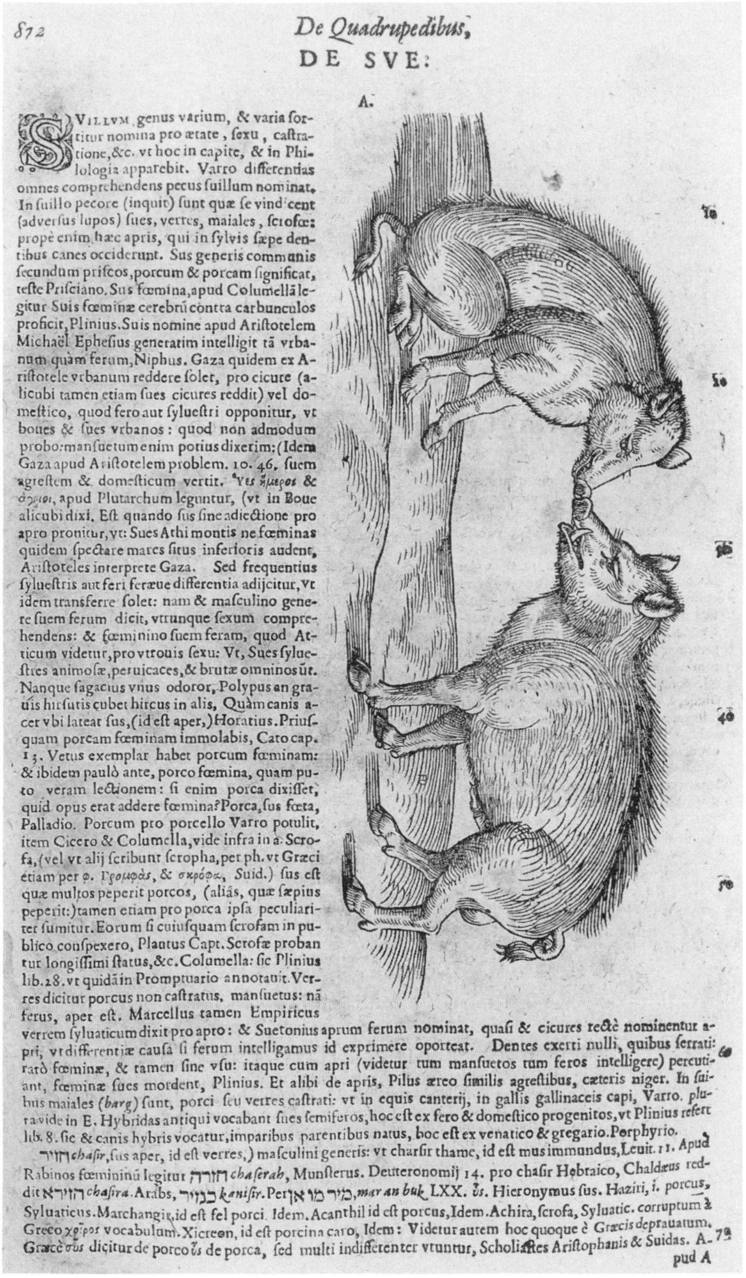
872 *De Quadrupedibus,*

DE SVE:

A.

SVILLVM genus varium, & varia ſortitur nomina pro ætate, ſexu, caſtratione, &c. vt hoc in capite, & in Philologia apparebit. Varro differentias omnes comprehendens pecus ſuillum nominat. In ſuillo pecore (inquit) ſunt quæ ſe vindicent (adverſus lupos) ſues, verres, maiales, ſcrofæ: propè enim hæc apris, qui in ſylvis ſæpe dentibus canes occiderunt. Sus generis communis ſecundum priſcos, porcum & porcam ſignificat, teſte Priſciano. Sus fœmina, apud Columellā legitur. Suis fœminæ cerebrū contra carbunculos proficit, Plinius. Suis nomine apud Ariſtotelem Michaël Epheſius generatim intelligit tā vrbanum quàm ferum, Niphus. Gaza quidem ex Ariſtotele vrbanum reddere ſolet, pro cicure (alicubi tamen etiam ſues cicures reddit) vel domeſtico, quod fero aut ſylueſtri opponitur, vt boues & ſues vrbanos: quod non admodum probo: manſuetum enim potius dixerim: (Idem Gaza apud Ariſtotelem problem. 10. 46. ſuem agreſtem & domeſticum vertit. Ὕες ἥμεροι & ἄγριοι, apud Plutarchum leguntur, (vt in Boue alicubi dixi. Eſt quando ſus ſine adiectione pro apro ponitur, vt: Sues Athi montis ne fœminas quidem ſpectare mares ſitus inferioris audent, Ariſtoteles interprete Gaza. Sed frequentius ſylueſtris aut feri feræue differentia adijcitur, vt idem transferre ſolet: nam & maſculino genere ſuem ferum dicit, vtrunque ſexum comprehendens: & fœminino ſuem feram, quod Atticum videtur, pro vtrouis ſexu: Vt, Sues ſylueſtres animoſæ, peruicaces, & brutæ omnino ſūt. Nanque ſagacius vnus odoror, Polypus an grauis hirſutis cubet hircus in alis, Quàm canis acer vbi lateat ſus, (id eſt aper,) Horatius. Priuſquam porcam fœminam immolabis, Cato cap. 13. Vetus exemplar habet porcum fœminam: & ibidem paulò ante, porco fœmina, quam puto veram lectionem: ſi enim porca dixiſſet, quid opus erat addere fœmina? Porca, ſus fœta, Palladio. Porcum pro porcello Varro potulit, item Cicero & Columella, vide infra in a. Scrofa, (vel vt alij ſcribunt ſcropha, per ph. vt Græci etiam per φ. Γρομφὰς, & σκρόφα, Suid.) ſus eſt quæ multos peperit porcos, (aliâs, quæ ſæpius peperit:) tamen etiam pro porca ipſa peculiariter ſumitur. Eorum ſi cuiuſquam ſcrofam in publico conſpexero, Plautus Capt. Scrofæ probantur longiſſimi ſtatus, &c. Columella: ſic Plinius lib. 28. vt quidā in Promptuario annotauit. Verres dicitur porcus non caſtratus, manſuetus: nā ferus, aper eſt. Marcellus tamen Empiricus verrem ſyluaticum dixit pro apro: & Suetonius aprum ferum nominat, quaſi & cicures rectè nominentur apri, vt differentiæ cauſa ſi ferum intelligamus id exprimere oporteat. Dentes exerti nulli, quibus ſerrati: rarò fœminæ, & tamen ſine vſu: itaque cum apri (videtur tum manſuetos tum feros intelligere) percutiant, fœminæ ſues mordent, Plinius. Et alibi de apris, Pilus æreo ſimilis agreſtibus, cæteris niger. In ſuibus maiales (*barg*) ſunt, porci ſeu verres caſtrati: vt in equis canterij, in gallis gallinaceis capi, Varro. *plura vide in* E. Hybridas antiqui vocabant ſues ſemiferos, hoc eſt ex fero & domeſtico progenitos, vt Plinius refert lib. 8. ſic & canis hybris vocatur, imparibus parentibus natus, hoc eſt ex venatico & gregario. Porphyrio.

חזיר *chaſir*, ſus aper, id eſt verres,) maſculini generis: vt charſir thame, id eſt mus immundus, Leuit. 11. Apud Rabinos fœmininū legitur חזירה *chaſerah*, Munſterus. Deuteronomij 14. pro chaſir Hebraico, Chaldæus reddit חזירא *chaſira*. Arabs, כנזיר *kaniſir*. Per. מר אן בוך *mar an buk* LXX. ὗς. Hieronymus ſus. Haziri, *i. porcus*, Syluaticus. Marchangir, id eſt fel porci. Idem. Acanthil id eſt porcus, Idem. Achira, ſcrofa, Syluatic. corruptum à Græco χοῖρος vocabulum. Xicreon, id eſt porcina caro, Idem: Videtur autem hoc quoque è *Græcis deprauatum*. Græcè σῦς dicitur de porco ὗς de porca, ſed multi indifferenter vtuntur, Scholiaſtes Ariſtophanis & Suidas. Apud A

27. Pigs, from Konrad Gesner, *Historiae animalium* (Tigur, 1558), p. 872. Courtesy of the Division of Rare and Manuscript Collections, Carl A. Kroch Library, Cornell University.

meat preparation first invented by the *Lucanians.* It is our bratwurst."[22]

Gesner noted, too, the term *botulus* (diminutive *botellus*) in Martial, which he described as a kind of mixture made from chopped pork. "Certain people judge that the name comes from the word *bolus* (choice bit, that is, choice bits of meat)."

Gesner provided Apicius's recipe for *botellus*, which was made not from meat or fat but from blood, and pointed to similar products of his own day: "Our intestines filled with blood are called *rosswurst*, or *bluswurst*. . . . Those that contain blood in addition to brain and chopped pork fat and are seasoned with spices are called *Weckerling*. Also pig's paunch, which is either cut in oblong pieces or cut up into very tiny pieces, and mixed together with [other] similarly cut meat, salt, caraway, and pepper and then stuffed into the large intestine, is called *schuling* or *magenwurst*."[23]

It is clear that the humanists could easily relate *lucanica* to the sausages of Europe. Some Renaissance philologists had more trouble with *insicia*. What were those chopped-meat mixtures that were not shaped like sausages? In reviewing Renaissance commentators of Apicius, Gesner dismissed their opinions on *insicia*. Working through Apicius carefully, he decided the key characteristic of *insicia* was that the meat was pounded after it was cut up. Apicius, wrote Gesner, "directs that the pounded flesh be molded into *insicia*. Stuck together in a mass, they are easily shaped with the hands into any form you may want. . . . They were eaten either fresh or smoked, as is made clear in Apicius."[24] But Gesner made no connection between these free-form pounded meat mixtures and anything he knew, as he had done for sausages.

Some of Nonnius's contemporaries, he said, believed that the third-century Roman emperor Heliogabulus, "that biggest spend-thrift of all, first gave these new delicacies to the world. . . . He first made *insicia* from fish, from ordinary oysters and smooth-shell oysters, and other kinds of shellfish of this sort—from lobsters, and sea crabs, and prawns." But Nonnius thought that fish *insicia* were being prepared before Heliogabulus, for he believed that the Apicius text preceded the emperor. Its Book II contains *insicia* recipes for sea crab, lobster, squid, cuttlefish, sea crayfish, scallop, and oyster. *Insicia* were to be reborn in Europe. A tradition grew up in Renaissance Europe of forcemeat or pounded fish balls (quenelles) and various pâtés of chopped meat. Nonnius emphasized that these chopped-meat mixtures were gullet teasers "rather than healthy food," and he was shocked to see that chopped-fish mixtures "were also creeping into diets for the sick."[25]

Succumbing to the ancients' passion for the pig, Renaissance Europe reveled with Pliny's compatriots in the parts of the

The Delights of Antiquity

animal proscribed by the sumptuary laws of antiquity. Adhering to the ways of their mentors, Renaissance men had their animals force-fed so that they might pluck huge, fattened livers from their bodies. Their pigs were behemoths, so larded with coveted fat that they were almost unable to walk. The cooks chopped and pounded and experimented until they felt they were truly preparing Heliogabulus's *insicia* or Martial's *lucanica*. In their quest to change cultures, people took pleasure in what had given pleasure to their ancient models. Overcoming an initial uneasiness, they put bloody meat in their mouths and devoured it like animals in the wild.

## In the Cookbooks

Pork appears repeatedly in the cookbooks. Apicius, the cookery texts of the High Middle Ages, those of the Renaissance and early modern period—all carry recipes for the flesh of swine. Indeed, it is difficult to tell from the cookery works alone that pork had taken on a new status. The cookbooks also disclose almost no information on high meat or the choices for roasted meats—rare, medium, well done.

But the cookbooks confirm the increase in the use of entrails and chopped meats and the reappearance of foie gras.

Apicius's text is full of chopped and pounded specialties. Its Book II is devoted to this form, for both meat and fish, and in

APICIUS (FOURTH CENTURY)
*Insicia* of squill or large prawns. The prawns or squills are taken out of their shells and pounded in a mortar with pepper and best *liquamen*, and rissoles formed from the meat.

*Insicia* in a caul. Chop up meat and pound with white bread without crust which has been steeped in wine. At the same time pound pepper, *liquamen*, and, if you like, seeded myrtle-berry. Make little forcemeat balls, inserting pine-kernels and peppercorns. Wrap in sausage-skin and cook gently in *caroenum* [reduced wine].

*Minutal Apicianum:* Oil, *liquamen*, wine, leeks with their white part, mint, small fish, tiny meat-balls, testicles of capons, sweetbread of sucking-pig. Let all this cook together. Pound pepper, lovage,

Flesh

fresh coriander or coriander seed, moisten with *liquamen*, add a little honey and some of the cooking liquor, blend with wine and honey, bring to the boil. When it boils crumble pastry into it to bind. Stir well. Sprinkle with pepper and serve.

Peeled cucumbers, another method. Stew with boiled brains, cumin and a little honey, celery seed, *liquamen*, and oil. Bind with eggs, sprinkle with pepper, and serve.

Grilled kidneys with the fat surrounding them: Cut them open, stretch them, and stuff them with ground pepper, pine-kernels and very finely chopped coriander, also ground fennel-seed. Then close the kidneys, sew together, wrap in sausage-skin and brown in oil and *liquamen*; afterwards roast in the oven [*clibanus*] or grill.

*Source:* Apicius, *Roman Cookery Book*, pp. 61, 65, 77, 113, 167.

other books *insicia*, or forcemeat balls, are found in casserole-like dishes.

The Arabs may have inherited this form of preparation from the Greco-Roman world. It is a dominant stylistic characteristic of both "A Baghdad Cookery Book" and the Hispanic-Moorish text. Though Europe borrowed heavily from the Arabs' food in the High Middle Ages, it evinced little interest in their finely chopped meat concoctions, except for such items as blancmange, which was made of pounded chicken and perhaps gilded kabobs.[26] The meat cuts that dominate the cookbooks of Italy, France, and England before the impact of the ancients are either largish sections of the carcass (our roasts), fowl cut up into their various

LE MÈNAGIER DE PARIS (FOURTEENTH CENTURY)
Stuffed piglet. . . . Hard boil twenty eggs. Peel some chestnuts cooked in water. Then take the yolks of the eggs, chestnuts, delicate old cheese, and meat from a cooked pork leg. Chop. Then pound with saffron and a great deal of ginger. Moisten with egg yolks if too solid.

*Source:* Ménagier de Paris, p. 226.

TWO ENGLISH COOKERY BOOKS (C. 1420)
Golden apples [gilded kabobs]
Take filets of raw pork and grind them well. Add salt and powdered pepper. Then take the white of eggs and put them in.

The Delights of Antiquity

> [The pork mixture] should be so firm that it may be roasted on a spit. Make the [kabobs] round as an apple. . . . Some people boil them in fresh broth and then spit them. [If you use this method], cool [the pork kabobs] before spitting them. Gild them with egg yolks mixed with the juice of hazel leaves.
>
> *Source: Two Fifteenth-Century Cookery-Books*, p. 38.

members, or meat cut into pieces—sometimes small but not finely chopped like our ground meat, although there are some sausage preparations. The interest in ground-meat mixtures increases in the writings of Platina (1475) and Messisbugo (1549). By 1570 Scappi was offering a profusion of these concoctions for the stuffing of various organs, pasta, and pastry, for all kinds of forcemeat balls, and for many sausages. The renowned quenelles and pâtés of France developed from this vogue.

BARTOLOMEO PLATINA (1475)

Parts of a cock in pastry. Cut the crests of a young fowl into three pieces and the liver into four and leave the testicles whole. Dice fatty salt pork and do not pound. Cut up very small two or three ounces of soft veal fat, or in place of the fat, beef or veal marrow. Take as much ginger, cinnamon, sugar as is necessary. And mix these with about 40 dried sour cherries. Place in pastry, which is most suitably made from flour. This can be cooked in the oven or under a covering in the hearth. When it is half cooked, pour over two beaten egg yolks, a little saffron and verjuice.

Calf's brain. From the cooked head take the brain and mix it together with two egg yolks well beaten, a little pepper, a little verjuice and enough salt. When all these things have been combined, place in a pan with *liquamen* and fry just until set, which is a short time. This food ought to be served quickly because when it is cold there is nothing more tasteless. It is for this dish that Palellus invites me frequently to dinner, where he prepares the dish in the same way.

*Source:* Platina, *De honesta voluptate*, bk. VI.

BARTOLOMEO SCAPPI (1570)

To make a pastry of veal sweetbreads. Immediately on killing a calf take out the sweetbreads and wash them well, taking off that blood which very often encircles them. Choose the best part,

Flesh

and cut in pieces the size of an egg, and sprinkle them with pepper, cinnamon, cloves, and nutmeg. Now take fatty and lean ham as well as beef marrow or the pounded fat that surrounds a veal kidney and cut in dice. Having prepared a large or small pastry rectangle according to the quantity of sweetbreads that there are, put in the bottom the beef marrow or pounded kidney fat and part of the ham; now put in the sweetbreads and cover with the rest of the ham mixture. Add gooseberries, verjuice berries, or raisins. Your choice will depend on the season. Cover the pastry and cook in the oven, and serve hot. If you want the pastry with a sauce, make it with raw egg yolks, sugar, pale verjuice, and if you have none, put in gooseberries, whole verjuice berries, or raisins. . . . In place of beef or pounded kidney fat, you can line the bottom of the pastry shell with a composition of *cervellata* or fine sausage meat in the autumn. And in the winter you may add raw cleaned truffles and in the spring *prugnuoli* [fungi] to the sweetbread pastry.

*Source:* Scappi, *Opera*, p. 338v.

Apicius's Book VII is devoted to "*polyteles*," expensive or sumptuous items. More than half of the recipes in this section are for wombs, skin, fillets, ribs, trotters, udders, livers, stomachs, kidneys, and lungs. This is the same section where the fungi and bulbs appear. Apicius has twenty-one recipes calling for brain, two for sweetbreads, and one for kidney. "A Baghdad Cookery Book" makes no mention of entrails or extremities except for one recipe for sheep's tripe and one calling for chicken livers and crops. The Hispanic-Moorish text—which, like "A Baghdad Cookery Book," is most concerned with red meat, mainly lamb and mutton—gives about the same attention to entrails as the Baghdad work does. It mentions brains twice, sweetbreads and kidneys three times each.[27]

In fourteenth- and fifteenth-century Italy, France, and England, brains, sweetbreads, and crests are very rarely mentioned. The *Libro di cucina*, for example, has one mention of brains—as a substitute for another ingredient. Occasionally the head may be called for, but the brains are not mentioned and perhaps were removed, as they are today when headcheese is made. At the beginning of the fifteenth century we see a change in the work of Platina, and by the time Scappi published his cookbook the new interest in viscera had become a strong current, soon to be taken up by the French and English.

The Delights of Antiquity

Among organs foie gras has become perhaps the most cele-brated. Any attempt to discuss this delicacy in the Italian cook-books involves a semantic problem. Latin has basically two ways of denoting liver, *jecur* and *ficatum*, the latter derived from the custom of feeding pigs and geese figs (*fici*) to fatten their livers. Apicius generally uses *jecur* for animal livers but twice employs *ficatum*, presumably to indicate a crammed liver. The Italian *fegato* comes from the Latin *ficatum* and so implies a fattened liver. Yet *fegato* has come to mean simply liver, and there is no reason to suspect that it did not have this meaning in the fourteenth century. The French and English cookbooks of that time do not pose a language obstacle: the only words that appear are

28. Jean-Baptiste Oudry, *Le Pate* (1743). Oil on canvas, 69½″ × 48½″. Courtesy of the Fine Arts Museums of San Francisco, Mildred Anna Williams Collection.

Flesh

"foie" in the French and "liver" in the English, with no adjective attached to indicate a fattened liver.

Again we see Platina start the discussion, but a commitment to fattened livers is not apparent in the sixteenth-century Italian cookbooks. Foie gras enters the French cookery works with La Varenne, and although the English books occasionally refer to

FRANÇOIS PIERRE DE LA VARENNE (1651)
Take your *beatilles*, which are crests, kidneys, and wings of pigeons. Cook them well, then season, and put them aside to drain. Take some eggs from which you have taken out more than half of the whites and beat them. Once they are well beaten, put in your *beatilles*.

Foie gras as a ragout. Choose the fattest and lightest-colored livers, clean them and throw them into hot water to take away the bitter taste, but take them out immediately. When you have wiped them off, put them into the pan and let them simmer with a little stock, parsley, and a whole onion. Once cooked, take out the onion and serve the sauce well bound. You may add truffles, fungi, and asparagus.

*Source:* La Varenne, *Cuisinier françois*, p. 92.

FRANÇOIS MASSIALOT (1691)
Beyond the part that cocks' crests play in the best ragouts and in *bisques*, they are also used as a dish on their own for an entremets, above all when they are stuffed either with foie gras or with champignons or morels, but also simply as they are.

There are a legion of different kinds of forcemeat. . . . We have seen, for example, . . . how one composes that for croquettes, veal and mutton chops, turkeys, shoulders of meat. . . .

*Source:* Massialot, *Cuisinier roial et bourgeois*, pp. 226, 249.

HENRY HOWARD (1726)
Stake Florendine. Take a Leg or a Neck of Mutton, cut it into Stakes; season it with Nutmeg, Pepper, and Salt: Put it into a Dish with three or four Shalots, a bunch of sweet Herbs, two or three Anchovies, twenty Balls of Forcemeat, half a Pint of Claret, as much fair Water; put in half a pound of Butter, cover it with Puff-paste; bake it.

*Source:* Howard, *England's Newest Way*, p. 22.

The Delights of Antiquity

VINCENT LA CHAPELLE (1736)
Pottage of Profitrolles with Crawfish. You must force your
Loaves, and boil your Crusts . . . ; put into a Stew-pan some
Cocks-combs and Sweetbreads, with some Mushrooms, Trufles
and Craw-fish Tails, Artichoke Bottoms, and a Bunch of sweet
Herbs, add some good Veal Gravy, and let it sweat gently; take
off all the Fat, and put to it a Cullis of Crawfish. . . . [Y]our
Crusts being boil'd in the dish you intend to serve the Pottage
up in, put the eight small Loaves in order upon your Crusts,
with the Artichoke Bottoms between each Loaf; garnish the rim
of your dish with Cocks-combs and Sweetbreads cut in long
pieces. Observe that your Ragout and Cullis of Crawfish be well
tasted, and not too thick; throw it on your Pottage, and serve
it hot.

*Source:* La Chapelle, *Modern Cook*, 1:42.

HANNAH GLASSE (1748)
To Force Cock's Combs. Parboil your Cock's Combs, then open
them with the point of a knife at the Grate-end; take the white
of a Fowl, as much Bacon, and Beef-marrow, cut these small, and
beat them fine in a Marble Mortar; Season them with Salt,
Pepper, and grated Nutmeg, and mix it up with an Egg; fill the
Combs and stew them in a little strong Gravy softly for half an
Hour; then slice in some fresh Mushrooms, and a few pickled
ones; then beat up the Yolk of an Egg in a little Gravy, stirring
it; season with Salt. When they are enough, dish them up in
little dishes or Plates.

*Source:* Glasse, *Art of Cookery*, p. 55.

it, the crammed goose liver becomes a motif from antiquity almost totally identified with France, as is the case with meat pâtés
(meats wrapped in pastry), spurred by a passage in Apicius.[28]

By the seventeenth and eighteenth centuries the whole gamut
of prestigious meat concoctions and body parts had entered the
composed dishes first of France, then of England.

# CHAPTER 7    Garden Produce

*I*t was obvious to anyone who pored over the ancients' texts that they honored gardening. Horticulture was a proper and moral activity—moral, that is, unless gardeners dug and hoed to provide delicacies for wantons both in and out of season. Pliny, a feisty favorite of many humanists, turned up his nose at some extremely lucrative crops. If beasts were chary of thistles, why did the Romans eat them? So many dainties were available in the market that no one needed to waste time on such stuff. Nature brought forth perfectly good asparagus in the wild, yet Romans yearned for cultivated varieties.

Sneering voices such as Pliny's led the lords of Renaissance villas—and the erudite humanists in their employ—directly to frowned-upon delicacies of the ancient garden. As a result, asparagus and two thistles, artichokes and cardoons, were once again cultivated. Renaissance gardens became mirrors of the ancients' plots. Lords demanded many varieties of cabbages dear to antiquity and various members of the genus Allium, the onion family. They looked with fresh eyes at common parsley. They changed the landscape of the manor by their vast plantings of fruit and nut trees to provide for Martial's dessert table. Humanists such as Porta, heavily dependent on the advice of the Roman agronomists and other ancients, aided the Renaissance virtuosi gardeners. The revival of horticulture was spurred

29. "Carduus vulgaris," from *Historia generalis plantarum*, by Jacques Dalechamps (Lyon, 1587), 2:1439. Courtesy of the History of Science Collections, Cornell University Library.

*CARDVVS Vulgaris, Matthioli.*

by imitation of antiquity before economic considerations entered the picture.

## THISTLES: ARTICHOKES AND CARDOONS

Pliny was instrumental in putting the thistle on the European table after centuries of neglect.

> It might be thought that all the vegetables of value had now been mentioned, did not there still remain an extremely profitable article of trade, which must be mentioned not without a feeling of shame. The fact is it is well known that at Carthage and particularly at Cordova crops of thistles [*cardui*] yield a return of 6000 sesterces from small plots—since we turn even the monstrosities of the earth to purposes of gluttony, and actually grow vegetables which all four-footed beasts without exception shrink from touching. . . . They are also preserved . . . so that there may be no day without thistles for dinner.[1]

Only two of the thistles that entered the European diet in the Renaissance became prominent—the artichoke and the cardoon. At the end of the fifteenth century Ermolao Barbaro wrote that "there is no magnificent . . . meal without [thistles]." Prospero Calano echoes Barbaro: "Because the artichoke figures frequently among delicacies of the palate, not a magnificent or solemn banquet takes place which lacks them." A Frenchman commented that artichokes "are reputed to be an exquisite food." One of Pierre de Ronsard's odes includes artichokes in a dream meal, and on the fictional Isle des Hermaphrodites they are served at feasts. In 1549 Catherine de' Medici was feted at a dinner where twelve dozen artichokes were consumed. In 1575 the queen became ill "from eating too many artichoke bottoms, cock crests, and kidneys, which she was crazy about." Bruyerin had cried, "It is agreed that artichokes were especially sought out and pricy long ago. There is no doubt that these hideous things are also worth a great deal now, in our age. Christians have turned them into food for gluttony, which cannot be said without shame." Seeking to mock King Lent, Rabelais said, "If he spat, it was basketfuls of artichokes." Rabelais was again being derisive when he had the "Gastrolaters" sacrifice artichokes "to their Ventripotent Gods."[2]

At the end of the fifteenth century artichokes were not

The Delights of Antiquity

always available in Italy. Barbaro observed that they were served only if "neither place nor time stands in the way." The artichoke, he wrote, "has not yet crept into Venice. Only one of this kind of plant is to be seen and that in the foreign gardens in the Moorish quarter." In the mid–sixteenth century Andrea Mattioli called the cardoon the most popular thistle in Italy, and by the 1580s Baldassare Pisanelli reported that cardoons were being grown all over Italy.[3]

By the sixteenth century the artichoke had clearly become the predominant thistle. About 1530 a French observer noted that "gardens [are] at present filled with them. . . . Indeed, I see not only the kitchens of princes loaded with them but also those of rustic and common people." Emmanuel Le Roy Ladurie has sketched their spread through France. From "1532 beds of artichokes are mentioned in Avignon by the *notaires;* from the main seat they diffuse into the market towns of the Comtat: artichokes at Cavaillon in 1541, at Châteauneuf-du-Pape in 1553, and at Orange in 1554. . . . Toward 1580 Languedoc in turn started cultivating them." In the 1580s artichoke cultivation accelerated. "Artichokes in the garden of the sexton, of the archdeacon, of Miss de Roques, at the forefront of gluttony; artichokes soon in the kitchen garden of the bourgeoisie: around 1640–1670 *l'artichaudière'* [a section set aside for artichokes] make up a quarter or a third of a Languedoc kitchen garden. Soon the artichoke is cultivated in the open field, which one encounters at Toulouse in 1640."[4]

In England the interest in artichokes dates from at least the time of Henry VIII. Toward the end of the sixteenth century Moffett wrote that "artichokes grew sometimes onely in the Isle of Sicil . . . and since my remembrance they were so dainty in England, that usually they were sold for crownes a peice; now industry and skill hath made them so common, that the poorest man is possessed of Princes dainties."[5]

By the 1620s the thistle production of western Europe far outdistanced that of ancient Cordova and Carthage. Nonnius observed: "In our age they are held in the highest culinary honor, and so in a very few years they have grown with manifold offspring, so that while in the age of Ermolao Barbaro they were seen only in a single garden in Venice, now they have taken over not only Italy and Spain, but also France, Germany, and Britain."[6] The cardoon had surpassed the artichoke and was the more widely available thistle of sixteenth-century Italy, but

*CARDVVS Altilis, Cynara sine capitibus acuta, Dod.*

30. "Carduus altilis," from *Historia generalis plantarum,* by Jacques Dalechamps (Lyon, 1587), 2:1440. Courtesy of the History of Science Collections, Cornell University Library.

CYNARA Non aculeata, Matthioli.

31. "Cynara non aculeata," from *Historia generalis plantarum,* by Jacques Dalechamps (Lyon, 1587), 2:1439. Courtesy of the History of Science Collections, Cornell University Library.

artichokes were also ubiquitous there by the end of the next century.

The *Encyclopédie méthodique* (1787) shows the scale of the artichoke grower's business in France by the second half of the eighteenth century: "The town of Laon . . . is able to produce in all 60,000 artichoke heads, not counting the small ones, of which 30,000 to 40,000 are brought to Paris, the rest being for Laon, Rheims, Châlons-sur-Marne, and Troyes. Paris receives a great quantity besides from its vicinity and Chauny and Noyon, but always under the name of artichokes of Laon."[7]

The large network of artichoke nurseries allowed Voltaire, off in Switzerland, to buy artichoke suckers and start a bed of his own, so that like the gourmands Pliny described, he never had to go a day without thistles. Voltaire wrote to Elie Bertrand, "I beg you to accept my thanks for admitting me to your Agricultural Society. My kitchen garden merits this place, if I do not. In the middle of winter I eat the best artichokes and all the best vegetables."[8]

The humanists gave credence to the idea that Renaissance society ate the same thistles as the ancients. Late in the fifteenth century Barbaro identified the artichoke as Pliny's *carduus,* and later Charles Estienne echoed his argument that its ancient name had been corrupted by the Arabs: "The *cinara* is a kind of cultivated *carduus* of which we eat the topmost fruit (which the Greeks call *scolymos,* and the Latins *strobilum*), because its prickly husk or seed capsule is like a pine nut. And in fact Hippocrates calls this fruit *cocalum,* to which word the Arabic article was prefixed, and so it was called *alcocalus.* Then, in fact, the article was corrupted and the word became *articocalus,* commonly *artichault* [artichoke]."[9]

Mattioli identified the cardoon with a thistle that Theophrastus had discussed "in chapter IV of Book VI of his *History of Plants.*" Mattioli cited Theophrastus as saying that the cardoon grew only in Sicily. Those thistles had wide leaves that were peeled before they were eaten and they had a rather bitter taste. Cardoons, "preeminent among domesticated varieties" of thistles in Italy, continued Mattioli, were taken from Sicily to Naples and thence to Tuscany. They "are blanched and made tender with considerable skill and served for the most part today at the end of the meal inasmuch as they are eaten raw with pepper and salt as the last food."[10]

Mattioli told his readers also how to go about eating an

The Delights of Antiquity

artichoke: "When one wants to eat the fruit, the downy seeds [the choke] . . . are cleaned out, and that which remains [the artichoke bottom], which is similar to the brain of palms [hearts of palm], is eaten." He noted various types of artichokes seen around Italy: "spiny, serrated, and open and nonspiny, round, long, open, and closed."[11]

## ASPARAGUS

Jacques Dalechamps compared the ancient gourmand's love of asparagus with that of his sixteenth-century contemporaries. "Gluttons made use of these young thyrsi for the pleasures of the gullet and gave first prize to those of Ravenna, which still enjoys the glory today." Asparagus, he wrote, "is amongst the delicacies of princes." At the end of the century Thomas Moffett claimed that asparagus was on every table: "Asparagus was in old time a meat for such Emperours as *Julius Caesar:* now every boord is served with them." Michel Bicais claimed in 1669 that all the wonderful attributes of asparagus "obliged the ancients to ferret them out greedily, and to attach a price to them, or to make them into something divine." John Parkinson wrote in 1629 that "the first shootes or heads of Asparagus are a Sallet of as much esteeme with all sorts of persons, as any whatsoever . . . and are almost wholly . . . for the pleasure of the pallate." The earl of Bedford's household bills for 1658 show a boosted consumption of vegetables in general and of asparagus in particular. The steep outlay for asparagus mirrors the expense he incurred for fish, especially for Colchester oysters.[12]

When Pliny scoffed at Ravenna's luxurious domestic asparagus —he preferred the wild varieties, especially those that grew on "the plains of upper Germany" and on "the island of Nisita off the coast of Campania . . . deemed far the best asparagus there is"—the humanists got the message that this green spear grew all around them for the taking. In imitation of Pliny, Platina claimed that the uncultivated varieties were preferable. Bruyerin wrote that the spears came forth abundantly in mountainous regions in France. At the end of the sixteenth century John Gerard, observing that "the ancients have set forth two sortes of Sperage: the garden and the wild Sperage," provided his readers with specific instructions for finding the wild plant in England.[13]

Asparagus may well have first been cultivated in modern

32. "Cactus," from *Historia generalis plantarum,* by Jacques Dalechamps (Lyon, 1587), 2:1438. Courtesy of the History of Science Collections, Cornell University Library.

Garden Produce

{113}

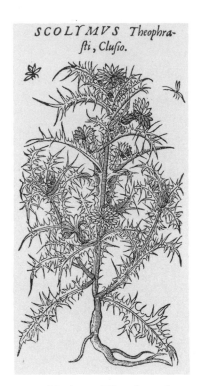

33. "Scolymus Theophrasti,"
from *Historia generalis plantarum*,
by Jacques Dalechamps (Lyon,
1587), 2:1438. Courtesy of the
History of Science Collections,
Cornell University Library.

times somewhere in Italy, though Georges Gibault found the first mention of its cultivation in the Renaissance in a 1469 description of a kitchen garden in Douai. Whether or not the asparagus was cultivated first in France, by the mid–sixteenth century it was being grown all over Italy, according to Mattioli. Asparagus does not seem to have been in English gardens as early as artichokes. But England's first book devoted to gardening (1568)—based, according to its author, on Pliny, Cato, Columella, Varro, Dioscorides, and other ancient sources— included instructions for raising asparagus as well as artichokes.[14]

Asparagus-producing regions in France, such as Epinay, Bezons, and Argenteuil, were already commercial producers of considerable size by at least the eighteenth century. The 1787 *Encyclopédie méthodique* says that Aubervilliers was "able to furnish Paris in a normal year 28,000 to 32,000 bunches of asparagus." The vintners around Orleans planted asparagus among the grapevines.[15]

Both domestic and wild spears were for sale in England. John Parkinson reported in 1640 that "the poore people doe gather the buddes or young shootes, and sell them in the markets of Bristow, much cheaper than our garden kind is sold at London." Retail greengrocers and markets such as Covent Garden offered asparagus, while pedlars hawked "ripe speragas" in the streets. One day Alexander Pope set out to buy a bunch of those green spears.

> At early Morn, I to the Market Haste,
> (Studious in ev'ry Thing to please they taste:)
> A curious Fowl and Sparagus I chose,
> (For I remembered you were fond of those).[16]

The forcing of asparagus and other vegetables was stimulated by the feats of antiquity. Athenaeus

recalled what the witty Aristophanes said in *The Seasons* when he praised the fair city of Athens in these lines: "You will see in midwinter, cucumbers, grapes, fruit. . . . You can see baskets of figs and of myrtle-berries together, covered with snow, and what is more, they sow cucumbers at the same time with turnips, so that nobody knows any longer what time of the year it is. . . . A very great boon, if one may get throughout the year whatever he wants."[17]

The Delights of Antiquity

Not to be outdone, the seventeenth-century French master gardener Jean de La Quintinie advised: "In case there be hot Beds, during the great Colds you may expect Novelties, Viz. Green Asparagus." Evelyn mocked the dandies who demanded fruits and vegetables out of season. Still, he shared with his readers information supplied by the *Transactions of the Royal Society* on how to force asparagus.[18]

SCOLYMVS Dioſcoridis, Cynara ſilueſtris, Pena.

## PARSLEY, ONIONS, AND GARLIC

Parsley, garlic, and onions, unlike artichokes and asparagus, had never fallen into neglect, but now their prominence in ancients' texts boosted their status.

In 1560 Bruyerin reported seeing parsley "swimming" in broths or sauces—a figure of speech that Pliny had also employed. Porta quoted Pliny directly: "Parsley is universally popular for sprigs of it are found swimming in draughts of milk everywhere in the country, and in condiments it enjoys a popularity all its own." Galen, too, had described parsley as "the most common and used condiment."[19]

In the sixteenth century it became a prime seasoning, used either cooked or raw, with boiled or roast meat, grilled fish, and eggs, and in a multitude of other preparations. In 1587 Pisanelli wrote that parsley was being used, as it had been in antiquity, "in almost all dishes that demand the seasoning of odoriferous and tasty herbs. Quite truthfully, because this herb is so much preferred to the others and enters into so many sauces, soups, stocks, dips, and all other condiments, it seems that we cannot cook without parsley." In England Henry Buttes agreed. By the end of the seventeenth century *L'Art de bien traiter* complained that chopped parsley was used too much; it advised readers to leave this herb for the parrots.[20]

34. "Scolymus Dioscoridis," from *Historia generalis plantarum*, by Jacques Dalechamps (Lyon, 1587), 2:1438. Courtesy of the History of Science Collections, Cornell University Library.

## THE ONION FAMILY: THE "BULBS" OF THE ANCIENTS?

The ancients loved to eat bulbs, and they often used only the generic term to refer to these morsels dug out of the ground. But when the ancients wrote about bulbs, borrowing from one another's writings, they often were ignorant of what an author in an earlier century had included among "bulbs." Some

Garden Produce

35. *Artischocke auf dreibeinigem Glutherd, Grünspecht und Wasserzuber mit Karpfen.* Oil on canvas, 54.5 × 73 cm. Courtesy of the Öffentliche Kunstsammlung Basel, Kunstmuseum.

thought that tulips, hyacinths, and lilies were edible bulbs. Others called all members of the genus Allium—what we now know as onion, garlic, chives, and so on—"bulbs." Renaissance humanists reflected this confusion, but nevertheless often took an emphatic stand, connecting the ancient "bulb" with something they knew. Charles Estienne wrote in 1536 that the Greeks called *bulbus* what "in Latin is called *Ascalonitas*, which is retained in the vernacular [French] name *eschalottes* [shallots]." The Italian physician Mattioli, however, insisted that a bulb was one thing and an onion another:

> There have been those [in our time] who think that the bulbs were the common shallots, or those onions which are very similar to them, called by us in Tuscany *cipolle maligie* [a type of very strong elongated onion]. But it is demonstrable that they are wrong. It may be seen in Theophrastus's *History of Plants*, Book IV, Chapter VII, that he numbers shallots and *Cipolle Maligie*, which he calls *Fissili*, among the ordinary species of onions, and not bulbs.[21]

The Delights of Antiquity

Those humanists who thought shallots were "the bulbs of the ancients" had an impact, all the same. Shallots captured a place in French seasoning.

Whether or not they associated onions with the ancients' "bulbs," sixteenth-century horticulturists developed a wide array of them. Those that could be directly linked to types noted in antiquity were accorded special status. Pliny had observed that "in our country we have two principal varieties, one the kind used for seasoning, the Greek name for which is *getion*-leek and the Latin '*pallacana*', and the other with a head." Apicius, in

36. "Ripe Speragas," from *The Cryes of the City of London Drawne after the Life,* by Pierce Tempest (London, 1711). Reproduced by courtesy of the Trustees of the British Museum.

Garden Produce {117}

*A P I V M Hortenſe.*

37. "Apium Hortense," from
*Historia generalis plantarum,* by
Jacques Dalechamps (Lyon,
1587), 1:700. Courtesy of the
History of Science Collections, Cornell University Library.

contrast, more often employed the headed variety as a seasoning. Renaissance readers thus had two differing models, Pliny and Apicius, for onions as seasoning. Passages in Estienne and Bruyerin show them identifying the *ciboule,* or green onion, as the *getion*-leek.[22] Although both the green onion and the headed onion continue to be used, the *getion*-leek triumphed in 1651 when La Varenne gave it a prominent place in his seasoning bouquet.

Garlic, too, climbed in status because some ancient writers, such as Celsus, had considered it a "bulb." This relative of the onion, which Athenaeus portrayed as a delicacy, was placed before the diner on a large tray bearing five plates in all, each holding a single ingredient. Besides the garlic were a sweet wine sop, ten cockles, a pair of sea urchins, and a piece of sturgeon. Garlic was not served only at ingeniously contrived offerings for the wealthy, Columella tells us, but also found a place in a "laborer's meal." In fact, Pliny reports that a certain kind of garlic "holds a high rank among the dishes of the country people, particularly in Africa."[23]

The socially respectable were meant to avoid any member of the onion family, however delicious and alluring they found it to be, because of its strong smell, especially when it was raw. Whether the ancients in fact did restrain themselves is a question. Pliny noted that "garlic as well as onions gives an offensive smell to the breath, though when cooked it causes no smell." Garlic had the worst reputation in this respect. Horace warned the lover against the odor of this small "bulb," and Plautus's characters show disdain by telling people they stink of garlic.[24]

This attitude toward garlic and the onions perhaps reinforced a bias that had lingered in Europe since antiquity. Bruyerin wrote that although onions "are eaten raw even by rather refined people, the more polished nonetheless prefer them cooked more, first of all because they are healthier that way and also because they do not give off such a strong odor." Evelyn remarked in 1699 that garlic "by Spaniards and Italians, and the more Southern People [is] familiarly eaten with almost everything. . . . [W]e yet think it more proper for our Northern Rustics. . . [and] absolutely forbid it entrance into our Salleting, by reason of its intolerable Rankness . . . which made it so detested of old." Men could partake of this little bulb if they were not courting, but "to be sure, 'tis not for Ladies Palats." For men who could not keep away from the stuff but

The Delights of Antiquity

expected to be in a woman's presence, he suggested "a light touch on the Dish, with a *Clove* thereof, much better supply'd by the gentler *Roccombo* [rocambole]."[25]

Despite such qualms, the flirtation with garlic continued. William King chortled at his compatriots' desire to copy the cooking of Paris, with its "rank" garlic, shallot, and rocambole.[26] The eighteenth-century journal *Common Sense* mocked an exchange on garlic in a fashionable English dining room:

> My Lord having tasted, and duly considered the Bechamele, shook his Head, and then offered as his Opinion to the Company, that the Garlick was not enough concealed, but earnestly desired to know their Sentiments, and begged they would taste it with Attention.
>
> The Company, after proper Deliberation, replied, That they were of his Lordship's Opinion, and that the Garlick did indeed distinguish itself too much: But the Maître D'Hôtel interposing represented, that they were now stronger than ever in Garlick at Paris; upon which the Company, one and all said,—That alter'd the Case.[27]

Garlic is often represented as the food of the "lower orders" or of country folk, just as Evelyn terms it the condiment of southerly climes. Yet from Apicius on and from north to south, the cookery manuals call for garlic, although other members of the onion family appear much more often.

## THE BLOOMING OF THE KITCHEN GARDEN

As the kitchen garden burst its medieval boundaries, a striking number of the new vegetables were linked to the texts of the ancients. In the south of France an explosion of horticultural interest, Le Roy Ladurie observes, transformed those "bleak collections of leeks, cabbages, and turnips" of the fifteenth-century garden into profuse collections of vegetables. By 1604 a garden at Nîmes had blanched lettuce, head or Milanese cabbage, headed endive, cauliflower, artichokes, turnips, parsley, fennel, and melons.[28]

This cultural preference for the produce of the ancients was reflected in the cookbooks as well. An occasional foray beyond the ancients' regimen led Scappi to use the eggplant, La Varenne to use the Jerusalem artichoke, and May to use the Virginia

38. Gaspari Traversi, *La Bancarella della verdura.* Courtesy of the Musei di Storia ed Arte, Trieste.

potato, but the scanting of these items in the vast majority of recipes underscores the common perception that they originated outside of Greco-Roman culture. The Arabs had been cultivating some vegetables lost to Europe during the medieval period and devising new varieties of old types, but though the Europeans were attracted by Arabic cookery, they were not drawn to these foods, perhaps because these vegetables never attained high status in the composite dishes of the Middle East or Spain.

Although the cauliflower was not known to the ancients and in fact originated in the Middle East, its appearance in the sixteenth-century garden is a striking instance of the general pattern of ancient revivals we have been witnessing. The cauliflower is in fact a form of cabbage, and the ancients loved their cabbage. Pliny noted that cabbage was esteemed in the gardens of his day: "Cabbages . . . which now have preeminence in gardens, I do not find to have been held in honour among the Greeks: but Cato sings marvellous praises of the head of cabbage. . . . He classifies cabbages as follows—a kind with the

The Delights of Antiquity

leaves wide open and a large stalk, another with a crinkly leaf, which is called celery cabbage, and a third with very small stalks; the last is a smooth and tender cabbage."[29] Later he mentions even more varieties. Since interest in horticulture was so great in the Renaissance, it is not surprising that numerous strains of cabbage were developed. "There are so many several sorts of Cabbages, that you shall hardly resolve to have them all in your Garden," said Nicolas de Bonnefons. In attempting to summarize the various strains of the cabbage family grown in France, he began with the cauliflower, the most precious, and presumably because he viewed it as a horticultural feat.[30] First produced in the Middle East, cauliflowers now appeared on European tables as part of the revival of the ancients' passion for cabbages.

### THE FRUIT AND NUT GARDEN

Fruits and nuts had furnished the ancients' "second table," or what we call the dessert course, which their Renaissance imitators took up with great enthusiasm.

"Ab ovo usque ad mala," from the egg to the apple, or from the beginning of the meal to the end, Horace wrote. Fruits and nuts graced his dessert table. Martial, too, promised diners, "When you have had your fill, I will give you ripe fruits." The ancients tended their orchards in order to have abundant fruit for their last course at table. "Anon the 'second tables' were loaded to the full," Athenaeus reported, "and upon them were pears and luscious apples, pomegranates and grapes, nurses of the Bromian god, and that freshly gathered grape which they call 'vine-bower.'" The virtuosity of the ancient horticulturist is apparent in Pliny's remark that the types and varieties of fruit could "scarcely be enumerated by their appearance or shape, let alone by their flavours and juices, which have been so frequently modified by crossing and grafting."[31]

Putting elegance briefly aside, Romans repaired to their country estates to dine rustically in their fruit houses (*oporothecas*), where they would use the products of all this ingenious pomology to enhance the scene by constructing still lifes of fresh fruit.

> Some people even spread a dining-table . . . to dine there [in the fruit house]; and, in fact, if luxury allows people to do this in a picture gallery, where the scene is set by art, why should they not

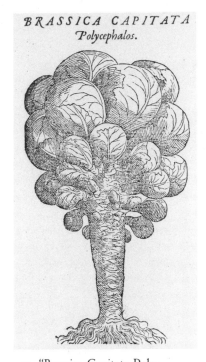

39. "Brassica Capitata Polycephalos," from *Historia generalis plantarum*, by Jacques Dalechamps (Lyon, 1587), 1:521. Courtesy of the History of Science Collections, Cornell University Library.

Garden Produce

enjoy a scene set by nature, in a charming arrangement of fruit? Provided always that you do not follow the example set by some, of buying fruit in Rome and carrying it to the country to pile up in the fruit-gallery for a dinner-party.[32]

Columella had said in the first century that there was no kind of fruit that could not be made into preserves. Thomas Artus's sixteenth-century traveler in the Isle des Hermaphrodites encountered so many preserves that he inferred that it was inappropriate ever to eat fruit in its natural state. The dessert course was so loaded with them and with cakes that the table, he concluded, must be as luxurious as Lucullus's. "And indeed," said our Renaissance traveler, "even when no one will be there but the master of the house, the table is laden profusely, and the reason for it is founded in antiquity, for they say that it is enough that Lucullus comes to dine at Lucullus's."[33]

Pietro Aretino certainly exaggerated when he claimed in 1537 that it was the Florentines who had revived the custom of serving fruit at the end of the meal. Fruit had been provided in the medieval period as well. But Aretino's words do capture a change in the status of fruit on the second table. The head of the manor showed off his fruit. It signaled not only the level of horticulture on his estate but his adherence to the culinary traditions of the ancients. Aretino called fruit not a food but, like truffles and oysters, a lure to the appetite, and people who offered Francis I truffles and oysters in the Midi accompanied them with peaches, which Pliny claimed fetched higher prices than any other fruit.[34]

In their zeal to put the correct thistles on the table, humanists *cum* natural philosophers carefully compared field specimens with ancient descriptions. Pliny in hand, they tracked the wild asparagus. Parsley now "swam" with new authority in sauces, and many varieties of onions and cabbages were developed and became widely available. Probably more fruit weighed down the trees in Renaissance orchards than Europe had seen since Pliny's day.

## IN THE COOKBOOKS

Apicius gives three recipes for *cardui*, but we cannot be certain which thistle he is calling for. Artichokes are found twice in the Hispanic-Moorish cookbook, but no thistle appears in the

APICIUS (FOURTH CENTURY)
Thistles (*cardui*): *Liquamen*, oil, and cut-up eggs.

Thistles, another method: Pound fresh rue, mint, coriander, fennel, and add pepper, lovage, honey, *liquamen*, and oil.

Thistles boiled, another method: Pepper, cumin, *liquamen* and oil.

Cold asparagus patina. Take cleaned asparagus, pound in the mortar, add water, beat thoroughly and pass through a sieve. Next put in a saucepan fig-peckers which you have prepared for cooking. Pound in the mortar 6 scruples of pepper, moisten with *liquamen*, grind well, add 1 cyathus each of wine and *passum*, put in a sauce pan 3 oz. of oil, and bring the mixture to the boil. Grease a shallow pan, and mix in it 6 eggs with *oenogarum*, add the asparagus puree, pour on the mixture described above, and arrange the birds [on top]. Cook, sprinkle with pepper and serve.

*Source*: Apicius, *Roman Cookery Book*, pp. 87–89, 97.

BARTOLOMEO PLATINA (1475)
Boiled asparagus are laid out in a shallow dish: salt, oil, and vinegar are added. There are those who sprinkle on aromatics [spices]. . . . There are those who cook them with wine added. . . .

*Source*: Platina, *De honesta voluptate*, bk. IV.

BRASSICA CAPITATA *Albida*.

41. "Brassica Capitata Albida," from *Historia generalis plantarum*, by Jacques Dalechamps (Lyon, 1587), 1:521. Courtesy of the History of Science Collections, Cornell University Library.

"Baghdad Cookery Book," nor does Maxim Rodinson mention any in his analysis of a thirteenth-century Arabic cookbook. No thistles are found in the fourteenth-century cookbooks of Italy, France, or England.

*Cardui* reappear in European cookery works with Platina's *De honesta voluptate* in 1475. We do not know if *cardui* here refers to

CRISTOFORO DI MESSISBUGO (1549)
Pastry of artichokes
    First make a rectangle of pastry. . . . Then in the bottom put butter and a little pepper, and *marzolino* (a cheese) cut very, very small.
    Then you will have three artichokes almost cooked and well trimmed of their spikes, with the heart well cleaned off of hay. Put into the pastry adding pepper, butter, and *marzolino* cut small in the same way.

Garden Produce                                          {123}

Then take two egg yolks, two ounces of sugar, and half a cup of verjuice, and a little bit of fragrant herbs cut fine with knives. Mix everything together and put into the pastry. Then put on its cover and put to cook. . . .

*Source:* Messisbugo, *Banchetti,* p. 130.

BARTOLOMEO SCAPPI (1570)
To make asparagus soup with meat broth:

Take some cultivated asparagus in season, which begins in the month of April and lasts through October (as the wild type in Rome begins in the autumn and lasts through April). Take the most tender part of your cultivated asparagus and without blanching put it directly into meat broth with some strips of ham. At the end of the cooking time add herbs beaten with a little pepper, cinnamon, saffron, whole gooseberries or verjuice, and serve hot in the broth. And if you want to mix the asparagus with eggs, cheese, and common spices, cook in the broth only until half done. Then pound the asparagus with a knife and finish cooking in fatty broth, adding gooseberries and verjuice. . . . You may cook wild asparagus in the same way after having first blanched it.

*Source:* Scappi, *Opera,* p. 80v.

42. Giambattista Ruoppolo, *Still Life with Fruit.* Courtesy of the Staatsgalerie Stuttgart.

The Delights of Antiquity

both cardoons and artichokes, but both can be found in Messisbugo's menus in 1549; the cardoons are offered with salt and pepper, presumably raw (the way Mattioli indicated they were eaten in his day), and the artichokes are either cooked or served raw, again with salt and pepper. Messisbugo gives only three recipes for thistles, and they call for artichokes as the main ingredients. Scappi (1570) includes cardoons cooked and raw in his menus, and artichokes now appear in his recipes not only as main ingredients but frequently in auxiliary roles. Cardoons, too, occasionally appear in minor roles.

Thistles are absent from French cookbooks until La Varenne's in 1651. They appear in those of England a few years

FRANÇOIS PIERRE DE LA VARENNE (1651)
Artichokes *à la poivrade*. Cut your artichokes into quarters, take out the hay, and blanch them in fresh water, and when you wish to serve, put them on a plate with pepper and salt.

Loin of veal as a ragout. The loin being well beaten, lard it with large pieces of pork fat and spit it. When it is half cooked put some good stock in and make a sauce bound with flour and sautéed onions. Garnish with champignons, artichokes, asparagus, truffles, and a kidney cut up. Serve.

Fried asparagus. Break them, cut them in pieces, and wash. Drain, fry with very fresh butter and season with salt, pepper, and chopped parsley. Once fried, put them to stew with an onion stuck with a clove, a drop of stock, and serve with nutmeg. You may also put in some cream if you wish.
    *Source:* La Varenne, *Cuisinier françois*, pp. 111, 44, 247.

ROBERT MAY (1660)
To fry Artichocks. Boil and sever all from the bottoms, then slice them in the midst, quarter them, dip them in batter, and fry them in butter. For the sauce take verjuyce, butter, and sugar, with the juyce of an orange, lay marrows on them, garnish them with oranges, and serve them up.

Another made Dish in the French Fashion, called an Entre de Table, Entrance to the Table. Take the bottoms of boil'd Artichocks, the yolks of hard Eggs, young Chicken-peepers or Pigeon-peepers finely trust, Sweetbreads of Veal, Lamb-stones blanched, and put them in a Pipkin, with Cock-stones and

43. Anonymous, *Still Life with Strawberries* (French, 17th century). 60 × 80.3 cm. The Metropolitan Museum of Art, Bequest of Harry G. Sperling, 1971 (1976.100.10).

later. In both France and England the artichoke bottom played an even more important auxiliary role than it did in sixteenth-century Italy. Artichokes were a staple in eighteenth-century England and France. An English cookbook writer proclaimed

The Delights of Antiquity

them to be "of great Use in Cookery throughout the whole year, for almost all Sorts of Ragoos, Soops, etc."[35] The first volume of the *Nouveau traité de la cuisine* (1739), which has four

---

FRANÇOIS MASSIALOT (1691)

Artichokes with a white sauce. Cook artichokes in water and a little salt. When they are cooked, sauté the *cus* [artichoke bottoms?] in a pan with parsley. Season with salt and black pepper. Make a sauce with egg yellows, a drop of vinegar, and a little stock.

Artichokes *au beurre blanc* [with white butter]. Your artichokes being cooked as above, taken out the hay and make a sauce with white butter, vinegar, salt, and nutmeg.

Source: Massialot, *Cuisinier roial et bourgeois*, p. 114.

VINCENT LA CHAPELLE (1736)

Another Pottage of Profitrolles. To consist of six Loaves, three forced with Ham, and three others with Capon, garnish with small Fricando's of Veal glazed, a rim of Cocks-combs, and a Ragout of Mushrooms, Artichoke bottoms, ends of Asparagus, all pass'd in a Stew-pan, with some good Veal Gravy a little thicken'd: Your Pottage being ready to serve, throw on your Ragout, and serve it hot.

A white Ragout of Asparagus. Cut and blanch some Asparagus as before, put them in a Stewing-pan, with a bit of Butter, fry them a little, powder them with half a Spoonful of fine Flower, moisten them with Broth, season them with Salt and Pepper, and then let them be stewed. Make a Thickening with several Yolks of Eggs, diluted with some Broth, and put there in a little Nutmeg. Your Asparagus being relishing, thicken them with the said Yolks, and make use of this Ragout to put under some larded Collops, or other sort of Meat.

Source: La Chapelle, *Modern Cook*, pp. 43, 299.

---

recipes for asparagus, one for broccoli, two for cabbage, two for cauliflower, and two for cucumbers, offers nineteen recipes for artichokes.

Asparagus appears in two of Apicius's recipes, both times as the main ingredient. It appears four times in the Hispanic-Moorish work and is found in Rodinson's texts, but not in "A Baghdad Cookery Book." In the Hispanic-Moorish work it is

Garden Produce

44. Louise Moillon, *La Marchande de fruits et de légumes.* The Louvre, Paris. Photo by Musées Nationaux.

mixed with meat, as are the artichokes. Asparagus is missing from Messisbugo's recipes, but he included a salad of asparagus in his menus.

Corroborating Bruyerin's and Porta's directions for the preparation of asparagus, Scappi used these garden spears both as salads and as the focus of other sorts of dishes. Yet, though he used it in soups and with eggs, asparagus is still perhaps best described as the main ingredient of those dishes; it does not really compete with artichoke bottoms as an adjunct ingredient. The seventeenth-century French school and its successors continued the Italian idea of asparagus on its own and used the tips also as an adjunct flavoring. The English did not use asparagus so pervasively as oysters in compound dishes, but it was a customary sight on the table, whether in a dish of fowl or fish or served on its own. The English cookbook writer Patrick Lamb reported that "Asparagus is a constant Dish in the Spring, while it is in Season," and the author of the 1767

The Delights of Antiquity

*Dictionnaire portatif de cuisine* observed that "everybody knows asparagus with butter sauce [*au beurre blanc*] and as a salad."[36]

Recipes in the fourteenth-century Italian *Libro di cucina* call
for onions, leeks, cabbage sprouts, and spinach, but those in the
French *Viandier* of the fifteenth century are still limited to onions, cress, white beets, peas, and beans. But along with thistles
and asparagus, carrots and cucumbers appear in Platina in 1475.
By 1549 Messisbugo prepared for a grand banquet by buying
not only the requisite thistles and asparagus but also lettuces,
endive, radish tops, cress, carrots, cucumbers, turnips, cauliflower and other cabbages, spinach, and squash of all sorts. The
same new vegetables appear in Scappi's menus and recipes,
where the variety of cabbages is now striking. La Varenne's 1651
*Cuisinier françois* contains lettuce, purslaine, chicories, turnips,
green peas, pumpkins and other squashes, parsnips, carrots,
salsify, beets, and cucumbers "of all sorts." The English cook
Robert May in 1660 used cucumbers, spinach, asparagus, cabbages, pumpkins, parsnips, turnips, and carrots.

# PART 3    The Salt-Acid Taste

They . . . invent new tricks, as Sausages,
Anchovies . . . Caviare, pickled Oysters,
Herrings, Runadoes, etc., innumerable salt-
meats, to increase their appetite.
  Robert Burton, *The Anatomy of Melancholy* (1621)

# CHAPTER 8    A Spur to the Appetite

As they plumbed the texts of the ancients, Renaissance scholars found salt treated as a sacred substance, as a medicine, and as a condiment.

Plutarch records a conversation that turns to the idea that salt was sacred for Homer and Plato. One of the participants remarks that "Homer goes so far as to say. 'He sprinkled with salt divine,' and Plato says that by the custom of mankind salt is regarded as of all substances the one most favoured by the gods." Since the gods were especially fond of salt, their devotees presented it as an offering, Pliny noted. He scoffed at the Romans of his own day who no longer thought salt good enough to give the gods, and offered perfumes instead: "Then reckon up the vast number of funerals celebrated yearly throughout the entire world, and the perfumes such as are given to the gods a grain at a time, that are piled up in heaps to the honour of dead bodies! Yet the gods used not to regard with less favour the worshippers who petitioned them with salted spelt, but rather, as the facts show, they were more benevolent in those days." Setting up a tension between salt and perfume (spices), Pliny implied his displeasure with intrusions of eastern customs and religions into the culture of the Greco-Roman world.[1]

Salt later acquired a medicinal value, and Galen recommended that one consume moderate amounts of salt food to encourage a flagging appetite.

Finally, salt was valued as a condiment: "First there is salt, without which practically nothing is eatable," writes Plutarch. "Salt is added even to bread and enriches its flavour; this explains why Poseidon shares a temple with Demeter." Salt has no peer, and it is requisite to good dining; "salt is the only relish that cannot be dispensed with. Just as colour requires light, so flavour requires salt to stimulate the sense; otherwise flavours are disagreeable and nauseous to the taste." Salt is "delicious as a seasoning, for salt is very nearly a seasoning and condiment to other seasoning," and "it serves as a kind of finishing touch . . . to the meal for the body, and adapts the food to our appetite."[2]

The power of salt as a condiment in the system Plutarch embraced is clear enough, but Renaissance readers could interpret this system as serving two ends, one moral and heroic, the other gluttonous and base. Homer's heroes sprinkled their meat only with salt and the straight-living citizens of Plato's *Republic* used salt and ate salted olives. Pliny thought a "civilized life . . . impossible without salt"; for him, salt was a proper and modest pleasure.[3] The gourmands, by contrast, ate salt to whip up their appetites during a dinner of delicacy piled upon delicacy. The Renaissance addiction to salt was fueled not by notions of its sacred quality or medicinal value but by the idea that it was the condiment of condiments for stimulating the appetite.

This new love of salt arose at a time when salt had long been suspect. The incidence of salt in recipes was considerably lower in the fourteenth century than it had been in antiquity. Even though it was customary to put salt on the table at the beginning of the meal, it was not necessarily being added to many foods. When salt began to dwindle in the European diet is not yet clear. Medieval Arabic cookery, with its leaning toward the sweet, certainly had an effect. But the Roman salty fish sauce known as *garum* or *liquamen* had been completely flushed from European cookery by the high Middle Ages, while it still lingered in the Arabic world.

Marsilio Ficino advised the melancholic against eating salty and brined food. Like Galen, he allowed the invalid a few salt morsels to stimulate the appetite, but he was against the salty diet of the ancient gourmands. Fear of salt ran high. At the beginning of the seventeenth century Joseph Duchesne urged his readers not to make the "popular error" of believing that salt was "more destructive than profitable to the health." Some people, he said, went so far as to avoid salted bread and never to put a grain of salt on an egg. The physician Tobias Venner chided those who thought salt so harmful that they believed that they could not "without danger put a crumme thereof to their pallats." But even Venner was convinced that an immoderate use of salt dried up the humors and diminished the *spiritus*, bringing on a shriveled-up old age. By this time, though, another segment of the population had forsaken medical prohibitions and, tempted by new culinary conceits associated with the Greeks and Romans, begun to eat a multitude of salty delicacies.[4]

### SALT DRIVES THE DINER

The ancient gourmands adored salty foods. Olives, jested Horace, were the poor people's food that still found a place at the feasts of kings. At Trimalchio's banquet a "donkey in Corinthian bronze stood on the side-board, with panniers holding olives, white in one side, black in the other." Martial called ham the dish of distinguished men and claimed that it was at its best when it was freshly cured. Lucanian sausages were a garnish of merit. Cato cried out that "certain persons had imported foreign luxuries into Rome; they had, he said, bought a cask of Pontic smoked fish for three hundred shillings." Near the Bosporus people cut sturgeon belly "into squares and make it into a pickle," wrote Athenaeus, and "of tunnies, pickled in the right season, Byzantium is mother." Gluttony was so connected with these foods that Columella stressed the simplicity of his salted products in an effort to dissociate his *De re rustica* from works devoted to the luxurious life. He was not, he claimed, like Gaius Matuius, who gave "instructions for urban dinner-parties and sumptuous entertainments . . . and . . . produced three books on which he inscribed the titles 'The Cook,' 'The Fish-monger,' and 'The Pickle-maker' (*Salgamarius*)." Nonetheless, Columella could not resist providing a recipe for a preserved olive mixture to be served at "sumptuous repasts."[5]

The ancients often added salt to a dish by means of fermented salt-fish preparations, which special ingredients and production could transform into luxury condiments. *Garum* was made from the refuse of fish that were "soaked in salt so that garum is really liquor from the putrefaction of these matters," Pliny explained. "Once this used to be made from a fish that the Greeks called *garos*. . . . Today the most popular garum is made from the scomber [mackerel]." *Allex,* another fermented salt-fish product, was at first simply the sediment of *garum* itself, Pliny reported. But then other fermented products were invented from "oysters, sea urchins, sea anemones, and mullet's liver," and also called *allex.* (Yet another kind of *allex* made in Roman times from tiny fish called *apua* would later have a greater impact on Renaissance Europe than all other ancient salt-fish preparations.) Horace described a luxurious dish of lamprey and shrimp in a sauce of *garum,* highly prized first-press olive oil from Venafrum, and select vinegar from Lesbian grapes—that is, a salt-acid-oil sauce.[6]

In imitation of the ancients, Renaissance Europe expanded its repertoire of salt-acid delicacies, as Rabelais is witness. Gargantua sat down to eat "and, being of a phlegmatic nature, began his meal with some dozens of hams, smoked ox-tongues, botargos, [and] sausages." He enjoyed his green salad, too. Picking lettuce—and unwittingly several pilgrims who had been hiding beneath the leaves—he went about the business of constructing a salad with oil, vinegar, and salt as an appetizer before his supper. A list of delicacies borne forth as offerings included salmagundi (a saladlike creation), sausages, smoked beef tongues, hams, salted venison, olives, and shoulder of mutton with salted capers. And on fast days these belly gods enjoyed among other delicacies preserved tuna, salted eels, salted salmon, salted whiting, and one hundred kinds of "salads" (*sallades*) for the first course (*entrée de table*). Rabelais called these fast days "*jours maigres entrelardez*" or "larded lean days," for the taking of salt-acid delicacies on a fast day was a hypocrisy. Renaissance diners baited their appetites with salt fish, salt meat, and salt vegetables.[7]

## SALT-FISH PRODUCTS

Platina, typically humanist in his treatment of delicacies, expressed himself as of two minds about salt fish. He insisted that salted tuna products, "like all salt-fish products, are the worst kind of nourishment." Yet Platina then set his better judgment aside and gave instructions for preparing salt-fish dishes: one from sturgeon, another from the sturgeon's eggs called caviar, and yet another from eggs other than the sturgeon's, which had the generic name botargo. Indulging himself with

The Salt-Acid Taste

other than proper pleasures, he savored the memory of having eaten "nothing more pleasant" than botargo. In May 1548 the raffish Aretino, who made little attempt to conceal his love of sensual living, sent his gratitude to a friend for a gift of botargo, which had "titillated [his] taste." Renaissance diners were so fond of gorging on salt fish and salted fish eggs that physicians condemned this passion.[8]

Salt fish, Bruyerin wrote in the mid–sixteenth century, "was in the highest repute among the ancients; nor do we find its reputation diminished in the least in our own age." So great was the interest in it, Bruyerin thought, that new delicacies were created: "Antiquity knew a great many salt-fish preparations of which our age is utterly ignorant. On the other hand, today some have been discovered which completely escaped the notice of the ancients, such as our herring, sturgeon eggs [caviar], and other items brought from Constantinople to Italy." Nonnius wrote that salt fish "was in time past not only in use but also counted among the highest delicacies. First the Greeks and then the Romans nearly went crazy because of their burning desire for these [salt-fish] preparations."[9]

Today most of the tuna available in Europe and America is preserved salted in cans. In 1719 Nicolas Delamare wrote that "tuna is unique among fish for being much better salted than fresh, as much for taste as for health." The ancients, too, did not serve it fresh. Athenaeus mentions it as present in all the magnificent meals he describes. He puts it among the most exquisite of dishes, those that are fit to be served to the gods, but always with the condition that it be salted.[10]

The rage for salt fish that started in Italy and bloomed in France soon journeyed to English soil. In the late sixteenth century, Tobias Venner took reluctant notice of "an Italian sauce called Caviaro, which begins to be in use with us. . . . But this and other such like noysome sauces, devised onely to allure the stomack and palate to meats and drinks, I leave to the beastly and Baccanalian meetings of drunkards and Apician belly-gods." Samuel Pepys seems to have enjoyed them, though. On June 6, 1661, he wrote in his diary: "We stayed talking and singing and drinking great draughts of claret, and eating botargo and bread and butter till twelve at night." Four days earlier, after the Sunday church service, he and a visitor had drunk wine and eaten anchovies in his chamber for "an hour or two."[11]

A Spur to the Appetite

In sixteenth-century Italy *garum* came to be associated with caviar and botargo. Guido Panciroli claimed, "Other types of *liquamen* [*garum*] called botargo and caviar now take the place" of the ancients' *garum*.[12] The cookbook of neither Messisbugo nor Scappi, however, provides any evidence that the Italians were using fish eggs as a *garum* substitute in composed dishes.

The French, not the Italians, invented a *garum* that in time found its way into the cookbooks. "Some people," Bruyerin wrote, "believe that the *smaris* (commonly called by some people *cerres* and by others *gerres*) . . . is the ancients' *garum* fish. Today at Antipolis in France this fish is called *garon*, and it is from this fish that the best *garum* is made, as all know who wish to try it." By the second half of the sixteenth century, then, a *garum* product seems to have been manufactured in the south of France from a fish that the French called *garon*. But another *garum* created in France was to become much more celebrated. Some people claimed, Bruyerin reported, that the little fish that Pliny called *apua* were the anchovies of their day. When anchovies are salted for preservation, he continued, "they turn into *garum*":

> If anchovies are treated with salt and exposed to the sun after gutting, their flesh will dissolve and make the best *garum* to be used for piquing and restoring an avid interest in food. . . . Certain people call [another kind] vinegar-oil *garum*, because the little preserved fish are prepared with them. The manner of making it is the following. The fish are taken out [of the brine] and not washed. Then they are thrown into a pan with oil, vinegar, and parsley. Afterward they are shaken over coals for as long as it takes for them to completely liquify. And these people think that this method of preparation is more outstanding than the one that antiquity favored.[13]

Melting the flesh of preserved anchovies into a sauce soon became a widespread practice. A half century after Bruyerin, the *Thrésor de santé*, having mentioned a dish of "mullet with *garum* sauce in the style of the ancients," described this *garum* as being converted from salted preserved anchovies. Randle Cotgrave made the same connection between anchovies and *garum* in his 1611 French-English dictionary. *Garum* or *garon* is a "pickle of fish or, the liquor wherein salt fish hath been resolved, or long soaked; also the little Anchova-like fish, *Garum*, whereof (being heated in a dish, with oyle or butter, and thereby melted) the best kind of that liquor is made."[14]

The melted anchovy started to appear in cookery works with the publication of La Varenne's *Cuisinier françois* in 1651, though the term *garum* never appears there or in the multitude of cookery books that followed its vogue. All the same, the connection was not lost. In 1668 Pierre Gontier wrote that anchovies "are put in salt in order that they may be preserved, and they become *garum*, or *liquamen*, which kitchens use for a great many sauces." Early in the eighteenth century Martin Lister, physician to the English queen, produced another edition of Apicius, in which he noted that melted anchovies were his age's *garum*. By 1727 John Houghton could write that *garum* was frequently used in England. Anchovies provided the "best sauce, for these salted fish, being put upon the fire, dissolve almost in any liquor, for which reason they are an ingredient in many delicates."[15]

## SALT MEAT

Martial loved hams and salty sausages. Galen singled out pork among meats as suitable for salting (he thought fresh pork should be relegated to laborers). Whether the advice came from an ancient connoisseur or from an ancient physician, the Renaissance gourmands turned it to their advantage. Baldassare Pisanelli wrote, "All the ancient writers agree . . . pork . . . conserved with a little salt for several days will be, as one says, short cured, and much better." Bruyerin concurred. "It is agreed from daily experience that fresh pork, i.e., pork recently slaughtered, and not sprinkled with salt, lies heavy in the stomach and is hardly digested." Butcher shops in Lyon cut lean pork up for commoners and rural folk, "but rarely is it served in important houses." Nonnius said, "To this day hams are held everywhere in the greatest honor." Bruyerin noted that the hams of Gaul had been worthy to be sent to Rome, and although the hams of his own day had not yet matched those of ancient Gaul, the secret of the excellent hams of Mainz had passed into France. By the seventeenth century the French Bayonne ham was competing with that of Mainz. The fame of both these hams traveled to England, where Alexander Pope would lift the Bayonne ham to the level of Périgord truffles.[16]

A Spur to the Appetite

A confluence of factors can be seen to have fostered the cured-pork industry: Pliny's report that the pig provided more meat to the cookshops than any other animal, Plutarch's story of the diner who was so surprised to learn that all the varied dishes at a banquet were forms of pork, the obvious popularity of pork with the Greeks and Romans, and the fact that "discriminating people" saw the ancients as adoring salted pork and sausages. Fresh domestic pork, wrote Delamare in the eighteenth century, had become food for the lower orders (*le menu Peuple*).[17] The cured-pork market was entrenched.

Though salted beef never attracted so much interest as salted pork, it had a certain following simply by virtue of being salted. Bruyerin insisted that "there is no time in which this food is not served at banquets . . . for the rich and famous for the first course. . . . Indeed, beef is more to be commended with moderate salting." Nonnius disagreed; by the next century he could report that much more fresh beef was eaten than fresh pork, which was not eaten by "elegant people."[18]

## SALT VEGETABLES

Bruyerin wrote of raw cucumbers macerated in salt and vinegar, enjoyed by both the powerful and commoners. The polished palate chose very tiny cucumbers (the kind Pliny had said were the most popular) to preserve. (The tiny preserved cucumbers called *cornichons* are still popular in France today.) Artichokes "ought to be eaten with oil, *garum*, and coriander," but "some eat artichokes with salt only." Nonnius observed, "Although [olives] supply us with little nourishment, their fame does not suffer that they pass unsung. For they are frequently served at magnificent banquets as an invention of prodigal men to stimulate the appetite and, moreover, to incite much drinking." Salted capers served the same function.[19]

## ELEVATING THE SALAD

Saline food took on new status not only because it was connected to salt but also because the salad could be linked to Pliny. The term "salad" rarely crops up before the sixteenth century, when the humanists claimed the salad to be Pliny's *acetaria*. By the early years of the seventeenth century, however,

The Salt-Acid Taste

Salvatore Massonio could write that the salad was eaten or at least known by everyone.[20]

The term *acetaria* appears only once in the texts of antiquity, and some scholars surmised from the context that it could mean only the produce gathered from the garden. *Acetaria*, they decided, must be derived from the verb *accipio* (to gather). Other philologists thought it must stem from *acetum* (vinegar), for the liquid with which the garden produce was treated, and this is the meaning that became accepted. Vinegar had obviously been highly valued in antiquity. Pliny himself had put it above salt. "No other sauce serves so well to season food or to heighten a flavour," he said, and Athenaeus remembered it as "the one condiment Attic writers called 'delight.'"[21]

In 1536 Charles Estienne pondered Ermolao Barbaro's earlier exegesis on Pliny and expressed ambivalence about the derivation of *acetaria*, but held that *acetarium* for Pliny was what was known in France as *une salade*. Whereas the French *salade* and the Italian *insalata*, continued Estienne, stemmed from the words for salt—in French *sel*, in Italian *sale*—the Latin term *acetarium* stemmed perhaps from the word for vinegar, *acetum*.[22]

In order to bring together the Latin *acetaria* and the vernacular "salad," said Massonio, "certain cultivated ingenious sorts have invented the term '*herbe salolacetaria*' . . . to express at the same time the ingredients of the salad and the ingredients of the dressing. The term *saloacetaria* reflects not only salt in *sal* and vinegar in *acetaria* but also oil in *ol*, for although "oil was not necessary . . . continued use has introduced it as a kind of necessity: nevertheless, a salad is a salad without it." He went on: "The ordinary seasoning of the salad is vinegar, oil, and salt and . . . he who eats it without the dressing . . . loses the point of its name, because in Latin it [the name] comes from vinegar, i.e., it is called *Acetarium* and in Italian it is called by the term *Insalata* [because] it is treated with salt."[23]

In his 1699 discourse on "sallets" John Evelyn defined *acetaria* as "salad" for his English public. "We are by *Sallet* to understand a particular Composition of certain *Crude* and fresh Herbs, such as usually are, or may safely be eaten with some *Acetous* Juice, *Oyl*, Salt." Like Massonio, he claimed that "the perfection of *Sallets*, and that which gives them the name, consists in the grateful *Saline Acid*-point." But he accepted the necessity of oil to counter the acid. Foods that were said to be "Pickl'd," he

A Spur to the Appetite

ARCHIDIPNO,
OVERO
DELL'INSALATA,
E DELL'VSO DI ESSA,
*Trattato nuouo, curioso, e non mai più dato in luce;*
DA SALVATORE MASSONIO
Scritto, e diuiso in Sessanta otto Capi;
Dedicato a' molto Illustri Signori fratelli,
LVDOVICO, ANTONIO, E FABRITIO
COL'ANTONII.

IN VENETIA, MDCXXVII.
APPRESSO MARC'ANTONIO BROGIOLLO,
*Con Licenza de' Superiori, e Priuilegio.*

45. Title page of *Archidipno, overo dell' insalata*, by Salvatore Massonio (Venice, 1627). Rare Books and Manuscripts Division, The New York Public Library, Astor, Lenox, and Tilden Foundations.

wrote, "challenge not the name of *Sallet* so properly here, tho' sometimes mention'd."[24]

As Massonio indicated, oil, although often used, was not necessary for salads. A product preserved in either salt, acid, or salt and acid was also a salad, or *acetaria*. Ben Jonson advised that "an olive, caper, or some better salad Ush'ring the mutton" would rectify the palate. "Your preserved Sallats are of two kinds," said Gervase Markham, "either pickled as are Cucumbers, Samphire, Purslan, Broome, and such like, or preserved

The Salt-Acid Taste

with vinegar as Violets, Primose, Cowslips, Gilly flowers." The eighteenth-century *Dictionnaire oeconomique* observed that there were two kinds of *salade*, "a mixture of different kitchen garden plants, which one ordinarily eats raw," and "preserves kept in salt and vinegar, such as those one makes with small cucumbers, otherwise called *cornichons, capucines*, capers, *cotons de pourpier*, etc." By the eighteenth century "pickle" had almost totally eclipsed "salad" for the popular preserved products in England. The 1728 *Collection of Above Three Hundred Receipts* calls for "whole Pickled Mushrooms, Capers or any Pickle you like."[25]

## THE TASTE OF THE SEA: MARINADES

The sixteenth century saw words that had been of limited importance at the fashionable table come to prominence: *misaltare, accarpionare*, and *marinare*, the latter becoming the base for the French *mariner* and the English "marinate," all denoting short salting. The traveler to the Isle des Hermaphrodites is bemused by the idea of marinated fish at the banquet: "Among these foods I noticed some dishes of fish: It was said that the fish was marinated. It seemed to me that this word was superfluous, for I remarked it was seafood, but the diners did not find it agreeable to their taste, if it were not disguised by this seasoning."[26]

In the late seventeenth century a French dictionary defined "marinade" as a "high seasoning of vinegar, salt, white pepper, and good herbs," and the 1767 *Dictionnaire portatif de cuisine* observed that to marinate was to give "a sea taste" to meat or fish. The eighteenth-century English cook John Nott defined marinades as "sorts of Sauces or Pickles, in which certain things are steep'd, the Taste of which we would have heighten'd and render'd more agreeable to the Palate."[27]

## TRADING IN SALT, ACID, AND OIL

Porta's sixteenth-century *Villa*, like other Renaissance works before and after it, noted the interest in olive groves and the production of quality oil shown by the likes of Cato, Columella, Varro, and Pliny, and discussed procedures for expanding olive cultivation in contemporary Italy. The market responded. Le Roy Ladurie has observed that "the agricultural renaissance was characterized, first of all, by a cycle of olive cultivation." This

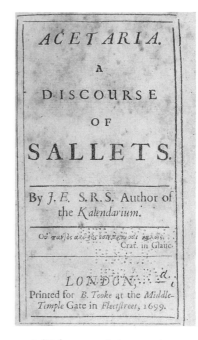

46. Title page of *Acetaria: A Discourse of Sallets*, by John Evelyn (London, 1699). Rare Books and Manuscripts Division, The New York Public Library, Astor, Lenox, and Tilden Foundations.

A Spur to the Appetite

crop was so important that "these Renaissance olive planters turn up on almost every page of the ancient registers." By at least the seventeenth century good olive oil from such places as Nice and Aremont was available in the Paris markets, and the 1674 *Art de bien traiter* advises readers to keep it on hand for food preparation.[28]

In England Lady Lisle was informed by her husband's clerk in 1537 that "a little barrel of sallett oyle" was to arrive by boat. But good oil was soon to be purchased in England. John Evelyn counseled his readers on distinguishing among olive oils, for some of lesser quality were often in the shops, as Richard Bradley noted in the eighteenth century. He agreed with Evelyn on the choice of Luccan oil, but noted that "excellent" oil also was available from France. The cheap kind from Genoa, however, was only for barbers.[29]

Households were to have both olive oil and olives on hand. Olivier de Serres urged estate owners in the non-olive-growing regions to keep a good supply so as not to be dependent on the expensive pickle dealers in the towns. Likewise in 1674 *L 'Art de bien traiter* advised readers to "have in storage some barrels of various good olives, as Spanish, Luccan, Veronese." Thomas Moffett identified three sorts of olives in England, those of Spain, those of Italy, and those of Provence, as did *The British Housewife* almost two centuries later. Records of the Lord Steward's Department spanning the seventeenth and eighteenth centuries show Lucan, Spanish, and Provençal olives imported for the royal household.[30]

Capers from Egypt and Apulia were in great demand in the late fifteenth century. The 1607 *Thrésor de santé* remarked that capers were coming north from Spain, Provence, and Alexandria. In the second half of the seventeenth century Bordeaux served as a distribution point for such products as capers and olives for the entire French Atlantic coast. According to *The British Housewife*, Toulon was the "principal Manufactury" for pickled capers, though some arrived from Lyon and a few from Majorca. Two kinds of capers appear in the lord steward's records in the second half of the eighteenth century—French and those referred to as "common," which seemed to mean simply that they were not of French origin. Some northerners contemplated growing capers, but Nicolas de Bonnefons advised in 1669 that capers were really not worth growing in the North when they were so easily raised in the South; "to Pickle them in

The Salt-Acid Taste

Salt . . . would cost you more than you may buy them for of the Oyl-men." In May 1760 Voltaire ordered one barrel of small capers and one of olives to have on hand.[31]

Salted meat products were widely available, and regional specialties grew in fame. In 1670 a British traveler found the Bolognese markets "exquisitely good for . . . Salsiccie [sausages] . . . which are a regalo [gift] for a Prince." Nonnius reported that hams from Mainz were especially prized in Italy and France. The French maître d'hôtel was advised to keep on hand "hams from Mainz, Bayonne . . . Bologna sausages: salted beef tongues," and salt beef. Four dozen hams that Lord Russel had purchased in Westphalia arrived in March 1671 at Woburn Abbey. London perhaps did not have meat of such high quality at its "ham shops." Henry Fielding concluded that "true nature is as diffi-cult to be met with in authors, as the Bayonne ham or Bologna sausage is to be found in the shops." The "Cheesemongers" sold these salt meats also, and Vincent La Chapelle, former cook to the earl of Chesterfield, advised house stewards to go to them for "larding Bacon," Westphalia and Bayonne hams, pork fat, sausages, "Andouilles," beef tongues, and "whatever . . . is requisite for Entremets."[32]

Salted products found far-flung markets, as they had done in centuries past, when Roman merchants had delicacies from all the empire available in their stalls. Capers and olives were trans-ported to northern countries, hams traveled from Westphalia at least as far as England, and Platina wrote that the best salt-fish products came from Greece. Scappi observed that Italian connoisseurs in Rome imported *buca* and sardines from Genoa, sturgeon and caviar from Alexandria, and salmon from Flanders, Burgundy, and various places in Italy. The Scotsman Fynes Moryson found the markets of Venice teeming with "great abundance of red herrings and pickled herrings, Sardelle, anchove, and like pickled fishes, of Caviale (a salt liquor made of fish) and Botargo (as I thinke the roe of a fish . . . all held for great dainties)."[33]

Tuna was a huge business in Italy, Portugal, Spain, Sicily, and other points. Konrad Gesner found it available at pickle shops in the sixteenth century. In the early eighteenth century Dela-mare reported that tuna was cut into slices and salted in tins or barrels in Provence and Languedoc and then sent to Paris, where it was sold with anchovies "not by merchants selling salt fish products but by grocers," who also carried the hams of

A Spur to the Appetite

highest repute. Traveling on the south coast of France later in the century, the English novelist Tobias Smollett was struck by the extent of the tuna industry: "A Company of adventurers have farmed the tunny-fishery of the King, for six years; a monopoly, for which they pay about three thousand pounds sterling."[34]

Anchovies, because of their use in sauces, may have had a bigger market still. Like olives and capers, they were stocked in shops in towns by the sixteenth century, and owners of estates kept large quantities of them on hand to avoid the high prices of the small retail dealers. In 1682 John Collins observed that anchovies came to England from Genoa in three-gallon barrels, and in 1727 John Houghton reported them very common not only in Genoa but in Venice, Rome, and Provence. Smollett noted that the immense quantities of anchovies caught in French waters were "salted, barreled, and exported into all the different kingdoms and states of Europe." If you lived in a rather isolated situation, you carried your anchovies with you, because even if you were willing to pay the retailers' prices, you could not always find these little fish. Richard Bradley wrote: "As the People in the Country have not always the convenience of a Market near them, and the Anchovy is often required for Fish-Sauce; so should every Family keep a quantity by them. They should be large and freshly brought over when we buy them."[35]

The Italians went to considerable trouble and expense to obtain caviar, bringing it not only from Alexandria but from as far as Russia. The Russians, Nonnius reported in 1627, prepared caviar "near the Black Sea from sturgeon roe which are collected, pressed together in huge lumps, packed into large vessels, and sent chiefly to Italy where it is much prized."[36]

From the same informant we learn that what we now call smoked salmon or lox was already coveted: "Among the Germans, French, and Belgians the most lauded salt fish (*salsamenta*) is prepared from salmon, for it is an oily fish and not tough." Herring "fill the establishments that process salt fish. From Belgium they are sent all over Europe." In England, Thomas Moffett tells us, this fish from the Baltic provided "an unusual and common meat coveted as much of the Nobility for variety and wantoness, as used of poor men for want of other provision."[37]

The Dutch took over the bulk of the herring trade in the

The Salt-Acid Taste

course of the sixteenth century and developed a boat specially designed to enable the crew to salt and pack herring on board. A ritual developed in Holland around the first salted herring delivery of the season, because short salting was considered to produce a delicacy: "The first of the catch always fetched a high price," J. H. Parry reports; "on the day when the first [boats] . . . arrived at Rotterdam or Vlaardingen the Dutch— usually no great horsemen—used every means of speed in a race to sell the first barrels of 'new herring' in the Hague and Amsterdam. Dealers kept light carts and fast horses for this purpose—as a matter of profit." This ritual race is reminiscent of the ancients' quest for newly salted fish, and of the people of whom Strabo and Plutarch tell, who put aside whatever they were doing when a bell sounded and rushed to meet the runners delivering fresh sea delicacies (*opsa*).[38]

As the taste for salty foods spread, the demand for salt itself rose. Bruyerin's assessment shows us the power of culture on the economy: "Almost nothing today brings more tax to the French king than salt."[39] Beyond the small amount of salt necessary for survival, convention determines how much of it one consumes; salty food is a taste one learns to like.

# CHAPTER 9     Salads in the Cookbooks

The most important salt product in Apicius's recipes is the fish sauce *garum*; it is present in so many of them that it was undoubtedly a characteristic taste of Roman food. Olives appear in a cabbage dish and in a leek dish, and are claimed to be good to stuff any bird. A dish of many ingre-

APICIUS (FOURTH CENTURY)
Another method [for leeks]. Cook the leeks with olives and serve as above.

Another method for [cabbage]. Dress as above, add fresh olives, and allow to come to the boil.

Horse-parsley or Alexanders. Make up into bunches. They are good eaten raw with *liquamen* [*garum*], oil, and wine, or you can eat them with grilled fish.

Sala cattabia. Pepper, mint, celery (seed?), dried pennyroyal, cheese, pine-kernels, honey, vinegar, *liquamen*, yolks of egg, fresh water. Have ready some pieces of bread soaked in water mixed with vinegar. Squeeze out the moisture, and arrange in a mould, followed by layers of cow's milk cheese, cucumbers, alternating with pine-kernels. Add finely chopped capers . . . alternating with chicken liver. Pour on the dressing, place over cold water [to cool], and serve.

> Another way to cook a bird. Stuff the bird with chopped fresh olives, sew it up, and boil. Afterwards remove the cooked olives.
>
> Boiled chicken in its own juice. Pound pepper, cumin, a little thyme, fennel seed, mint, rue, asafoetida root; moisten with vinegar, add Jericho date, and pound this too. Blend with honey, vinegar, *liquamen*, and oil. Pour over the cooled and dried chicken and serve.
>
> Source: Apicius, *Roman Cookery Book*, pp. 81, 83, 93, 149, 153.

dients has chopped capers and other Lucanian sausages. A mixture of brain, livers, cheese, and eggs contains salt fish.[1]

Although Arabic food was much sweeter than it was salty, it still used salt products. The recipes call for a fermented sauce, *almorí*, sometimes made with a fish base.[2] "A Baghdad Cookery Book" uses *almorí* less than the Hispanic-Moorish text, perhaps because of the Roman influence in Iberia. Roman influence probably also accounts for the Hispanic-Moorish text's reliance on olive oil, whereas "A Baghdad Cookery Book" uses fat from the tail of the lamb.

"A Baghdad Cookery Book" employs no capers, olives, or salt meat as auxiliary items in composed dishes but gives a few recipes for salt fish. The Hispanic-Moorish text calls for no capers or salt meat, and uses olives only four times. Maxim Rodinson noted conserves of olives, capers, and a few other vegetables in a contemporary cookery work from the Middle East. A passage in *Meadows of Gold* describes a platter of olives and salt fish and capers in a vermilion sauce. These salt items were part of the culinary culture but they certainly did not dominate it.[3]

The fourteenth- and fifteenth-century European cookery works also show a limited use of salt products. The *Libro di cucina* uses salt pork (*lardo insalato*) four times in composed dishes and offers a recipe for mortadella, a spiced pork sausage. *Le Ménagier de Paris* considers salt to be primarily a preservative: tongues are salted for keeping and salted fish are to be eaten when fresh are not to be had. It makes an exception for ham, though: a ham is to be salted for three days so that it will be good.[4]

Our first sight of change comes in a mid-fifteenth-century Italian cookery work that mentions caviar, botargo, and salt

The Salt-Acid Taste

tuna. By 1475 Platina had advanced the place of salt with his mentions of caviar, botargo, salt tuna, olives, capers, green salads, hams, and Roman sausages. Messisbugo's menus in 1549 and Scappi's in 1570 contain a large number of salads of olives, capers, asparagus, artichokes, mushrooms, greens, lemons, and oranges. A profusion of salt meats (*salami*) such as ham and various types of sausages are offered, and an abundance of salt fish—anchovies, sardines, herring, botargo, sturgeon, caviar, salmon—are suggested for fast days. Scappi gives instructions for preparing "various salt fish . . . [which] are served on the proper tables of great princes," and recipes for ham and sausages such as *mortadella gialla* and *salcizza gialla*.[5]

In 1570 Scappi accompanies duck and partridge with capers and roast meat with olives. This use of salt vegetables as condiments had not yet emerged in Messisbugo's 1549 work, but we find it in Apicius's text. The Italian works almost never mention

BARTOLOMEO SCAPPI (1570)

To cook . . . partridges . . . on the spit and other ways. . . . They are able to be served, after being roasted and cut up, with capers, sugar, and cinnamon on top, or with slices of small very acid lemons and sugar on top.

To stew any sort of capon and domestic fowl. Once the capons and fowls have been plucked and cleaned and their innards removed, they can be filled with a composition found in chapter 116. After having been stuffed, they may be put in a stewing pot with a pound of ham cut in slices, half an ounce of whole cinnamon, a quarter of an ounce of ginger, half an ounce of nutmeg, sufficient saffron, a half-pint of white wine, a tumbler of pale verjuice, and four ounces altogether of dry plums and sour cherries, and four ounces of raisins. Now put in enough water to cover the capon and cook with the vessel closed and sealed so that no vapor may escape. When it is cooked, serve with the mixture over it. . . .

To roast and prepare turtledoves and quail in several ways. . . . Sometimes fat quail are half-salted with salt and fennel and left to stand in a wooden or earthenware vessel three or four days, and then fried in pork fat with onion. . . .

*Source:* Scappi, *Opera*, pp. 59v, 52r, 56r.

Salads in the Cookbooks

salt fish as a condiment. Messisbugo once uses finely cut-up botargo in a dish of artichokes, and Scappi twice uses salt eel in a stuffing. Of all the salads in sixteenth-century Italian composed dishes, however, salt meat is by far the most extensively used—in marked contrast to Apicius's usage. Scappi boils capons with "salami" (salt meat); slices of prosciutto (ham) appear in a beef dish; cardoons or artichokes are prepared with "diverse salt meats." Sometimes the recipe gives a choice—ham or *gola de porco*, say, or ham or *cervellato*. Ham is by far the salt meat most frequently mentioned. This Italian twist on Roman food, the addition of the salt meats beloved of the ancients as condiments, was again not yet prominent in Messisbugo's 1549 work, although he sometimes recommended the use of "good ham or salt meat" and "ham for odor."[6]

Scappi uses half-salting extensively. Soak the belly of a fresh pike in water and salt for three hours, then cook with salt so that it remains "tasty." Leave beef to marinate in summer for four days and eight in winter. And if you need salt beef quickly and the animal has just been slaughtered, boil the meat in water with a very large amount of salt until the meat is cooked. Marinated meat and fish dishes abound. Twenty years earlier they were not prominent in Messisbugo's recipes.[7]

A 1591 English cookbook shows a "Sallet" and a boiled "Sallet" with spinach, vinegar, and sugar. By the early seventeenth century salads had begun to play a prominent part in English menus as dishes on their own, but not as condiments. In mid-sixteenth-century France the *Grand cuisinier de toute cuisine*'s menus show some plates of orange and lemon salads, sausages, green salads, olives, cucumbers, and hams from Mainz.[8]

In the mid–seventeenth century La Varenne, like the Italians, continued to recommend salad platters, including salt meats, which he suggested should be kept on hand. He gave instructions for half-salt or marinated fish and chicken and directions for preserving lettuce, artichokes, cucumbers, purslane, asparagus, chicory, and cabbage. Salt products are prominent in his composed dishes. The melted anchovy, or *garum*, makes its debut, linking La Varenne closely with Apicius. In contrast to the Italians, he gave no kind of salt meat any prominence in composed dishes. The mid-seventeenth-century French twist on Roman food is the caper, which now makes its appearance in dishes of every sort.[9]

The Salt-Acid Taste

47. Pieter Claesz, *Still Life* (c. 1651). Oil on panel, 59 × 79.5 cm. Rijksmuseum Kröller-Müller, Otterloo, The Netherlands. Reproduced by permission of the Kröller-Müller Stichting.

FRANÇOIS PIERRE DE LA VARENNE (1651)

Capon with oysters. Your capon being dressed and barded with lard and buttered paper, roast it over a pan to catch the drippings. After you have cleaned your oysters, blanch them if they are old. Once they have been cleaned and blanched, sauté them with what has fallen into the dripping pan. Season them with champignons, onion stuck [with a clove], and a bouquet. When they are well fried, lift out the bouquet and put the remainder of the mixture you have sautéed into the cavity of the capon. Now simmer the capon with a few capers and serve.

Ramequin of onion. Take your onions and pound them in a mortar with salt and a great deal of pepper. You may put in well-melted anchovies with a little butter. Pass a red-hot iron over the top and serve.

Cucumbers. Take very small ones. Blanch them and stick them with a clove. Then put them in a vessel with salt, pepper,

Salads in the Cookbooks

vinegar, and a bay leaf. Cover them so well that no air comes in. Serve them as a salad.

Fried and marinated tench. Once you have cleaned them, split them in half, then marinate them with salt, pepper, onion, and lemon peel. When the marinating has been completed, take them out and wipe them off. Coat them with flour or with two or three eggs beaten with a little flour and some salt. Fry them with mature butter. When they are cooked, pour in your marinade, let it bubble up, and serve. Garnish with what you have.

*Source:* La Varenne, *Cuisinier français*, pp. 51–52, 105, 270, 179.

François Massialot's menus, reflecting the meals served by the duc de Chartres, show much the same preference for salted foods. The only real difference between Massialot's and La Varenne's recipes is Massialot's greater stress on ham as a condiment. He offers salt beef topped with a chopped mixture of ham, roasted hare with a ham sauce, artichoke hearts with a ham sauce, sweetbreads stuffed with ham, chicken with ham. Yet this use of ham never approaches Scappi's.[10] In time to come, though, small pieces of *petit lard* or *salé* (salt pork) were to play major roles in French recipes.

Massialot continues the use of anchovies in, for example, a stuffed fish with an anchovy sauce and a sauce for roast meat with anchovies and shallots, and he suggests salads of sole, turbot, brill, oysters, smelts, salmon, trout, skate, whiting, stingfish, tuna, anchovies, sardines, salmon, shrimp, and crayfish. Chicken and any kind of game bird, he says, may be prepared with olives. We find combinations with names still familiar to us, such as a remoulade composed of parsley, green onion, anchovy, salt, pepper, nutmeg, oil, and vinegar. He urges the use of all garden vegetables as salads.[11]

The English cookbooks of the eighteenth century, like those published in France, seem to be full-blown expressions of Pliny's *acetaria*. Hannah Glasse included recipes for pickled walnuts, gherkins, large cucumbers, asparagus, radishes, French beans, cauliflowers, beetroot, onions, fungi, fennel, nasturtium berries, artichokes, and cabbage in her *Art of Cookery*. In 1731 Patrick Lamb said, "We dress with Olives in the same manner [as ducks] Teals, Pullets, Capons, Chickens and Partridges." For a stewed rump of beef Glasse called for "two spoonfuls of Capers

The Salt-Acid Taste

48. Jan Jansz den Uyl the Elder, *Still Life with Ham* (ca. 1640). Oil on panel, 25½″ × 20¼″. Courtesy of the Wadsworth Atheneum, Hartford, Conn., Ella Gallup Sumner and Mary Catlin Sumner Collection.

or Astertion [nasturtium] Buds pickled, or Broom Buds." She recommended the addition of "white Walnut Pickle, or Mushrooms, in the room of Capers, just to make your Sauce a little tart." Elizabeth Raper, daughter of a merchant in the East India Company and wife of a Hertfordshire physician in the second half of the eighteenth century, included a "sauce for any meat broiled on spits" in her collection of recipes: "Mix oil, vinegar, a little pepper and salt . . . parsley, a little pickled cucumber and some shallot, all chopt very fine." In addition the English took up a variety of eastern pickles not seen in the French or Italian works. "Indian pickle" or "Picca Lillo" (piccalilli), with its salt-acid taste, fitted easily into the model of salads taken from antiquity.[12]

The English pickled as much fish as they did vegetables. Like the French, they embraced the melted anchovy. In 1743 Sarah

49. Jan Davidsz de Heem, *Still Life with a Lobster* (c. 1645–50). Oil on canvas, 79.2 × 102.5 cm. Reproduced by permission of the Trustees of the Wallace Collection, London.

Harrison claimed that the recipe for stewed carp with melted anchovy in her *House-keeper's Pocket Book* was the one devised by the cook at Pontack, a well-known London eating establishment. By the end of the seventeenth century the English were not only using the anchovy as a *garum*, as in France, but were often incorporating it in a mixture they began to make in imitation of a product that was at first imported from somewhere in the East: "And now we have a new Sawce called Catchup, from East India, sold at a Guiney a Bottle."[13]

For the English, as for the French, salt meat was relatively unimportant as a condiment, with the exception of an occasional piece of ham or salt pork. Like the French, they continued to offer large platters of salt meats and give recipes for them: Robert May suggested in 1660 that "roast Beef, Chine, Surloin, Rib, Brisket, Flank, or Neats Tongues" be pickled. Nathan Bailey offered a recipe "to salt a Ham in imitation of Westphalia." Madam Johnson's cookery work includes a recipe

The Salt-Acid Taste

59

50. "Delicate Cowcumbers to pickle," from *The Cryes of the City of London Drawne after the Life*, by Pierce Tempest (London, 1711). Print Collection, Miriam and Ira D. Wallach Division of Art, Prints, and Photographs, The New York Public Library, Astor, Lenox, and Tilden Foundations.

for "Pickle for Pork, that is proper to be eaten in a Week, or ten Days time."[14]

The English paid more attention to the composed salad than either the Italians or French had done in the sixteenth and seventeenth centuries. Scappi reported having prepared "tuna mixed with caviar" for the meal celebrating the coronation of Pius V on January 17, 1566. Elsewhere he mentioned an *Insalata di mescolanza* in his list of menus, which may have been a mixed green salad, perhaps the kind Massonio described in his salad book sixty years later: "Some salads that we eat are called

Salads in the Cookbooks          {157}

'mixed' because they are made up of different sorts of greens put together and made into a salad. [And they are mixed] either because they are more useful in medicine, or because they stimulate the appetite more." A few pages later he remarked that another kind of mixed salad could be made with lettuce, very thin slices of lemon, olives, salt sardines, onion, salt tuna, parsley, and similar materials. "But this kind of salad is little in use." A French cookery book published in 1654 describes an arrangement of ham, tongue, and sausage of various sorts with some little "Ragouts & Sallades" in the middle. That assortment was probably the stimulus for such English contrivances as "Bal-

51. "Fair Lemons & Oranges," from *The Cryes of the City of London Drawne after the Life*, by Pierce Tempest (London, 1711). Print Collection, Miriam and Ira D. Wallach Division of Art, Prints, and Photographs, The New York Public Library, Astor, Lenox, and Tilden Foundations.

The Salt-Acid Taste

lonia Sausages, Anchovies, Mushrooms, Caviare, and pickled Oysters, in a dish together."[15]

By the late seventeenth century the English made "grand salads" in several forms; "some all sorts of pickles laid orderly

E. SMITH (1739)

To make English ketchup. Take a wide-mouth'd bottle, put therein a pint of the best white-wine vinegar; then put in ten or twelve cloves of eschalot peeled and just bruised; then take a quarter of a pint of the best Langoon white-wine, boil it a little, and put to it twelve or fourteen anchovies wash'd and shred, and dissolve them in the wine, and when cold put them in the bottle; then take a quarter of a pint more of white wine, and put in it mace, ginger sliced, a few cloves, a spoonful of whole pepper just bruised, let them boil all a little; when near cold, slice in almost a whole nutmeg, and some lemon-peel, and like wise put in two or three spoonfuls of horse-radish; then stop it close, and for a week shake it once or twice a day; then use it; 'tis good to put into fish sauce, or any savoury dish of meat; you may add to it the clear liquor that comes from mushrooms.

To hash a Lamb's Neck. Boil the Head and Neck at most a quarter of an hour, the Heart five minutes, and the Lights half an hour, the Liver boil'd or fry'd in slices (but not hash'd), slice all the rest very thin, put in the gravy that runs from it, and a quarter of a pint of the liquor they are boiled in, a few spoonfuls of walnut liquor, or a little elder-vinegar, a little ketchup, pepper, salt, and nutmeg, the brains a little boiled and chopped, with half a spoonful of flour and a piece of butter as big as a walnut mixed up with them; but before you put in the butter, put in four middling cucumbers sliced thin and stewed a little time, or you may fry them in butter before you put them into the Hash, and shake them up together; but they are excellent good if only stew'd. . . .

To fricasy Fish. Melt butter according to the quantity of fish you have; melt it thick; cut your fish in pieces in length and breadth three fingers, then put them and your butter into a frying or stew-pan; it must not boil too fast, for fear of breaking the fish, and turning the butter into oil; turn them often until they are enough: put in a bunch of sweet-herbs at first, an onion, two or three anchovies cut small, a little pepper, nutmeg, mace, lemon-peel, two or three cloves; when all these are in, put in some claret, and let them stew all together; beat up six yolks of eggs and put them in, with such pickles as you please, as oysters, mushrooms, and capers, shake them well together that they do not curdle: if you put the spice in whole, take it out when it is done. The seasoning ought to be stewed first in a little water, and then the butter melted in that and wine before you put the fish in. Jacks do best this way.

Source: Smith, *Compleat Housewife*, pp. 91, 42, 28.

HENRY HOWARD (1717)

Salamongundy. Take Chicken or Veal minced very fine, then lay a Layer of it, and a Layer of the Yolks of hard Eggs, and a Layer of the Whites; a Layer of Anchovies, a Layer of Limon; then a Layer of all sorts of Pickles, or as many as you have; and between everyone of these, lay a Layer of Sorrel, Spinage and Chives shred very fine, as the others; and when you have laid your Dish all round, that it's full, only leave a place a top to set an Orange or Lemon; Garnish with Horse-radish, Limon and Barberries: This is proper for a second Course Side-dish, or a Middle-dish, for Supper: You must take two Dishes and lay the uppermost dish to build the Salamongundy on, it being out of fashion to mix it all together, but everyone mixes it on their Plates; some like it with the Juice of Limon, and some with Oil and Vinegar beat up thick together.

Source: Howard, *England's Newest Way*, p. 64.

in a great Dish, with a Tree or some device set in the middle of it, others of sorts of Souced Meats cut in slices, and others with all sorts of coloured Jellies." Another is a proto-version of the salmagundi that often appears in the eighteenth-century cookbooks.[16] In the course of that century the influence of the grand salad moved from England back to the Continent to become the progenitor of today's so-called *salade niçoise*. The 1742 *Nouvelle cuisine* has a recipe for a cold leg of lamb garnished with artichoke hearts, olives, anchovies, beets, cornichons, capers, chervil, and carrot, the whole platter "seasoned with good oil and tarragon vinegar." A cooked rabbit is sliced and mixed with anchovies, capers, onions, salt, oil, pepper, and vinegar.[17]

The salt-acid taste was the heart of the new food, whether it was a platter of salt meat, a composite dish with pickled products, a grand salad—almost a meal in itself—or, as we shall see, the entire meal, in fact, up to the dessert.

The Salt-Acid Taste

# PART 4  The French Synthesis and Design

Is it less strange, the Prodigal should waste
His wealth, to purchase what he ne'er can taste?
Not for himself he sees, or hears, or eats;
Artists must chuse his Pictures, Music, Meats.
Alexander Pope, Epistle IV, "To the Earl
of Burlington" (1731)

# CHAPTER 10   Inventing the Modern World

With the publication in 1651 of *Le Cuisinier françois* by François Pierre de La Varenne, the French broke with Italian Renaissance food and launched modern cooking. By the end of the seventeenth century all of Renaissance Europe, even the Italians, recognized that the French had dramatically changed their cuisine and were beginning to follow their example.[1] The French, the new mentors, had set what would become for the Western world the correct attitude toward eating and gained an authority in cooking which they have yet to lose. This radical transformation of cookery was part of a major cultural shift that reached into all aspects of living and learning, both on the Continent and in England.

The establishment of modern cuisine and modern science as normative during the seventeenth century had a common basis. The freeing of food and of natural philosophy from the web of the occult universe was part of the process that sought to rid the Western world of the magus, that symbol of supernatural power whose increasing grip on Protestant sectaries and many others posed a threat to entrenched powers. Assumptions about a connection between the occult and food came to be rejected in a social and political context that ushered in a new mentality, one that permitted the scientist, the artist, and the hedonist to sit more comfortably side by side.

To understand more clearly the steps the French took to create a new food, let us review the course food took up until the seventeenth century. Highly spiced and golden food had taken root in medieval Europe primarily for two reasons. It had been viewed as the basis of a culture that acknowledged sensuality openly, in a way that Christendom did not. Spice thus connoted luxury and indulgence in a pleasurable table. At the same time, fragrance and golden hue, elements linking humans to the divine in the Plotinian universe, were essential components of cordial, alchemical, and astrological medicine.

Some sixteenth-century French took from the Italians the idea of including in their dishes motifs derived from Greek and Roman texts, and followed their mentors in giving fungi, fish, salt pork, chopped meat, artichokes, asparagus, and other specialties honored places on their tables. Throughout the century, however, the golden-spice framework remained paramount. While Europeans were under the influence of the Italian Renaissance, they embraced contrary notions about food; the magically spiritual and the voluptuously earthy appeared on the same banquet table. Fragrant golden mixtures incorporating sensual and spiritual values took their place next to sensual salads; alluring composite dishes with Greco-Roman motifs often had a sweetly perfumed base and golden tint.

In the seventeenth century the French created and promoted a new style of cookery that broke with the Italian model. The French did three things. First, they all but eliminated sweet odors and the color of gold from their food, thereby wrenching the aspect of the divine from Renaissance food; the fact that gold, spicy food also had a sensual side did not save it. Second, the French took one voluptuous aspect of Italian Renaissance food, the salt-acid taste, and adapted it to build a framework in which they incorporated other motifs from antiquity. Third, they *tamed* the concept of alchemical quintessences by lifting them out of the realm of the mysterious and placing them in the realm of the sensual. In the new sauces built on these essences, they interpreted harmony as the condition in which each ingredient loses its particular identity to merge with the whole.

## FRENCH PROTESTANTS: HEALING THE HUMAN AND POLITICAL BODIES

The Catholic church had always turned a suspicious eye on proponents of occult ideas—that is, mysteries not associated

The French Synthesis and Design

with its own. It had not coped well with the influx of magic from the Arabic world; many of its clergy, such as Ficino, were swept up by these notions that competed with the church's magic. Though from time to time the church leveled aspersions and threats at magi of all sorts, in general an uneasy peace prevailed. With the rise of the Protestant forces in the sixteenth century, however, the tide turned decisively against the occult. Threatened with major revolt, the church took a determined stance against heretical magic, and by the end of the century the edicts of the Council of Trent brought Giordano Bruno to the stake, Tommaso Campanella to prison, and the works of Paracelsus to their place on the Index. Now Catholics in France were wary of openly acknowledging Neoplatonism and the Plotinian universe, but many Protestants still stood resolutely behind the divine medicine of Paracelsus. Thus, when open civil war erupted, France found itself riven not only by politics and religion but also by medical philosophy.[2]

The Galenic Catholic medical faculty of the University of Paris had begun to strike at its foe in the 1560s. They were particularly enraged when Henry IV, though he had converted to Catholicism, surrounded himself with a ring of Protestant physicians who practiced alchemical medicine. The friction between the two medical groups was to continue for fifty years.[3]

In the 1630s the medical faculty pounced on Theophraste Renaudot. Born a Protestant in 1586 at Loudon, Renaudot went to Paris and converted to Catholicism, probably to increase his opportunities. Conversion did little to dampen either his passion for occult subjects or his devotion to public welfare for the indigent, both commitments of his mentor, Paracelsus. Renaudot was dedicated to purifying both the corrupt world and the corrupt human body. At the Parisian Bureau d'Adresse, where he ministered to the poor without charge, he held discussions on the occult thinking of Geronimo Cardano, Guillaume Postel, Paracelsus, Ramón Lull, and Tommaso Campanella, and also aired his views on skepticism. By the late 1630s the discussions had become so controversial that the faculty accused him of Paracelsianism, Protestantism, and witchcraft.[4]

Gui Patin, spokesman for the faculty, claimed that he could cure more people by his Galenic means "than the Arabs, with all their syrups and opiates." Renaudot insisted that "there was nothing irreligious about Arab, i.e., chemical medicine." If Patin could argue that Hippocrates and Galen could have been good

Inventing the Modern World

Christians, "why not also Arab physicians, and by association, the physicians of Montpellier?" (The university at Montpellier, a Protestant stronghold, backed alchemical medicine.) Renaudot did not emerge the victor from this debate. When Richelieu, who had patronized him, died in 1642, Renaudot's mystical vision of repairing the political and human bodies died with him.[5]

Renaudot was not the only Catholic physician to maintain close ties to the radical medical thinking associated with Montpellier. Many Catholics circumspectly sought out alchemical healers, as did Richelieu himself. A diverse group of French Protestants, too, remained interested in alchemy in the seventeenth century. What the people in power found especially unnerving was the call to social and political action issued by Protestants imbued with the alchemical vision. A 1635 emblem by Abraham Bosse indicates the ideological challenge that this group was disseminating, and merits our close attention.

Bosse, a Protestant engraver known for his portrayals of French society, moved to Paris in 1632, about the time Renaudot's Bureau d'Adresse was beginning to blossom. The emblem he produced in 1635 (Figure 52) shows forth his radical Protestant views and the occult philosophy with which they were entwined. The motto of Bosse's emblem is "Taste" (*Gustus*, *Goust*). The device depicts a scene of wealth in a typical Renaissance architectural setting. A man and a woman are dining with three persons in attendance. At the center of the table is an artichoke holder containing a large artichoke, from which the woman is plucking a leaf. Below, two poems, one in Latin and one in French, comment on the device. The Latin reads:

> Whatever seeps from the land, whatever flows down from the
>  stars, whatever sails on smooth waters,
> All these things are untiringly laboring for me without end.
> Rightly I am called the King of the senses and of men.

The French poem reads:

> How taste without excess has honest charms.
> How nature takes pleasure in reasonable things.
> And how it well shows that the luxury of tables
> Makes us starve in the midst of the meal.

The French Synthesis and Design

The two poems are critical comments on food. Our palates may be stimulated and our stomachs feel full, yet we perish morally in following false taste and pursuing the trifles of a sumptuous board. The artichoke, symbolic of the hedonistic follies of antiquity, has no place in a judicious life. The French verse could have been written by any of the moralists of antiquity or their humanist followers; the Latin poem is alchemical and Christian. The moral humanist position enhances the Christian alchemical one. Alchemical literature insists that the adept be a good and righteous person. The alchemist who is not righteous cannot purify the world. The French offers a negative comment on voluptuous dining and the Latin forcefully sets out the "true" path. The speaker, Taste, claims to be king of the senses, and the path to enlightened taste is through alchemy. All spiritual forces work for this true Taste: the spirit over the water, the celestial rays that shoot down from the heavens, and the seepage

52. Abraham Bosse, *Taste* (in the series *The Five Senses*) (1635). Engraving, 25.7 × 32.6 cm. Courtesy of the Smith College Museum of Art, Northampton, Mass.

or exhalation from the earth, capable of producing metals and minerals, as Aristotle said in a passage that is a root of alchemy. True Taste is in things that nourish the *spiritus*, not in things that feed corporeal pleasure, such as artichokes. For a man, wrote Paracelsus, is a beast when he "finds his food in the earth. But he ought not to be like a beast; his essence stems from the eternal and he should therefore feed on things eternal. For he was created not beast, but man, in the image and likeness of God."[6]

The tapestry behind Bosse's diners depicts an entourage of two unveiled women on horseback accompanied by two turbaned riders carrying shields bearing crescents. Two men on foot accompany the party. One has no head covering; the other wears a presumably European soldier's helmet and carries a shield that also bears a crescent. One of the turbaned men holds the Roman standard. The symbolism implies an exchange of culture between Europeans and Muslims. The tapestry bears the message of irenic religious toleration—ostensibly for Muslims but by implication for Protestants as well. The idea of the *prisca theologica*, an occult body of knowledge passed from one sage or prophet to the next, which had served to bring together Plato and Christ, could now be used to underwrite a union of all religions. Bosse's device pleads for peace with the menacing Turk and argues against a narrow chauvinistic stance. Like Renaudot, he was inspired by the twofold alchemical program— the purification of the human body and the transformation of human society.[7]

## PROTESTANT SECTARIES AND SOCIAL UPHEAVAL

Ideas of social justice developed rapidly in the spirit of liberalism that prevailed in England in the 1640s. Samuel Hartlib was one of many Europeans who crossed the Channel in the hope of helping to create an alchemical revolution and a new society. His ideas, however, would seem tame by the next decade, for he aimed merely to establish an institution such as Renaudot's, which would redress social ills and cure disease. In the course of the two English civil wars of the 1640s, the regicide of 1649, and the eleven-year interregnum that followed, Protestant politics moved far to the left. God, the sectaries insisted, gave no person the right to direct another's life. Thus the state was by its very nature corrupt, any church hierarchy

The French Synthesis and Design

was evil, and Puritan presbyters were as bad as Anglican bishops or the pope himself. Moreover, men could not claim to own women, there was nothing sacred about marriage, and men and women could lie with whomever they would. Social decorum, the sectaries said, was the artifice of a sinful society that had been driven from Eden. The prophets of the radical sectaries preached that the millennium would arrive sometime in the 1650s; then the poor would inherit the earth and all material wealth would be shared. Private property, in their view, contradicted the tenets of the Christian faith.

These and other radical claims spread in sectary meetings and in a press that was virtually free of constraint. Packed together in warrenlike circumstances, London's poor drank in this kind of talk, and far from the hubbub of the city itinerants brought news of the latest urban sectary demands and preached to radical sects in the forests and countryside. When this flood of words began to be translated into deeds, it seemed to many people that a social revolution was at hand, that the poor were literally attempting to take over the earth. In various parts of the country, sectaries seized and cultivated common land. Their most celebrated foray came in 1649, when a Digger colony tried to work St. George's Hill, not far from London.

The creed that emboldened the sectaries to act as they did was permeated by occult premises. Radical magi took to heart notions of popular pantheism and human divinity, which in their view empowered them to act as prophets and miracle workers. They could draw down power from the planets, which were linked to earth through the Plotinian universe. In their laboratories they could produce wondrous essences—potable gold for transforming all around. They claimed to foresee future political events, and gained influence by promising the people wonders of all kinds. Striking out at one of the sects, a foe said that they "are very confident that by knowledge of astrology and strength of reason they shall be able to conquer over the whole world." Through all these sects ran a thread of Christian alchemy—a vision of a return to the primordial state. Alchemy became so entrenched among the mystical sects that to be a sectarian was almost by definition to be a believer in alchemy. Sectaries wished to wipe away the dross of the here and now and return to the golden era of the Garden of Eden, which they envisioned as a Christian utopia.[8]

As the Protestant movement became increasingly radical,

people with power and assets grew ever more nervous about both the dissenters' actual demands and the cosmology that emboldened them. Even some sectarians were uncomfortable with the more radical aspects of the movement and sought to dissociate themselves from the most notorious of the radicals. George Fox, founder of the Society of Friends, withdrew his Quakers from the "scabrous" Ranters. Earlier in the century, the German Andreas Libavius (d. 1616), a systematizer of alchemy, had in a sense predicted the social and political consequences of the alchemical vision. He had recoiled in fear from the "madmen" Paracelsus and Oswald Croll and the "phantasies of their imagination." To him Paracelsus's "enthusiasm" (inspiration by the divine) was a threat to the "fabric of society." Now, in mid-seventeenth-century England, Robert Boyle, a wealthy scion of a prominent family that had been intrigued by the idea of a Christian utopia and by alchemical healing, turned against the Paracelsian vision. However alluring alchemy's promise of enduring youth and a life free of sickness, it was not worth the accompanying social upheaval. A year before the restoration of Charles II, Christopher Hill writes, "a pamphleteer noticed 'the old spirit of the gentry brought in play again', opposing an 'earthly, lordly rule' to 'the growing light of the people of God'." It was this "growing light," Hill maintains, that made "the most considerable" of people forget their old objections to the Anglican church and bishops. The sectaries who survived, such as the Quakers, made concessions, the primary one being that earth was anything but heaven, and for the time being, anyway, the poor would inherit neither power nor land.[9]

## THE FALL OF THE PLOTINIAN UNIVERSE

The English pandemonium sent tremors through the Catholic establishment in France. With the Treaty of Westphalia (1648) France was at last done with a bloody and exhausting conflict; though a victor, it stood as raw and vulnerable as any other participant in the Thirty Years' War. The next year the French court witnessed the regicide in England, a powerful image to the royal family in Paris, which now faced its own civil war. In this highly flammable situation radical mysticism could underwrite profound social and political dissension, as it had done in England. This was the setting, then, in which the French esca-

The French Synthesis and Design

lated their war on the Plotinian cosmology that fed the claims of the alchemists, astrologers, and prophets. Mysticism was effectively swept from its prominent position by a variety of tactics. "Enthusiasm" was discussed less openly. The "cultivated" hoisted high a new cosmology that made God less accessible. Taste dictated an indulgence in earthly eroticism rather than the ecstatic variety celebrated by such mystics as Saint Teresa (1515–1582). The medical establishments denied the power of mystical medicine, and the academies now expelled metaphysics, the occult, and "inspired" art. Cooks turned from spice and saffron to Greco-Roman motifs.

Mysticism was, in a sense, blotted out. One of the most innovative features of the assault on the occult in the seventeenth century was an engulfing silence. Magic was deliberately ignored. Our view of the transition from the Renaissance world to the modern world is still clouded by this hush, as it was intended to be. Though this was one of the major transformations in history, the old forms seem simply to fade away.

As Hugh Trevor-Roper points out, by 1697, "in Pierre Bayle's great *Dictionnaire historique et critique*, that marvelous repository of the learning of the past two centuries—or rather, perhaps, that capacious acid tank in which that learning was quietly dissolved —there is no entry for Paracelsus: indeed, in all that vast work, he is only mentioned once." Like Bayle in the face of Paracelsus, the eighteenth-century *Encyclopédie* closes off a part of history by omitting discussion of fragrant golden food. By the end of the seventeenth century, the scientific academies of Europe had little to say about the *spiritus* or its ability to extend life and wipe out melancholy through alchemical medicine. Sir Isaac Newton, who continued to think about occult philosophy and do alchemical experiments, kept this aspect of his work secret. An exchange of letters between Newton and John Locke after Robert Boyle died reveals that they and Boyle—perhaps the last men of Restoration England to be thought by historians forty years ago to have engaged in such activities—exchanged alchemical information and pledged one another to silence.[10]

In public all of these men endorsed the mechanical philosophy. The occult philosophy explained the universe in terms of a divine web of correlated influences—saffron, for example, was said to draw down solar power; the mechanical philosophy cut the web by removing the divine from anything but the cosmogony of the deanimated universe. By the end of the seven-

Inventing the Modern World

teenth century, melancholy had been incorporated into the transformation and given a mechanical causation, so that vitalistic medicine became useless. By advertising its support of the mechanical philosophy and insisting on witnessed experiments, the Royal Society pushed the magus and his claims from center stage, where they were not to be seen again until Anton Mesmer came forward to enchant his contemporaries in the second half of the eighteenth century. His opponents immediately noted a connection between "mesmerism" and past occult practices.[11]

Some historians have argued that the ascendancy of the mechanical philosophy resulted only in part from the social and political circumstances of the day.[12] In support of this position it can be said that Galileo's mechanical universe and the atomistic theories of Epicurus and Democritus were genuinely interesting and stimulating to Descartes, Boyle, Newton, and a slew of others. Nevertheless, the question remains why the idea of a mechanistic universe became publicly normative only in the second half of the century, after a period of radical turmoil. The physician Robert Fludd fought against a mechanical universe because it did not square with his belief in Neoplatonism. We might dismiss Fludd and others of his persuasion as blind reactionaries, but what do we do with the secret interests of Boyle, Locke, and Newton? Obviously they did not find the mechanistic universe completely satisfying, though in public they embraced it. Is it not possible that many people jettisoned the notion of a vitalistic universe *primarily* as a way of squelching the cosmology that supported the social and political radicalism of the time?

## THE MODERN EPICUREAN

Epicurus was important to developments in the seventeenth century in a variety of ways. His theory of an atomistic universe was part of the authority used to support a mechanical universe. Matter for him was inanimate, in contrast to the vitalism of the Platonic system. He argued against astral influences and superstition, and for some followers was the model of a moral man and an ideal way of life. In the seventeenth century Pierre Gassendi extolled him in these terms. Epicurus's gods sat detached from the workings of the natural world; instead of anxiety over retribution from the heavens, Epicurus offered a

The French Synthesis and Design

life of detached pleasure in a universe where the gods lived yonder and did not interfere in human affairs.

Epicurus's cosmology was the antithesis of the Plotinian universe, which had provided the base for the occult virtues of spice and color, and his ideas—or at least a latter-day version of them—provided part of the basis for the transformation of food. Since antiquity this philosopher, who emphasized the importance of the senses in the acquisition of knowledge and the life of pleasure as the ideal, had been distorted into a caricature. In this version of his thought, Epicurus came to stand for voluptuous living—for sensuous indulgence in the pleasures of the moment.

Much of the Epicureanism of the second half of the seventeenth century was of this kind. The publication of the *Puttana errante* in 1650 marked the flowering of a sexually explicit literature in France. Such works were soon available in translation in England, and in their emphasis on sex they are not unrelated to Restoration comedy. La Varenne's *Cuisinier françois* (1651) reflects the same voluptuous orientation. The new French cuisine—that is, modern cooking—was the food of the modern Epicurean, the *honnête homme*, the proper gallant, at once polished, playful, detached from cosmic spiritual and mystical concerns, and exceedingly hedonistic. In its shift of ingredients, the new cooking represents the substitution of revived notions of the earthly sensual for the mystical.

In sum, there were two versions of Epicurus, and each left its mark on the new cooking. The Epicurus who opposed the animate universe helped to topple the spice-sugar-saffron complex, and the parodic Epicurus of the lushly sensual garden was enlisted in support of cookery based on voluptuous motifs revived from antiquity. The "rational" joined hands with the luxurious and sexually alluring to displace the occult. It is no happenstance that Restoration comedy and the Royal Society appeared at the same time.

The Epicurean milieu was characterized by an ever-increasing desire to satisfy the palate. An eighteenth-century satire that appeared first in England and then in France sneered at the male connoisseur at the height of his culinary powers:

The Meal is now at once the most frivolous and most serious Part of Life—The Mind is bent to the utmost, and all the attention

Inventing the Modern World

exerted, for what? The critical Examination of compound Dishes, and if any two or three People happen to start some useful or agreeable Subject or Conversation, they are soon interrupted, and over-powered by the extatick Interjections of, Excellent! Exquisite! Delicious! pray taste this, you never eat a better Thing in your Life: Is that good! Is it tender? Is it season'd enough? Wou'd it not have been better so?[13]

In 1757 a wife moaned in the London *Connoisseur* that the magnificent feasts of Athens could not compare with the attention her husband paid to detail and "exquisite taste."[14] Pope in mirthful wit wrote:

> Our Courtier walks from dish to dish,
> Tastes for his Friend of Fowl and Fish;
> Tells all their names, lays down the law,
> 'Que ça est bon! Ah goutez ça!'[15]

## PHARMACY CHASTENED

An Epicurean environment was not a place in which miraculous medicines could thrive, and in both France and England the medical establishments cast them out. Dr. Steven's water, a cordial that appeared in many books of secrets, had been included in the London *Pharmacoepia* since 1618, but in the 1740s the Royal College of physicians dropped it and most other waters of this nature, claiming they contained too many ingredients. Since their decision does not seem to have been based on data obtained from experiments, their action might be taken as a blow to the system of which these cordials had been so long a part—a foreign system built on sweet fragrance and color. The deletion of the cordials from the pages of the *Pharmacoepia* echoes Pliny's disparagement of the compounds and "mysterious mixtures" from Arabia and India which were supposed to renew vitality.[16]

Despite the denunciation of these miraculous fragrant waters, belief in them did not fall away in a day. Not surprisingly, a market remained for the cordials. They came to be associated with quack medicine, and in England the Royal College of Physicians was lax in scrutinizing such products as Dr. Radcliffe's Famous Purging Elixir. The French Société Royale de Médecine, however, exercised its power to license or reject such

The French Synthesis and Design

medicaments quite strictly. One committee looked into and rejected a "potable gold" that was being peddled in Paris.[17]

If you were the king, however, these potions were probably readily available to you. Louis XIV, in any case, supervised his own alchemical-cordial regime. "On rising instead of a little bread, wine, and water, for quite some time he had taken only two cups of sage and veronica [herbal waters]," the duc de Saint-Simon reports. "Often between meals and always before going to bed he used to take glasses of Water . . . with a little orange flower water mixed in." He drank this orange water also at his meals. Between meals he took only cinnamon pastilles. "His soups, of which he ate several in the evening and in the morning . . . were filled with *jus* [the meat cordials of Avicenna] and of a great strength, and everything that was served to him was full of spices, double at least of what one ordinarily puts in, and very strong."[18] In private the great could interest themselves in hermetical medicine and dining; publicly they backed the new cooking.

## The Rout of Mysticism

With its web of connections, the Plotinian universe had been a powerful force behind demands for the establishment of a single academy to treat knowledge as a whole. Richelieu— his private sympathies with elements of the alchemical movement notwithstanding—curtailed the implementation of a pansophic academy when he established the Académie Française in 1635. The academicians were to make the French language and literature conform to "rules," which were so interpreted as to be, for all intents and purposes, the taste of the poet and critic François de Malherbe (1555–1628). Malherbe, whose ideas had languished in the early years of the seventeenth century, now shot to fame. Under his authority condemnation awaited authors who took inspiration from the imagination, that part of the faculties which "rageth" in the melancholic and empowered the magus. The academicians set aside metaphysical speculation and occult ideas as they labored to create a normative dictionary of the French language.[19]

Under Louis XIV more academies were established for painting, dance, music, architecture, and science. With this splintering of the academy into separate disciplines, science was cut off from what would be known in the eighteenth century as

Inventing the Modern World

the "arts" or "fine arts" (beaux arts). Charles Perrault's *Parallel des anciens et des modernes* (1688–96) did place "the art of cooking" among the sciences, but as the new century progressed, cooking moved steadily toward the arts, and thus away from medicine. Because of the low status of cookery, no formal academy could be established for food, but the new French cooking heralded by *Le Cuisinier françois* was upheld by a kind of unchartered academy, which still can be detected in France today. As early as 1674 the cookbook writer designated only as L. S. R. acknowledged that La Varenne had given cookery "rules and method," and a persistent theme in the eighteenth-century cookbooks is the importance of the "rules."[20]

## COOKING BY THE RULES

All of these early modern academies were intended to enforce an intertwining set of vague and fluctuating precepts—the so-called rules of order, of reason, of judgment, of refinement, of propriety, of harmony, of art's relation to nature, and so forth—that had wound their way through the ancients' writings on philosophy and the arts, which included the preparation of food. (In the Renaissance "taste" would be added to the group of teachings.) In imitation of antiquity the Italians had revived interest in these aesthetic discussions, although they certainly had not disappeared completely during the medieval period. The French and English were stimulated by the Italians to create art within rules—and this was the founding charge of the new academies.

Some of the ancients had mocked attempts to bring such a lowly activity as cooking within the realm of the arts. Horace, for one, drew a wry portrait of an "erudite" gentleman, one Catius, who used Aristotle's theory of flavors to explain the art of dining. In a comical scene Athenaeus describes a master cook who taught rules to ignorant whippersnappers whose "pickled sauce of fish of contradictory qualities" had not been built, as it ought to have been, according to the rules that governed musical harmony. Cookery, he insisted, was an art, and like all such pursuits, it had its rules.[21]

It is not surprising that some Renaissance writers read these passages literally and concluded that a theoretical framework was as appropriate to a meal as to poetry, drama, and architecture. The burgeoning aesthetic of food faced the same problems that confronted painting and landscaping, for none of these fields could boast of any work of the stature of Aristotle's *Poetics*, Horace's *Art of Poetry*, or Vitruvius's *On Architecture*. Painters and landscape artists were forced to create a set of rules based on those of the other arts. Horace's celebrated "ut pictura poesis" (a poem is like a picture) came to govern landscape art as if the simile were "ut poesia hortis" (a garden is like poetry).[22] The same approach applied to cooking. And following the ancients, some moderns poked fun at people who dared to treat cookery as art.

Platina discussed the need for "order" in a meal, and Erasmus directed his ironic wit at the same idea in a dialogue between Apicius and Spudus. Spudus asks how often he must change the dishes, and Apicius replies that the number of changes of dishes is the same as the number of parts of a rhetorical oration or acts of a play. Questioned on the order of the meal, Apicius explains again that it should follow the plan of an oration.[23]

But many instructions to serve food in accordance with rules were offered seriously. The master cook, Scappi wrote, must act like a "judicious architect, who, after making a well-considered design, establishes a strong foundation, and upon it gives to the world a useful and wonderful edifice. The design of the master cook must be of beautiful and certain order." A French cookbook writer expressed the same sentiment in 1655.[24]

The term "composition" was used to denote a harmonic arrangement, or balance among the parts. In 1537, Pietro Aretino thanked Girolamo Sarra for a perfectly constructed bunch of salad greens: "I gape open-mouth at the way you compensate for the sharpness of one herb with the sweetness of another. It takes no small skill to match the pungency and the bite of one leaf with the savor, neither pungent nor biting, of a different one until the whole is a mixture [*componimento*] so tasty that it would satisfy satiety itself."[25]

In 1549 Messisbugo called his recipe section "Compositions of the Most Important Dishes." Five years later Scappi wrote of "milk tortes of diverse compositions," and in fact "composition" appears throughout his work. At the end of the sixteenth century an English observer wrote, "The Italian (as all the world knowes) is most exquisite in the composition of all sortes of Condiments." At the beginning of the seventeenth century a Scottish traveler noted that the French "sup . . . on sumptuous

Inventing the Modern World

compositions." To achieve the balance promised in a composition, the French cook was advised to use "reason" and "judgment" in the choice of ingredients. Nicolas Boileau-Despreaux ridiculed the host who said, "When they speak of sauces, they must point up the subtleties; as for me, above all, I like pepper to dominate."[26]

In England, Robert May also advised harmony, temperance, and discretion:

> Learn of this Cook who with judgment and reason,
> Teacheth for every Time, each thing its true season:
> Making his compounds with such harmony,
> Taste shall not charge with superiority
> Of Pepper, Salt or Spice, by the best Pallat,
> Or any one Herb in his brothe or Sallat,
> Where Temperance and Discretion guides his deeds;
> Satis his Motto, where nothing exceeds.[27]

John Evelyn provided passage after passage on the harmony and balance of a salad's composition. "Thus, by the discreet choice and mixture of the *Oxoleon* (*Oyl, Vinegar, Salt,* &c.) the Composition is perfect; so as neither the *Prodigal, Niggard,* nor *Insipid,* should (according to the *Italian* Rule) prescribe in my Opinion." Sounding much like Aretino, Evelyn described the subtle counterpoint of a salad, bringing in Athenaeus's master cook for support:

> In the Composure of a *Sallet,* every Plant should come in to bear its part, without being over-power'd by some Herb of a stronger Taste . . . like the *Notes* in *Music,* in which there should be nothing harsh or grating. . . . Reconcile all Dissonancies, and melt them into an agreeable Composition. Thus the Comical *Master-Cook,* introduc'd by *Damoxenus,* when asked . . . *What Harmony there was in Meats?* The very same (says he) that a *Diatessaron, Diapente,* and *Diapason* have one to another in a Consort of Music. . . . The whole Scene is very diverting, as *Athenaeus* presents it.

Evelyn drew on the passage in which Milton ("our Paradisian Bard") introduces Eve, "dressing of a *Sallet* for her *Angelical* Guest":

> What choice to choose, for delicacy best;
> What Order so contriv'd, as not to mix
> Tastes not well join'd inelegant, but bring
> Taste after Taste, upheld by kindliest change.[28]

In the next century the same passage appeared as an epigraph on the title page of Ann Schackleford's *Modern Art of Cookery Improved.*

Calling on the authority of the theoretician J. P. de Crousaz, whose 1714 treatise on aesthetics was widely influential, and of the mathematician-philosopher Louis-Bertrand Castel and his comparison of aural and ocular effects, the author of the 1749 *Science du maître d'hôtel cuisinier* encouraged his readers to "push [their] contemplation of nature further. The diversity of tastes would mean little . . . if it were not accompanied by unity. . . . Would it be wrong then to put forth the idea that there is a harmony of flavors, like the harmony of sounds, and perhaps that of colors and smells?" This eighteenth-century text gives no hint that the arts should simulate the harmony of the heavens, as the aesthetic discussion of the fifteenth and sixteenth centuries had often insisted.[29]

The burlesque poet William King, like some of his French contemporaries and Erasmus before him, made sport of such serious culinary discussions:

> Tis a sage Question, if the Art of Cooks
> Is lodg'd by Nature, or attained by Books.

For the final word King suggested turning to a learned "authority."

> We must submit our Treats to Critiks View,
> And every prudent Cook should read Bossu.[30]

The eighteenth-century gentleman was so consumed by questions on food, a journalist wrote, that "it is really not to be imagined with what profound Knowledge and Erudition Men of Quality now treat these culinary Subjects, and I cannot but hope that such excellent Criticks will at last turn Authors themselves, nay I daily expect to see a Digest of the whole Art of Cookery by some Person of Honour."[31]

## THE END OF HERMETIC DINING

The year after the promoters of the new cooking had brandished *Le Cuisinier françois* before the Parisian public, a satiric work called *A Hermeticall Banquet* appeared in London. This trenchant piece of foolery—a comedy of despair, in all probability —posed a question that must have been discussed in France during the 1640s. Should hermetic dining continue or should it be extirpated and displaced? In France foes of the occult had proffered a new style of cooking. What would now happen in England? The anonymous author of the *Hermeticall Banquet* very probably had *Le Cuisinier françois* in mind when he composed his parody.

A *Hermeticall Banquet* lampoons both sides of the Paracelsus-Galen debate, which appeared in England in milder form than in France, and both of the styles of food that the Italians had embraced to produce the eclectic cooking of the Renaissance. In the *Hermeticall Banquet* alchemical medicine and dining are represented by numerous recipes filled with fragrant spices, roses, rose water, lemon, almonds, white sugar, tincture of gold, and tincture of saffron. The spiced wine known as hippocras is called a hermetical claret. Spices, odoriferous herbs, and minerals are altered "by an Essentiall Fire" to become "Quintessences, Elixars, Extracts, Tinctures, Balsams, Magistralls, Spirits [and] Arcani"—all medicaments found in Paracelsus.[32] On this side of the divide, the *Hermeticall Banquet* provides recipes much like those of earlier centuries.

An Italian dish, *bianco mangiare*, or blancmange, is similar to *brouet blanc* (see p. 3). One begins the recipe by mixing rice flour with milk:

> Then take the Pulpe of a young *Capon* tender boyld, sweet Almonds number xiiij. Beat these well in a Mortar, then mix them with the Milk, and Rice: pass all through a Course Cloath, adding thereto what quantity of Sugar you please: Then boil it on a soft fire, still stirring it, untill it coagulates into the consistence of a strong Gelly: when it begins to cool adde thereto of Amber, and musk dissolv'd in Rose Water as much as shall render it a grateful Odour.[33]

Ingredients for a hermetical gelatin and instructions on how to make it are also given:

> *Geladina*
> $R_x$ A capon of two years old,
> the flesh of a leg of Veal,
> four Calves feet,

The French Synthesis and Design

White Wine,
Fair Water.

The cook is to boil these ingredients together and skim the fat from the liquid, then add sugar, cinnamon, and cloves and boil the broth again with the whites of two eggs (to clarify it). The broth is then filtered through a cotton bag. Musk and amber dissolved in rose water are now added to this liquid, the transparent spirit of the flesh.[34]

The author insists that "galenicall potions" be cast out and is adamant that those foods—which exacerbate the ill effects of melancholy, according to writers on medicine of various persuasions, including Galen—be excluded from the dining table. *A Hermeticall Banquet*'s alchemical cook facetiously says to his guest: "Look from one end of my table to the other and you shall not see either gross, flatulent, unctuous, vaporous, nauseous, or crude and indigestible meats such as are 'Old Beefe Milk, Fat Broths, strong Wines, Butter, Black Olives, Nuts, Onions, Cabbage, Raw Sallads, Beans, Pease, Rochet, or any such Cephalick Enemy.'" In the same vein the cook observes, "The Stomack hath many particular enemies, whome he abhors with that detested *Nauseo*, that when he finds them in his kitchin, he is never well till he hath frighted them out with hot Waters." These enemies include raw onions, radishes, garlic, cucumber, brains, much oil, salt fish, butter, and cream.[35] Many of the foods that the melancholic wizard was supposed to avoid, then, were also those that had played prominent roles in the sensuous cooking of ancient Greece and Rome and in its Renaissance revival.

The author of *A Hermeticall Banquet* is in effect calling down a pox on both houses engaged in the medical war as well as on sensual banqueting. In 1652 he could not have known that his curse would soon be borne out, at least as far as medicine was concerned: the Neoplatonic cosmology that supported Paracelsian medicine and the Aristotelian cosmology that supported Galen's both began to crumble before the onslaught of the new mechanical philosophy. Nor could the author have known that the very foods from which the alchemical cook drew back in horror would triumph on English soil, as they would in France. When La Varenne gave a cold shoulder to melancholic magi and their problems, all Europe followed his lead.

Inventing the Modern World

Threatened by the radical Protestant occult cosmology, fearful of anarchy and civil war after thirty years of bloody international conflict, the French brought off a coup. They invented a food that transformed disruptive elements from the past and reassembled ancient forms to make something entirely new, insisting on a sense of harmony not seen before in food. Had the author of *A Hermeticall Banquet* lived into the eighteenth century, he would have seen the French style of food dominate all western Europe.

The French Synthesis and Design

# CHAPTER 11   In the French Style

*T*o create a new food the French elevated pepper and parsley to vaunted positions; proclaimed native herbs to be superior to spices; stressed butter on the authority of Dioscorides; reintroduced Apicius's herb bouquet; embraced all the revivals as seasonings; used essences based on cordial-alchemical medicine for their most "refined" (pun intended) dishes; and then wrapped the whole package in the salt-acid taste.

Whereas Renaissance food had had both sensual and spiritual aspects, the reformed French cooking intentionally emphasized secular, sensual motifs and called for a complete surrender to the body's desires at table. Here were Rome and Apicius. Here were Greece and Archestratus, that hedonist who, Athenaeus tells us, "made a voyage round the world to satisfy his stomach and appetites even lower." The primary goal of the new French food was to stimulate desire. The task of cooks was now exclusively to stave off satiety. When we think of the French in the seventeenth century creating ways to accomplish this feat, we might think back to Montaigne's Italian steward and his concern with "the differences in appetites: the one we have before eating, the one we have after the second and third course; the means now of simply gratifying it, now of arousing and stimulating it."[1]

Some of the Renaissance revivals had been considered particularly potent sexual stimulants. Truffles brought on lust, as did oysters and artichokes. But none was thought to contribute more to prurience than salt. Moffett saw a moral in Plutarch's story that the Egyptian priests abstained from salt. "No doubt they did wisely in it," he opined, "for of all other things it is very effectual to stir up Venus, whom Poets fain therefore to have been bred in the Salt Sea. . . . Finally remember, that lechery (Latin) is not idly, or at adventure termed *Salaritas, Saltishness;* for every man knows that the salter our humours be, the more prone and inclinable we are to lechery."[2]

## THE SALAD ENGULFS THE MEAL

The French took the salad—that is, food seasoned with salt and acid—as the framework of their new, stimulating cuisine. They derived the notion of extending the salad throughout the meal—that is, of making the salt-acid taste a kind of umbrella —from the ancients and the Renaissance Italians, both of whom had served salads at various points during their banquets.

From Plutarch Renaissance scholars learned that salt-acid foods were commonly set out before the meal: "It is conventional before a main course to take appetizers that are sharp or briny, and in general anything that has a highly salty character. For these relishes act as charms to entice the appetite towards the other delicacies." These briny vegetables seem to have been offered among other lures such as raw oysters. But Plutarch noted that the positioning of this course was a recent change: "The 'cold course,' as it used to be called, with oysters, sea-urchins, and raw vegetables, has like a body of light-armed troops been shifted from the rear to the front, and holds first place instead of last." Plutarch's contemporary Martial posed a question that pointed to the same shift: "Tell me, why is it that lettuce, which used to end our grandsires' dinners, ushers in our banquets?" Athenaeus noted the same change: "As to the ancients, however, none of them had the custom of serving swine's paunches or lettuce or any other like relish before a banquet, as is done to-day. Archestratus, at any rate, the inventive genius of cookery, speaks of it after the dinner, the toasts, and the smearing with perfumes."[3]

In the century before Plutarch and Martial, Fundanius tells Horace of dishes served before all of the others: "First there was a wild boar. . . . Around it were pungent turnips, lettuces, radishes—such things as whet a jaded appetite—skirret [water

The French Synthesis and Design

parsnip] [and] fish-pickle [*allex*]." Yet Horace observed elsewhere that the diner is freshened, or restimulated, by ham and sausages, indicating that these goads were taken at the end of the meal as well, or so later scholars interpreted his observation.[4]

Renaissance Italians, intent as always on copying the ancients, served salads before and after the meal. But ambiguity of the ancients' placement of salads sparked a debate on the proper place or time for them—a debate that continues today, though we have lost sight of its ancient origins. In the late sixteenth century William Harrison wrote, "I might here take occasion to set down the variety used by antiquity in their beginnings of their diets, wherein almost every nation had a several fashion, some beginning of custom (as we do in summertime) with salads at supper and some ending with lettuce." Harrison's observation may imply that the English ate salads only in summer, or more likely that they ate them at some other point in the meal. In *Henry IV, Part I* (II.iv), Falstaff's jottings of his outlays for food include 2s.6d. for anchovies "after supper." In 1645 Nonnius described a similar practice. Ham was being offered first to stimulate the appetite and at the end to arouse the tired stomach, in much the same way it had been used in Horace's time.[5]

This debate relativized the position of the salad, and in time the Italians developed an alternative of their own: they made salads available throughout the meal. This practice can be observed in Scappi's and Messisbugo's menus. Not only olives but other kinds of "salads" were kept on the table. Massonio noted in 1627: "Some salads that pass under the name of plain food are put on the table at the beginning of the meal and left there to the end, and acquire the name 'salad' because of some condiment that stimulates the appetite even though the food does not have this power without the condiment."[6] In other words, salt and pepper on a piece of plain chicken turn it into a "salad." The French idea of engulfing the meal in the salad came principally from this Italian practice of making salads of various kinds available throughout the dinner.

In their radical revision of food, the French took the idea of the salad and reshaped the whole meal up to the sweet course so that it would stimulate the appetite. Every dish was to become saladlike, whether it was called a salad or not. The entire meal outside of the dessert served the function of a salad. Salt

In the French Style

coupled with acid became the signature of many a sauce, just as it had become the stamp of a salad. The acid might be vinegar, wine, verjuice (juice of unripe fruit), lemon, or orange (or much later the tomato). Bonnefons wrote that salt, verjuice, and orange juice made the optimum sauce for a capon; for a duck, salt and the juice of a sour orange was "the best of all Sauces."[7]

Of the two crucial parts of a salad, the French gave the palm to salt. The touch of acid was important, but not so critical as salt. In fact, salt would become the most necessary condiment. Its use increased steadily, but it was not until well into the eighteenth century that salt per se (and not simply a pickle) began to be added to dishes as a matter of course. By the time Voltaire invoked the image of a salty sauce swimming over a little sweetbread, such sauces had held center stage in French cookbooks for at least a century.[8]

La Varenne's mentors knew what they were driving at. They were clearing a road down which the curious appetite could travel unimpeded. The Italians had left saladlike dishes on the table throughout the meal but served sugared dishes at the same time. With clarity of vision the French conceived of a salt-sweet divide—a separation they observed ever more strictly as the seventeenth century wore on. They sundered the meal into an extended salad and a dessert. For the first time in the West salty and sweet dishes were strictly separated. The French marshaled sugared items at the end, where their supposed power to extinguish the appetite would shut down any further desire to eat and bring on a feeling of satiation.

### SUGAR SPOILS THE APPETITE

The French alighted on the Italian salad as a framework for their new food not only because they thought salt was peerless in stimulating the appetite but also because one of the notable features of the Italian salad in its many forms was the almost total absence of sugar or any sweet taste. The Italians had created this genre without sugar for two principal reasons. First, the ancients served, as Plutarch said, a first course of highly salted items with no honey (at least, the descriptions made no mention of it). Second, since antiquity sweetness had been thought to dull other tastes. The ancients saw honey as toning down salt. In Apicius we read, "If [the dish] is too insipid [*fatuus*], add *liquamen*; if too salty, add a little honey." But of all

The French Synthesis and Design

sweeteners sugar was the most powerful in its ability to mask other tastes. An early-sixteenth-century French edition of Platina's *De honesta voluptate* maintained that "granulated sugar softens and tempers all dishes and hot and aromatic spices." In Bruyerin's view, sugar "mitigates biting foods, blunts sour ones, makes salty things sweeter, takes away harshness, mellows bitter things, and gives flavor to insipid food: in a word, it can be considered the conqueror of all flavors. For what is more powerful than the acid strength of vinegar? Nevertheless, it is broken by the sweetness of sugar." The 1715 English translation of a work by Guido Panciroli said much the same thing, and Evelyn spoke directly to the issue when he observed that "now *Sugar* is almost wholly banish'd from all, except the more effeminate Palates, as too much palling, and taking from the grateful *Acid* now in use." In short, the commonly accepted view was that because sugar vitiated the force of the appetite stimulants, it blunted the appetite.[9]

In fact, anything sweet was thought to interfere with the appetite. In 1627 Massonio wrote that "if [the sour orange] is taken with other foods and if these be fish or meat . . . the taste will be stimulated and the appetite awakened," but if the sweet orange "is eaten with other foods, it will not add any grace to them, but by its sweetness will produce a sated feeling rather than an appetite for eating. The first then by its sourness serves as the peculiarly appropriate condiment to any salad . . . and the second serves him who desires appetite less." Evelyn had much the same to say.[10]

In France, then, all sweets became suspect, for they were thought to destroy the appetitive qualities of salt, acid, and other goads. Over the course of the seventeenth century sugar, almond milk, and fruits were rooted out of all but the dessert dishes, not only because they were part of the Arabic style of cooking but simply because they were sweet. Those sweet fruits still served as a first course were now accompanied by a stimulant such as ham. Nonnius reminded his readers of Galen's suggestion that figs be eaten with *garum,* and credited him with influencing his own age's delight in taking figs with salt and pepper.[11] The notion of eating fruit accompanied by a salty stimulant at the beginning of the meal is the source of today's figs or melon with prosciutto.

The salt-sweet divide was basically in place by the mid-seventeenth century, yet some remnants of the old system lingered for a time. By the eighteenth century they would look decidedly anachronistic. In 1651 La Varenne suggested that "if your kids are small, put them into pastry; and separate them, putting sugar into one and a ragout [a stimulating ensemble of the revivals] into the other." By 1674 a French cookbook writer—a follower of La Varenne's style—castigated cooks who served a sweet sauce with meat, but then relented and provided a recipe for one. By the next century a prolific writer of cookbooks warned his readers to use caramel syrup in place of meat extract only when time was short, for the sugar would make the taste of the sauce disagreeable.[12]

From France the new views on the avoidance of sugar and the emphasis on salt, acid, and the other revivals were carried to England. In 1709 William King employed his customary buffoonery to jeer at compatriots who had stopped sweetening their meat in order to embrace the new French fashion:

> Perhaps no salt is thrown upon the Dish,
> Or no fry'd Parsley scatter'd on the Fish;
> Shall I in Passion from my dinner fly,
> And hopes of Pardon to my cook deny.

King seized the opportunity presented by the recent publication of Martin Lister's annotated edition of Apicius to write some satiric lines on the subject of the new English passion for the salt-acid taste:

> Dispatch [a copy of Apicius] . . . therefore to us with all Speed, for I expect Wonders from it. Let me tell you; I hope, in the first place, it will, in some measure, remove the Barbarity of our present Education: For what hopes can there be of any Progress in Learning, whilst our Gentlemen suffer their sons at *Westminster, Eaton,* and *Winchester* to eat nothing but *Salt* with their Mutton, and *Vinegar* with their *Roast Beef* upon Holidays?[13]

In the Preface to her 1728 *Collection of Above Three Hundred Receipts,* Mary Kettilby ranted against the "Master" who had decreed the new code that impinged on her freedom in the kitchen:

> Some great Master having given us Rules in that Art so strangely odd and fantastical, that 'tis hard to say, Whether the Reading has

The French Synthesis and Design

given more Sport and Diversion, or the Practice more Vexation and Chagrin, in spoiling us many a good Dish, by following their directions. But so it is, that a Poor Woman must be laugh'd at, for only sugaring a Mess of Beans; whilst a Great Name must be had in Admiration, for Contriving Relishes a thousand times more Distasteful to the Palate.

Kettilby's recipes, make no mistake, were for the most part unsugared, for the book had to sell. Nevertheless, in a recipe "to make a pasty of beef or mutton as good as Venison," she not only included sugar but stoutly defended her choice: "Let no one dislike the laying [the meat] in Sugar, 'till they have try'd it, for how preposterous an Ingredient soever it may seem in a savoury Pye, I must beg leave to assure the Reader, that nothing gives so certain a shortness and tenderness to the Meat as Sugar."[14]

The English balked more than the French at the new code and deviated from it more often, but many of them were firmly committed to the French style. Richard Bradley thought the decree against sugar was not being enforced strictly enough. He wrote *The Country Housewife* in part, he claimed, because he had met "with good Provisions, in many Places in England, which [had] been murder'd in the dressing. I could mention many Instances as bad as the common story of Bacon and Eggs strewed with brown Sugar." He complained, too, of "Sugar with a pickled trout."[15]

Households dedicated to the new cuisine probably served sweets not only at the very end of the meal but at the end of each course. A "course" consisted of numerous dishes, all put on the table at one time. Most of these dishes were savory, but some obviously sweet ones were often included, or at least this seems to have been the case at elaborate dinners. One course described in 1691 included ham and sausage and a confection with apricot marmalade in it.[16] The progression of dishes in a course perhaps derived from the same theory that relegated the dessert to the very end of the meal: a diner would eat the savory dishes first and finish with the sweet ones. After the first course came a break, when entertainment was sometimes provided. The second course, which had many savory and some sweet dishes, then appeared, and the process began again. The sweet dishes in each course, we may surmise, were intended to dampen the appetite at the end of that portion of the meal.

In the French Style

In some cases, however, the diner was not meant to stop at the dessert. In these instances, salad was offered with the dessert, or served alone after the sweets had been eaten, as a goad to further drinking, à l'Archestratus. The salty item might be a dish of olives or a ham. (Notice the ham among the fruits on the dessert table in Figure 53.) In 1674 a French cookbook writer offered ham and tongue with the fruits for dessert. In the princess Palatine's description of a typical meal, Louis XIV finishes with an egg. The egg, we may presume, was served with either salt or a salty condiment. "I have often seen the king eating four full plates of soup, a whole pheasant, a partridge, a big dish of salad, two big slices of ham, some mutton with *jus* and garlic, a plate of pastry, and fruit and some hard-boiled eggs." In England Elizabeth Raffald suggested various ices, fruits, nuts, and olives as an ending to an elaborate meal. Parson Woodforde recorded in his diary that he occasionally took olives with his dessert, as on July 13, 1792: "Desert, french Olives, Raspberries, Cherries, three sorts of Strawberries and White Currants, Mountain and Port Wines"; and on May 22, 1794: "Desert, Almonds and Raisins, Oranges, and Olives."[17]

## PEPPER

Of all the spices, pepper had been the most popular among the Romans. Pliny conveyed his indignation that this stimulant should have such success:

> It is remarkable that the use of pepper has come so much into favour, as in the case of some commodities their sweet taste has been an attraction, and in others their appearance, but pepper has nothing to recommend it in either fruit or berry. To think that its only pleasing quality is pungency and that we go all the way to India to get this! Who was the first person who was willing to try it on his viands, or in his greed for an appetite was not content merely to be hungry?[18]

Other voices in antiquity indicated the kind of expense people were willing to incur in order to obtain this condiment, which could turn a common food into a "delicacy."[19]

In 1627 Salvatore Massonio had written that salads are "gracefully" seasoned by pepper.[20] The Italians used salt and pepper together on thistles, truffles, and other dishes that came

The French Synthesis and Design

53. Alexander François Desportes, *Still Life with Silver.* 261.6 × 187.3 cm. The Metropolitan Museum of Art, Purchase, Bequest of Mary Wetmore Shively in memory of her husband, Henry L. Shively, M.D., 1964 (64.315).

to be seen as "salads" in the extended meaning of the word, but they did not set pepper alone on the table. Other golden dishes were present to counteract the effect of its blackness.

This was not the case in France. Gold-colored food was not interspersed with the many peppered dishes on La Varenne's table. Judging by the frequency with which his recipes call for pepper, his readers may have presumed that he had no fear of the substance long connected with Saturn. The French had done an about-face on the dark spice that had been thought to induce melancholy. They transformed it from a rarely used spice—sometimes colored with a yellow agent to mitigate its evil effects—into the open consort of salt, a position it has

In the French Style

retained to this day. In the mid–eighteenth century, Menon, the most prolific cookbook writer of his time, said, "As to salt, everyone knows that it is indispensable, while pepper is only a little less so."[21]

## FINES HERBES

Spices were portrayed as inferior to herbs, even as vulgar. Saint-Evremond claimed, "Fine herbs are wholesomer, and have something in them more exquisite than Spices." But he still cautioned that "they are not equally proper for everything." By the eighteenth century, however, the *Dictionnaire portatif de cuisine* noted that "if one cannot do without strong seasonings, it would be better to choose delicate and aromatic herbs [*herbes fines & aromatiques*] than spices."[22]

Parsley—the herb that Galen and Pliny had noted was so often employed—understandably held a premier position in the new food. In 1654 Bonnefons called parsley "our French spice, which seasons countless preparations and is used almost everywhere in food," and in 1669 he noted that parsley often served "instead of Pepper and spice." Nevertheless, Bonnefons, a follower of La Varenne, used a considerable amount of pepper. Even though parsley was indigenous and thus "better" to Bonnefons's mind than foreign spice, pepper gained preeminence. In effect the new French cooking came to divorce pepper from its foreign origin, since it had been such an important Roman condiment. When Bonnefons spoke of "pepper and spice" as of two separate categories, he was expressing a characteristic attitude. Over time pepper became for the French and their followers an almost indigenous condiment, like parsley—a naturalized citizen, so to speak.[23]

## BUTTER

Both Galen and Dioscorides discoursed on the uses of butter in medicine, but the humanists' knowledge of the ancients' use of butter as a food depended on just one line of Dioscorides. Its many translators and commentators interpreted it in various ways. Gesner, for example, read it to mean that butter "is added to delicacies in place of oil and to sweets in place of fat." Mattioli saw the passage as saying that "fresh butter is put into

The French Synthesis and Design

foods in exchange for oil and into sweet foods, which are eaten at the end of the meal, instead of fat." An English translator said: "That which is new [fresh and without salt] is put in sawce for meates instead of oyle, & in cakes instead of fatt." Bruyerin made it out to mean that "fresh [butter] is added to delicacies instead of oil and to fungi eaten at the second course instead of fat." His own age, he remarked, had begun to use butter in the most special foods, presumably because of Dioscorides' observation. Recall Bruyerin's remark that some people thought fungi cooked in butter a dish for connoisseurs.[24]

Butter is not found in recipes for sauces in fourteenth- and fifteenth-century cookery works from England, France, or Italy, but it does begin to appear there in the first half of the sixteenth century. Eight percent of the recipes for sauces in *Le Livre fort excellent* contain butter. As the new French style spread, so did the use of butter. It appears in 39 percent of La Varenne's sauce recipes and climbs to 55 percent of Menon's in *La Cuisinière bourgeoise*.[25]

## ESSENCES IN CUISINE

The French, as we have seen, followed the Italians in establishing academies and formulating rules for the arts, among which they included cookery, and in the sixteenth century they followed along again by conceiving of food compositions as harmonious structures exhibiting a balance among their parts.

But then the French took quite a different path: they reinterpreted harmony in sauces, now taking it to mean that whatever the initial ingredient, only its essence would be left in the final product. They rid sauces of the body, or solid components, as alchemy had believed it rid medicines of corporeal elements. The only kind of food in which something similar had happened was gelatin. Just as the alchemical physician sought to rarefy the *spiritus* and make it more subtle through rarefied and subtle medicines, so the cook now created rarefied and subtle sauces that would puzzle and tease the tongue at sensual banquets. The French reined in alchemy to serve the sensual table, literally debasing the spiritual essences. Similarly, the new science reined in and coopted alchemy by taking over its technological base while jettisoning its cosmological assumptions. Cookery forced Paracelsian ideas into sensual submission, much as science checked them by cutting the occult web of influences.

What "science" remained in cooking was now subsumed under the "art" of cookery. In the Preface to his eighteenth-century cookbook François Marin describes cookery as a kind of "chemistry." Cooking changes "solids foods into a sort of artificial chyle, as one sees by extracts and restoratives." Be aware that "nothing leaves the hands of the cook that has not, so to speak, been assayed and that has not been purified. The coarsest meats by virtue of heat divest themselves of their earthly qualities and taste, to take on qualities and a taste completely opposite to their endowed ones."[26]

In the fullest expression of the new French art, harmony is no longer a balance of parts, with one ingredient playing off another, but a whole in which the parts have lost their identity. This is the harmony that Seneca urges the writer to achieve, but more important for the period, it is the mystical concept of all things flowing into a cosmic whole. Again sensual French cooking has coopted spiritual intention. Marin writes:

> The union and rupture of colors that make for the beauty of colored things represent very well . . . this mixture of tastes and ingredients from which the cook composes his ragouts. These ingredients and essences must be blended and merged in the same way that the painter blends his colors, and the same harmony that in a painting strikes the eyes of connoisseurs should make itself felt to refined palates in the taste of a sauce.

This "rupturing" process occurs easily with *jus* or essences, as these "purified extracts" stream into one another: "The science of the cook consists today of breaking down and extracting the quintessence from the meat, drawing out the nourishing and light juices, mixing them and mingling them together so that nothing dominates and yet everything makes itself felt." Again Marin emphasized that the science of cookery was indeed an art, developing an elaborate analogy between the harmony achieved by the cook in the sauce and the harmony achieved by the painter on canvas: "Finally [cooks] give to [sauces] the union that painters give to colors, to render them so homogeneous that there will be only one delicate and piquant taste resulting from their combined flavors . . . [and] a harmony of

The French Synthesis and Design

all their tastes united together." A pregnant line follows in the 1750 edition: "There lies the whole object of the art, and the making of gold in cooking." Marin makes clear the analogy between alchemy and cooking with the reference to gold and the pun on the word "art." "Art" was the word commonly used to denote alchemy. A sensual art had captured and tamed cordial-alchemical medicine.

Across the Channel, the English adopted the new French sauces founded on essences that intermingled so thoroughly that they perplexed the diner as to their true identity. Horace Walpole wrote to Horace Mann in June 1749:

Sunday and Monday next are banquets at Cambridge for the installment of the Duke of Newcastle as Chancellor. The whole world goes to it: he has invited, summoned, pressed the entire body of nobility and gentry from all parts of England. His cooks have been there these ten days distilling essences of every living creature, and massacring and confounding all the species that Noah and Moses took such pains to preserve and distinguish.[27]

A writer to *The Connoisseur* jested that "the ordinary distinctions of fish, flesh and fowl, are quite destroyed; and nothing comes upon table under its proper form and appellation."[28]

The French produced the *jus* (that is, the essences or quintessences) they needed for their subtle sauces by sweating or pressing various meats or by pressing fungi. Such a large amount of meat or mushrooms was needed to produce a small amount of essence that the sauce made with it was a luxury. The idea of putting such costly liquids into sauces vexed a writer for the *London Journal:* whereas "twenty Legs of Mutton would have made a Marriage Feast for our Ancestors; we now mangle them to furnish out a Dish, and that but a small one." *Fog's Journal* asked whether "there [is] a Man in London, who has not heard of Trimalchio and his Cook?—of the Sauce for a Brace of Partridges extracted from two Dozen? of twenty-five Legs of Mutton for the Composition of a small Assiette." Exaggerations? To be sure. But this branch of the new salt-acid cuisine was indeed beyond the reach of most people and a drain on the pockets of those who served such sauces at great dinners: "It is impossible to conceive, what vast sums are melted down into sauces!" wrote a commentator in *The Connoisseur.* "We have a cargo of hams every year from Westphalia, only to extract the

Essence of them for our soups; and we kill a brace of bucks every week, to make coulis of the haunches."[29]

## THE APICIAN HERB BUNDLE

The herb bundle beloved of Apicius usually contained a member of the onion family (often leeks) as well as an herb or two, perhaps coriander, savory, dill, or oregano. The idea of putting herbs into a dish in retractable form appears in "A Baghdad Cookery Book," where condiments are occasionally tied up in a little cotton sack. The early cookbooks of western Europe very seldom mention a bound bundle of herbs, and in the sixteenth century Messisbugo and Scappi chop up the herbs and place them directly in the sauce. In seventeenth-century France, however, the herb bundle becomes an important unit of seasoning, as it had been to Apicius.

"To make a bouquet," said La Varenne, "take scallions [*siboulles*], parsley, and thyme and tie them together." Here the scallion (Pliny's *getion*-leek) is knotted with parsley (praised by Pliny and Galen) and thyme (used by Apicius and Pliny) to form a cornerstone of the new French cooking. In 1656 Pierre de Lune included a piece of pork fat in his bundle. To Louis Liger, a "packet of delicate herbs" consisted of parsley and a scallion tied together. Vincent La Chapelle, the French cook who plied his trade in England, called for a "Bunch made of green Onions, Parsley, sweet Herbs and Cloves." Menon's *Cuisinière bourgeoise* says that "a bouquet is made with parsley, scallion, garlic, clove, thyme, bay leaf, and basil." The ingredients of the bouquet vary from cookbook to cookbook.[30]

When the herb bouquet was lifted from the cooking liquid, it left behind only an "impression" of itself. Alchemy had again left its mark. The important part of the condiment was not its body but its essence. Instructions in a 1674 cookbook were to "take a bouquet of delicate herbs and tie them together well, so that you can pull them out when they have imparted their taste to the dish." Early in the eighteenth century Louis Liger observed that one inserted the herb bouquet during the cooking and then removed it instead of chopping herbs "into ragouts because the majority of refined people like only the taste of these herbs, without finding them in the sauce." In 1742 Menon removed both the herbs and the salted ingredient: "When [the dish] is cooked and seasoned as it should be, take out the bouquet

The French Synthesis and Design

and the slice of ham, and arrange the ragout on the serving plate." With the body—that is, the solid matter—removed, the supposed essence of the herbs and salt meat flowed into the sauce in the same way that a *jus* or essence of meat made separately melted into the general, unified taste when it was added to a sauce. In his popular *Tableau de Paris*, Louis Sébastien Mercier said that *la nouvelle cuisine*—the new, simple, and light cooking of the late eighteenth century—had eliminated the stimulating and caustic ragouts, and the *Nouveau Dictionnaire* remarked that "today in France . . . it is expected that the seasoning of dishes will be almost imperceptible."[31]

These new French sauce creations were unique in the history of Western cookery. Apicius had stipulated that the bundle of herbs used to flavor a dish be removed, but he had placed no restriction on chopping other herbs into the same sauce. The French sauces are also a far cry from sixteenth-century Italian notions of harmony and the balance of parts. Italian cooks added chopped herbs in the belief that they could play each herb off against the other to create a harmonic whole. So long as the dish contained other substances to balance the sugar and cinnamon (or salt and pepper) that they sprinkled on it after it was cooked, the Italian cooks were convinced that they had achieved harmony. French cooks took a very different route to harmony, but it must be noted that this blending of tastes into a unified whole pertained to only one strand of the new French salt-acid cuisine. Many dishes in the French cookbooks retained herbs, bulbs, anchovies, capers, salt pork, and other stimulants, and these recipes, though they are now associated with Provence, cannot be passed off as provincial cooking. They were a Parisian conceit, as much a part of the new salt-acid food as were the "refined" sauces of smooth and unified taste.

## New Words for New Tastes

The French conceived a cookery seasoned with the revivals and essences. They invented new words—ragout, *haut goût*, garnish—for the tastes meant to seduce the diner. In 1694 the *Dictionnaire de l'Académie française* defined "ragout" as that which baits or "irritates" the appetite; *haut goût*, used far less often, has the same meaning. "Ragout" has something of the Latin *irritamentum*, which Pliny used to characterize certain fungi that he laughingly described as the latest enticements, *irritamenta*, to the

In the French Style

appetite. The French used "ragout" to designate a set of alluring ingredients, the ancient revivals, used singly or in combination. The word can also be applied to a whole dish that is considered a stimulating creation. "Garnish" designates something decorative. If the ragout entices, the garnish amuses and dallies with the diner. Thus lightly and erotically teased, diners indulge themselves with increasing pleasure.

"Ragout," *haut goût*, and "garnish" are interchangeable with "seasoning." La Varenne wrote, "Season with capers and champignons"; "Simmer well seasoned with salt, butter, chopped capers, and an anchovy"; "All sorts of pastries for meat or fast days . . . are seasoned" with a "garden garnish [ *garniture* ] such as champignons, truffles, asparagus, egg yolks, artichoke bottoms, capers, cardoons, pistachios. To meat pastries besides the garden garnishes, you may add sweetbreads, kidneys, crests, etc."; "Fill with small ragouts such as truffles, artichokes, asparagus, and fried champignons." L. S. R. wrote that "*coulis, liaisons,* and *jus* [all built on essences or broths] . . . season, garnish, crown all soups, light as well as dark [brown], galimaufries, fricasees, stews, daubes, fried foods, gelatins." *Le Cuisinier roial et bourgeois* observes that "one garnishes [birds] with champignons, foie gras, truffles, pounded pork fat, and other seasoning." To the most prolific of eighteenth-century French cookbook writers truffles were among the best "seasonings," as they were to the author of the *Dictionnaire portatif de cuisine.*[32]

The English cooks were soon hard on the heels of the French. "Seasoned very high" and "high relish" are equivalent to *haut goût.* A marinade was a "high seasoning of vinegar, salt, white pepper and good herbs." John Evelyn talked of garlic as an *haut goût* and claimed that he had no interest in being thought an excellent cook in the style of "*Mithacus* a *Culinary Philosopher,* and other *Eruditae Gulae;* who read Lectures of *Hautgouts,* like the *Archestratus* in *Athenaeus.*"[33]

To Robert May, "seasoning" included "Pepper, Salt, Nutmegs, and boil'd sparagus." He "garnished" carps with "Horse-radish, fried Parsley, Oranges and Lemons." A fricasse of "mushrooms" calls for "a quarter of Pint of that liquory they were stewed in, with as much white Wine and strong Gravy [ *jus* ] . . . whole white Pepper, Mace and Nutmeg . . . Anchovies . . . Thyme, [and] a Shalot or two." Take care to "season it very high to your taste with these things." La Chapelle "season'd" a turkey with "Salt, Pepper, sweet Herbs, all Spice,

Mushrooms, Parsley, Chibbol [green onions]." Into the turkey's cavity, he advises, put a "Ragout with Sweetbreads, Champignons and CocksCombs, which [you should] moisten with good Gravy, good Cullis [*coulis*] and good Essence." E. Smith used "claret, gravy, sweet-herbs, and savoury spice . . . lamb-stones, cock's combs . . . oysters, mushrooms, truffles and morrels" in her "Ragoo for made Dishes," the sauce to be thickened with brown butter (butter fried with flour). Hannah Glasse advised her readers (Samuel Johnson was one) to "garnish" a calf's head "with fry'd Oysters, Brains, Lemon, and Force-Meat Balls [quenelles]."[34]

## THE FATE OF THE GOLDEN SPICES

It is apparent that as mid-century approached, spices and saffron had begun to be despised. The authors of the Introduction to the modern edition of La Varenne's *Cuisinier françois* report that "John the Husbandman, who accompanied Princess Marie de Ganzague, new wife of King Ladislas IV, from France to Poland in 1648, complained many times in his voyage that in Germany and in Poland the dishes were so full of saffron and various spices at the magnificent banquets that had been given for them that no Frenchman would be able to eat them." And the distaste continued: "In Spain the countess d'Aulnoy in 1691 tells us of being tantalized several times on seeing herself offered sumptuous meals of which she could eat not a thing, everything being seasoned with spices and saffron." And at the beginning of the eighteenth century a German "warned his compatriots that those who much appreciated spiced food would be disappointed in France."[35]

La Varenne's *Cuisinier françois* reflects the dislike for spices and saffron that can already be seen in the remarks of John the Husbandman. But their cookbooks tell us that the French did not eradicate every vestige of the golden, fragrant spices. For a time, two of them—nutmeg, thought to be an appetite stimulant, and clove, considered to have the powers of pepper—were often included alongside pepper. A second contraction of the spice gamut occurred in the 1730s, and henceforth salt and pepper were the common (though not exclusive) condiment unit. Nutmeg and clove retained a place, though not as large.[36]

Golden spices other than clove and nutmeg are occasionally

included in the recipes of the seventeenth and eighteenth centuries, but they are usually clustered under the term "spice" and provided in ready-prepared spice mixtures. (This practice continues to this day in France in a mixture called *quatre épices*.) Ginger and cinnamon, so important from the High Middle Ages through the sixteenth century, are now relegated to the general rubric "spice." La Varenne's *Patissier françois*, which appeared shortly after *Le Cuisinier françois*, contains a passage that augurs the steady erosion of spices after the mid–seventeenth century: "Note also that a number of people use only pepper in place of the other spices, even though the spice mixture is sweeter than pepper alone."[37] The French could use sugar with a far less troubled mind than spice, for the sweetness of sugar fed the body, whereas the fragrance of spices nourished the *spiritus*, as Avicenna had said.

In the second half of the seventeenth century the English began to follow the French in limiting the spices they would use, but this is a transitional period in England so far as spices are concerned. Cinnamon and ginger still appear in many recipes, and such cookbooks as Robert May's (1660) retain strong affinities to the sixteenth-century Italian cookery works. By about 1700 the spices in the English cookbooks are very similar to contemporary French ones: pepper, clove, nutmeg, and mace (the aril of the nutmeg) reigned as in France. The English books, however, do not indicate that a second spice contraction occurred there during the 1730s. Here, as in the case of sugar, the English proved less orthodox in the implementation of the code of modern cookery. Allspice and cayenne were common in the second half of the eighteenth century, along with clove, nutmeg, and pepper. Nonetheless, "allspice" functions for the English like "spice" for the French,[38] and allspice was made even more acceptable when in the eighteenth century it came to be called Jamaica pepper. Cayenne functioned like pepper, as an appetite stimulant.

As for saffron, it had all but dropped from French cooking by the middle of the seventeenth century. Other coloring processes, such as brushing with egg yolk or roasting or frying "until golden," although not stressed, managed to survive. Some cookbook writers went to great lengths to avoid calling foods yellow or golden, as when they called a sauce made with butter and egg yolks a "white sauce," but they had an interesting

The French Synthesis and Design

precedent in Apicius, who also has "white sauces." We rarely find food noted as gold-colored in the seventeenth and eighteenth centuries. Soon after La Varenne's work appeared, Bonnefons commented that putting saffron in food was bad form. "In the countryside they put saffron in to give it the color and the taste to which they have long been accustomed, although it is a bad thing." Saffron managed to continue in France only in minor ways. Under "saffron" the mid-eighteenth-century *Dictionnaire portatif de cuisine* commented that "the French kitchen makes little use of it," and it was now relegated to a few liqueurs and sweets.[39]

At the end of the sixteenth century William Harrison could still write that saffron had many uses in the English kitchen. By the end of the seventeenth century, however, it had all but disappeared. When Evelyn reported on its use in foods in Germany, Italy, and Spain, he described it as a foreign custom. In 1726 Richard Bradley observed that the once thriving saffron trade at Saffron Waldon had collapsed.[40]

Rose water is almost nonexistent in *Le Cuisinier françois*, and though it appears more often in *Le Patissier françois*, it loses ground steadily in both French and English kitchens until it all but disappears.

By suppressing golden fragrant food and enveloping the revivals and essences in a salt-acid taste, sometimes in a freshly conceived harmonic whole, the French invented a modern food for the Western world. We can sum up this revolution in French cooking with a blunt claim put forth in the 1776 *Nouveau Dictionnaire:* "Today in France . . . spices, sugar, and saffron, etc. are proscribed."[41] So far as spices are concerned, the author overstates the case, but his rhetoric does convey the clear impression of a style that shuns sweet fragrance. As for sugar, the pronouncement of course refers to those dishes served before the dessert, when sugar was provided in abundance to check the appetite that had been so artfully stimulated.

Saffron had the roughest ride of all, and it was to regain respectability only much later, when it resurfaced as an ingredient in such supposedly Provençal dishes as the fish stew we know as bouillabaisse. Platina had set saffron apart from the other spices because of its special power to impart a golden hue to anything it touched. By the eighteenth century, however, the Dutch physician Hermann Boerhaave had to remind his readers of the virtues once attributed to the orange-red stigmas of the crocus. Commenting on Paracelsus in his *Elementa chemiae,* one of the most popular works of chemistry in France in the first half of the century, Boerhaave noted that the alchemists had once called saffron the "scent of the philosophers" because of its golden color.[42]

# Some Postprandial Remarks
# on Acquiring Taste

*I*n calling his book *Le Cuisinier françois*, La Varenne was claiming to be the French cook and his cooking to be French cooking. This cookbook was part of the design for the new France, which was to lead the rest of Europe in the new direction it had chosen. The publisher wrote that since Paris was the "Capital, and the seat of our Kings," the food would first be offered there in the hope that if Paris accepted it, it would readily be received in the provinces and abroad.[1]

To think of the formation of the new French food, or modern food, as elitist dabbling is to misunderstand the intent of its designers. Modern food was offered as an alternative way of eating, intended to draw all people away from food with mystical connections. The aim was to effect a change in the eating patterns of those who dined lavishly as well as those whose diet was close to the subsistence level. The message was this: Forsake the spirit-filled universe and perfumed, golden food, whether you be rich and accustomed to costly foreign fragrances and dyes or of limited means and accustomed to redolent yellow plants plucked from a garden or nearby field. Turn to the sensual and ribald side of life. Eat salt, which brings on hunger for food and for sex.

Depending on their income, people could incorporate the new system in their daily lives in various ways. The well-to-do could afford great quantities of salt to pickle all sorts of vegetables, meats, and fish. The less well off could at least sprinkle their food with a few grains of it. The poor obviously could not afford meat essences, but the subtle sauces were but one part of the new cooking. *If you could afford to eat, you could afford to eat in the new French style.* The Preface to the 1702 *Court and Country Cook*, an English translation of François Massialot's *Cuisinier roial et bourgeois*, first published in 1691, is explicit about spreading the gospel of the revolutionary style to everyone. The recipes, it announces, are for the tables of the titled as well as all other tables, including those of "indifferent ordinaries." The reader is to study the recipes, for once the principles of the new cooking are grasped, the food will be seen to be adaptable to any table. "It is also to be hop'd, that *The Court and Country-Cook*, will be as acceptable here, in an English Dress, as in that of [Massialot's] native Country; where three several Editions of his Work have been printed and sold, in a short space of Time."

The cookbooks functioned in the same way as architectural books that peddled new ideas. The baroque, with its mystical intentions, was not allowed to mature in the second half of the seventeenth century in France or past the early eighteenth century in England, where the earl of Burlington and his associates, John Summerson tells us, were so "distressed by Baroque deviation" that they used "every device of persuasion and performance to fix a standard of architectural taste." Using his clout and money, Burlington made certain that "under George II Palladianism conquered not only the high places of architecture —the great patrons, the government offices—but, through the medium of prints and books, the whole of the vernacular, finding its way ultimately into the workshop of the humblest carpenter and bricklayer." This third earl of Burlington, Richard Boyle (1695–1753), was born just four years after the death of his celebrated kinsman Robert Boyle, younger brother of the first earl of Burlington. As Robert had worked to crush the claims of the alchemists, Richard, inspired by Andrea Palladio's revival of Roman architecture in Italy, labored to eradicate the baroque.[2]

The seventeenth-century baroque architect had orchestrated a purifying and mystical experience for the people who entered his church, much like the one the alchemists had planned for those who drank their elixirs. The elements that delineated space, no longer discreet, flowed into a cosmic whole. Undulating and deeply shadowed walls and twisted columns, such as those in Bernini's Baldacchino in St. Peter's, evoked a strong feeling of movement, flux, and even disintegration, as in the

Postprandial Remarks on Acquiring Taste

initial stage of the alchemical process. At strategic points light was introduced to dissipate the melancholy-inducing shadows and bring on a golden resolution, as in the final stage of Christian alchemy. The sun's rays might stream down through a dome, or a worshiper might ascend vicariously through a painted apotheosis into blinding light. Despite the Council of Trent, the high baroque dwelled on the Neoplatonic conception of a mystical union with immaterial effulgence, the kind of union with light that a Gothic cathedral had provided. The antidote was Palladio—or at least one side of him. In 1759 the well-known architect William Chambers called Palladio's style "correct and elegant" and his architecture of "happy" disposition.[3] Palladio became the epitome of the sanguine, cheerful artisan as opposed to the brooding, melancholic genius.

La Varenne and his followers held their audience in the material world in the same way that the Palladians did theirs. A promise appears in this bit of doggerel on the frontispiece of Caroline Butler's *New London and Country Cook* (1770):

> If in the Modern Taste, you'd learn to Cook,
> Study the Perfect Method in our Book.
> Then the Best Table you may serve with ease,
> And the nice Appetite exactly Please.

The new food could never have taken hold if powerful people had not backed it. No matter what the men and women of the *haut monde* ate in private during the transition period, they publicly stood behind a sensual food based on the ancients. Instructed from a tender age on the horrors of heresy, Louis XIV did not become the sun king of a religious hermetic empire of the sort Campanella had envisioned in his *City of the Sun*. The role he played instead was similar to the one played by Augustus, another ruler associated with the sun. Although Augustus had himself succumbed to ideas that were to influence Plotinus's conceptions, he sought to flush the foreign mystery cults from Rome.[4]

A question remains as to who originally backed the *Cuisinier françois*. La Varenne claims in his Preface that he learned the principles of cooking from the marquis d'Uxelles. Who were the marquis's close allies? Who formed the circle that conceived of the ingenious new code? Who were the Frenchmen who led the assault on the fragrant golden food of the spirit-filled universe in the way Burlington and his coterie later led the crusade against the baroque in England? We do not know their names, but we know they exorcised the spirit of the mystic from a Europe haunted by a fear of chaos and anarchy. The French response to that threat was absolutism. Absolutism often brought hideous acts of repression, but it was not always implemented cruelly. When it reached into the arts to establish academies and rules, it sanctioned a food that was to draw people to it because of the sensual pleasures it was said to afford.

It has been estimated that 90,000 copies of cookbooks were in circulation in France in the second half of the seventeenth century and 273,600 in the years between 1700 and 1789.[5] Menon, the best-known French cookbook writer of the eighteenth century, prefaced one of his works with a quip on the growing number of cookbooks on the market: "What! Perhaps it will be said, Yet another work on cookery. For many years the public has been inundated with a deluge of writings in this genre."[6] *Le Cuisinier françois* was translated into English and published in London in 1653, just two years after it first appeared in Paris. In the eighteenth century England produced even more books on the new French synthesis and design than France.[7] Such books went into multiple editions on both sides of the English Channel. A sixth edition of Mary Kettilby's *Collection of Above Three Hundred Receipts* ran to 2,000 copies, and three years later a seventh edition was a large seller.[8] Through these books the ladies and gentlemen of the household passed the new ways to their servants. The caption under the frontispiece of one of these books (Figure 54) reads: "A Lady presenting her Servant with the UNIVERSAL FAMILY COOK who diffident of her own knowledge has recourse to that Work for Information."

As one country after another adopted the new French system, they called it now English food, now American food, now Italian food. Eventually the French base went unacknowledged. In England it was even adamantly denied. The *Connoisseur* snidely remarked that the cook at White's was no doubt a Frenchman who would "oblige the world by a treatise on the art and mystery of sauces."[9] All the same, recipes for the new sauces were being published continually in what were being called English cookbooks. Hannah Glasse ranted about the absurdities of French cooking, yet her own cookbook was obviously built on the French model.

Postprandial Remarks on Acquiring Taste

*Collinger delin et sculp.*

≈Explanation≈

*A Lady presenting her Servant with the* UNIVERSAL FAMILY COOK *who diffident of her own knowledge has recourse to that Work for Information. On the right hand a Person Instructing a Young Man in the* ART OF CARVING *by referring to a print on that Subject. In the front Ground various Articles of Cookery, Confectionary, Brewing &c emblematical of the various useful information contained in this Work.*

54. Frontispiece of *The Housekeeper's Instructor, or Universal Family Cook,* by William Augustus Henderson (London, 1795). Courtesy of the Cambridge University Library.

In the *Critical Review* for October 1759 Tobias Smollett appraised a book in which William Verral claimed that he had been influenced by the duke of Newcastle's French cook, Chloe.

If you are really ambitious of culinary fame [Will,] . . . we advise you to reject the pernicious slops, sauces, and kickshaws of the French, which serve only to irritate the appetite . . . and rather endeavor to contrive dishes of substantial food, upon true British principles. . . . But you will say, the English cookery will not furnish hints enough for variety to please the fickleness of modern palates. If that be the case, learn Latin, Will, and study the antients; study the cookery of the Romans. . . . Study the famous Apicius. . . . In lieu of your *marinade*, what say you to the famous *liquamen*, or pickle called *garum*, made of the gills of a mackerel, with salt and vinegar, and sometimes of the sturgeon of the Nile? How should you like to make force-meat, or rather farce-meat in the way of *Chabob*, with lobsters, crabs, or cuttle-fish, beat up with pepper, cumin seed, and the root of the laser, which some naturalists suppose to be the plant that yields the assafoetida? or pork sausages, called *vulvulae & botelli*, seasoned with leeks, pepper, pinetops, and the pickle *garum*? . . . These, and an hundred more delicious dishes, are to be found in the works of Apicius, which we advise you, Mr. Verral, to peruse for your improvement in the *ars coquinaria:*—and so we bid you, heartily, farewell.[10]

By his injunction to learn Latin and comprehend the principles of the cooking of antiquity, Smollett was ironically seeking to detach the label "French" from contemporary food. By whatever name it is called, however, the modern cooking of the Western world is a French invention. For all the minor rebellions against it, the design the French set in motion in the mid—seventeenth century still largely determines the way we eat. Like the earlier style, it is an acquired taste.

Postprandial Remarks on Acquiring Taste

# Notes

1. "Eat and Drink with Relish": An Islamic Anticipation
of Paradise

1. Apicius, *Roman Cookery Book.*

2. Hitti, *History of the Arabs,* pp. 602–10; Asín-Palacios, *Islam and the Divine Comedy,* p. 241. The Arab traveler is quoted in Runciman, *The Sicilian Vespers,* p. 10.

3. Asín-Palacios, *Islam and the Divine Comedy,* pp. 241–44.

4. Runciman, *History of the Crusades,* 2:101.

5. The following discussion is drawn from Peterson, "Arab Influence on Western European Cooking"; Taillevent, *Viandier de Guillaume Tirel; Libro di cucina del secolo XIV;* "Ein Buch von guter Speise"; *Ménagier de Paris; Two Fifteenth-Century Cookery-Books;* Platina, *De honesta voluptate* (1475); Messisbugo, *Banchetti* (1549); Granado, *Libro del arte de cocina* (1599); *Eenen Nyeuwen coock boeck* (1560); Scappi, *Opera* (1610).

6. Deerr, *History of Sugar,* 1:73; Platina, *De honesta voluptate,* bk. 2; *Thrésor de santé,* p. 407.

7. Balducci Pegolotti, *Pratica della mercatura,* pp. 434–35; Bennett, *Pastons and Their England,* p. 57; *Ménagier de Paris,* p. 217; *Two Fifteenth-Century Cookery-Books,* p. 8; Platina, *De honesta voluptate,* bk. II, *De saccharo;* "Baghdad Cookery Book," p. 29; Balducci Pegolotti, *Pratica della mercatura,* p. 435; *Thrésor de santé,* p. 403; Moffett, *Healths Improvement,* p. 250.

8. Platina, *De honesta voluptate,* bk. VI; Barbaro, *In Dioscoridem corollariorum libri quinque;* bk. 2, p. 51v; Pisanelli, *Traité de la nature des viandes,* pp. 193–94; Bruyerin, *De re cibaria,* pp. 560–62.

9. Harrison, *Description of England*, p. 129; Moffett, *Healths Improvement*, p. 251; Buttes, *Dyets dry dinner*, n.p.; Serres, *Théâtre d'agriculture*, 2:633.

10. Granado, *Libro del arte de cocina*, p. 40; "Baghdad Cookery Book," pp. 195, 35.

11. *Ménagier de Paris*, pp. 210, 217, 227, 263; *Libro di cucina*, pp. 3–4; Taillevent, *Viandier de Guillaume Tirel*, p. 66; Scappi, *Opera*, p. 103v; *Traducción española*, p. 40.

12. Pliny, *Natural History*, p. 99, bk. XIII, chap. I, "Perfume ought by right be accredited to the Persian race"; Aristotle, *Parva naturalia*, 8:253. The Loeb translation reads, "Those who 'doctor' drinks in this way develop an acquired taste for them, until pleasure arises from two senses as if it were a single pleasure from one."

13. Theophrastus, *Enquiry into Plants*, 2:337; Pliny, *Natural History*, 4:25, 113; Plutarch, *Moralia*, 12:553.

14. Apicius, *L'Art culinaire*, pp. 123, 125–32. The *Excerpta* consists of thirty-one recipes. Twenty-six of them call for pepper. Here are some of their other ingredients, with the percentages of pepper they represent, when that figure can be calculated.

| Ingredient | Percent of pepper | Ingredient | Percent of pepper |
|---|---|---|---|
| Sugar | — | Cumin | 8% |
| Honey | 8% | Fennel | — |
| Saffron | 4 | Galingale | — |
| Cinnamon | — | "Herbs" | 8 |
| Clove | — | Hyssop | — |
| Ginger | 4 | Lavender | — |
| "Grains" [cardamom?] | 4 | Lovage | 46 |
| Nutmeg | — | Mastic | — |
| Mace | — | Mint | 8 |
| Cubebs | — | Oregano | 8 |
| Sumac | — | Parsley | 4 |
| "Spices" | — | Rosemary | — |
| Anise | 4 | Rue | 23 |
| Asafetida | 27 | Sage | — |
| Caraway | 4 | Sandalwood | — |
| Celery seed | 4 | Thyme | 4 |
| Coriander | 38 | Dill | 15 |

15. Flückiger, "Note on Costus," p. 121.

16. Taillevent, *Viandier de Guillaume Tirel*, pp. 34, 96. Cf. Rodinson, "Recherches sur les documents arabes," p. 147. Bruno Laurioux is mistaken in his assertion that the spices the Arabs were consuming were very different from those of the Western world: *Moyen Age à table*, p. 40. For a numerical analysis of the relative use of spices and other

key ingredients, including sugar and saffron, in extant cookbooks from Apicius through those of the sixteenth century, see Peterson, "Arab Influence on Western European Cooking," pp. 334–37.

17. *Traducción española*, p. 85; Ashtor, "Essay on the Diet," p. 145; *Libro di cucina*, pp. 4, 58, 63; Taillevent, *Viandier de Guillaume Tirel*, pp. 10, 123; *Ménagier de Paris*.

18. *Libro di cucina*, pp. 3, 63; *Ménagier de Paris*, p. 186; Messisbugo, *Banchetti*, p. 146.

19. "Baghdad Cookery Book," pp. 192, 195, 31 (Arthur Arberry, the book's translator, does not specify whether his ounce equivalency to a dirham is a medieval weight); *Traducción española*, pp. 35, 172.

20. Dioscorides, *Dioscoride*, p. 74.

21. Bruyerin, *De re cibaria*, p. 500; Serres, *Théâtre d'agriculture*, 2:421, 1:xxxi; Saffron Walden Museum, "Some Notes on Saffron"; Holinshed, *Chronicles of England*, p. 113; Balducci Pegolotti, *Pratica della mercatura*. For an extensive discussion of the place of saffron in medieval commerce, see Bardenhewer, *Safranhandel in Mittelalter*.

22. Platina, *De honesta voluptate*, bk. 3; "Ein Buch von guter Speise," p. 17; Messisbugo, *Banchetti*, p. 191.

23. "Baghdad Cookery Book," pp. 203, 29 (see also pp. 36, 40, 41, 44); *Traducción española*, pp. 22–23, 47–48, 78.

24. Harvey, *Mediaeval Gardens*, pp. 22, 32, 66, 120, 122; Apicius, *Roman Cookery Book*, p. 229; "Baghdad Cookery Book," pp. 37–38; *Two Fifteenth-Century Cookery-Books*, p. 31; "Ein Buch von guter Speise," p. 19; *Ménagier de Paris*, p. 201; *Traducción española*, p. 38; *Libro di cucina*, p. 19; Scappi, *Opera*, p. 44v.

25. Lemons and oranges: Tolkowski, *Hesperides*, pp. 269–70; Runciman, *Sicilian Vespers*, p. 5. Rose water: "Baghdad Cookery Book," pp. 34–41; *Traducción española*, pp. 37–38, 41, 44, 46, 51, 62, 69, 72, 74, 77, 79, 221–23, 239–44; *Libro di cucina*, pp. 4, 5, 28, 30, 44; Taillevent, *Viandier de Guillaume Tirel*, pp. 57, 66, 67; *Two Fifteenth-Century Cookery Books*, p. 27; Granado, *Libro del arte de cocina*, pp. 24, 45, 57, 61, 79, 83, 108; Messisbugo, *Banchetti*, pp. 178–79, 190, 214, 216; *Eenen Nyeuwen coock boeck*, pp. 31, 53, 65, 109 (the index records rose water 34 times throughout the text).

26. *Libro di cucina*, pp. 23, 38, 68; Messisbugo, *Banchetti*, pp. 176, 198, 200; Scappi, *Opera*, pp. 15, 20, 22, 26; Granado, *Libro del arte de cocina*, pp. 24, 45, 57, 61, 79, 83, 108; Platina, *De honesta voluptate*, bk. 2; *Ménagier de Paris*, p. 229.

27. *Libro di cucina*, p. 23. See also Bennett, *Pastons and Their England*, p. 58.

28. Pisanelli, *Traité de la nature des viandes*, p. 24. Rodinson, "Romania," pp. 434–37; Granado, *Libro del arte de cocina*, p. 31; Balducci Pegolotti, *Pratica della mercatura*, p. 420.

29. Brown, *Body and Society*, pp. 223–24, 238, 441, 443; Augustine, *Confessions*, p. 197.

30. Dickie, "Islamic Garden in Spain," p. 90.

31. Rodinson, "Recherches sur les documents arabes," pp. 144–45; "Baghdad Cookery Book," p. 32.

32. Kritzeck, *Peter the Venerable and Islam*, pp. 3, 37, 42, 97, 207; Petrus Alfonsi, *Disciplina clericalis*, pp. 8, 35.

33. Metlitzki, *Matter of Araby*, p. 213; *Escala de Mahoma*, pp. 355–60.

34. Vaanen, "'Fabliau' de Cocagne," pp. 22–23; Metlitzki, *Matter of Araby*, p. 213.

35. Riddle, "Introduction and Use of Eastern Drugs," pp. 186–92.

## 2. FOOD AS DIVINE MEDICINE

1. "Baghdad Cookery Book," pp. 21, 24. Hereafter page references are given in the text.

2. Avicenna, *Treatise*, p. 548.

3. Avicenna, *Avicennae liber canonis*, pp. 562–65.

4. Avicenna, *Treatise*, p. 548, and *Avicennae liber canonis*, p. 566r. Aromatics were not used only to buoy the *spiritus*; they were used in sundry compounds for specific ailments. The Greek physicians, especially from Galen on, inspired by the use of perfumes in medicine in Asia and Africa, began to include many aromatics in their own pharmaceutical preparations. Aromatics had been key ingredients in Middle Eastern pharmacy as far back as Mesopotamian times. See Martin Levey, *Early Arabic Pharmacology*, pp. 7–8.

5. Avicenna, *Treatise*, pp. 123, 535, 538, 547, 549. For a discussion of a mystical dimension of Avicenna's work, see Nasr, *Science and Civilization in Islam*, pp. 297–304. See also Nasr, *Introduction to Islamic Cosmological Doctrines*, pp. 252–59.

6. Multhauf, *Origins of Chemistry*, pp. 106–7.

7. Ibid., p. 125; Taylor, *Alchemists*, pp. 32–33; Hopkins, *Alchemy*, p. 65; *Turba philosophorum*, pp. 170, 257.

8. Holmyard, *Alchemy*, pp. 29–30.

9. For a discussion of the Chinese elixir of life in the Islamic world and the West, see Sheppard, "Alchemy," pp. 83–84; Partington, *History of Chemistry*, 1:33; Gruman, *History of Ideas*; Crosland, *Historical Studies*, p. 15.

10. See Sivin, *Chinese Alchemy*, pp. 25–26, 169–214; Darmstaedter, "Per la storia dell'aurum potabile," p. 30; Sheppard, "Alchemy," p. 73. Darmstaedter was unable to establish the ingestion of gold anywhere except in China before its use by the Arabs. Sheppard found that in India the Atharva Veda of perhaps the eighth century B.C.E. "mentions the use of a gold talisman to prolong life." Again, "In the *Satapatha Brahmana* [c. seventh century B.C.E.] it is said that 'gold is indeed fire, light and immortality.'" Nothing, however, is said about taking gold into the body.

11. Yates, *Giordano Bruno*, pp. 50–51; Majrīṭī, *"Picatrix"* (1962), pp. lxvii, 157–63, 167–68, 228–29; cf. *Picatrix* (1986), pp. 91–95, 128–35.

12. Holmyard, *Alchemy*, p. 95.

13. Ferguson, *Religions of the Roman Empire*, p. 153.

14. Smith, *Porphyry's Place*, chaps. 6, 8, 9. For a general discussion of this late form of Platonism see Wallis, *Neoplatonism*.

15. Augustine, *City of God*, p. 386.

16. Barb, "Survival of Magic Arts," pp. 105, 110, 114. See also Brown, *World of Late Antiquity*, pp. 104–8.

17. Kristeller, *Renaissance Thought*, p. 53.

18. Dionysius the Areopagite, *Works*, pp. 115–16.

19. Quoted in Rudolph, *Gnosis*, p. 244.

20. Hippolytus, *Philosophumena*, 1:161; Budge, *Egyptian Magic*, p. 185; Atchley, *History of the Use of Incense*, pp. 108–9. See also Budge, *Book of the Opening of the Mouth*, 1:26, 213; *Book of the Dead*, 1:66, 69, 70. For the same concept in Babylonian and Persian religious views see Thompson, *Devils and Evil Spirits*, 2:17, 43.

21. Atchley, *History of the Use of Incense*, pp. 82–96, 117, 133, 208. See ibid., chap. 4, and Tertullianus, *Apology*, p. 153.

22. Multhauf, *Origins of Chemistry*, p. 207. See also Sarton, *Introduction to the History of Science*, 1:728: "Mesuë the Younger. Masawaih al-Mardini, from Mardin in Upper Mesopotamia. Flourished in Baghdad, later at the court of the Fatimid caliph al-Hakim in Egypt, where he died in 1015 at the age of ninety. Physician. Jacobit Christian. He wrote books on purgatives and emetics (*De medicinis laxativis; De consolatione medicinarum et correctione operationum earundem*) and on the remedies relative to each disease (*De egritudinibus*), but his main work is a complete pharmacopoeia in 12 parts called the *Antidotarium sive Grabadin medicamentorum compositorum*, based on Muslim knowledge. The last-named work was immensely popular. It remained for centuries the standard text-book of pharmacy in the West, and Mesuë was called 'pharmacopoeorum evangelista.'" A note adds: "But as no Arabic text of his work is extant, it has been suggested that Mesuë was simply a Western writer living in the eleventh or twelfth century, who had assumed the name to increase his popularity(?)." This suggestion has been disputed.

23. Alderotti, *Consilia*, p. 132. On Alderotti see Siraisi, *Taddeo Alderotti*.

24. Yates, *Giordano Bruno*, pp. 12–13; Walker, *Spiritual and Demonic Magic*, p. 23. See also Field, *Origins of the Platonic Academy*, p. 193.

25. Seznec, *Survival of the Pagan Gods*, p. 52; Garin, *Astrology in the Renaissance*, p. 24.

26. Klibansky, Panofsky, and Saxl, *Saturn and Melancholy*, pp. 188, 198; Ficino, *Three Books on Life*, pp. 365, 367, bk. III, chap. 22.

27. Ficino, *Three Books on Life*, p. 23. Hereafter page references are given in the text. I do not agree, however, that Ficino provides a

sufficient key to *Melencolia I.* See the discussion in Klibansky et al., *Saturn and Melancholy,* pp. 317ff.

28. Ficino, *Three Books on Life,* pp. 16, 19, 28, 45–47. See also Copenhaver, "Scholastic Philosophy," p. 551, and "Hermes Trismegistus," p. 85.

29. Walker, *Spiritual and Demonic Magic,* pp. 32–33.

30. Avicenna, *Treatise,* p. 539.

31. Ficino notes (pp. 221–23) that even though the kinds of nourishment required by the heart and by the liver are at variance, the heart can use some sweet substance and the liver some aromatics. Avicenna had said that because the liver produced one part of the *spiritus,* the liver required aromatics: *Treatise,* p. 548. Ficino claimed (p. 424n) that Galen, too, felt that the spirits were nourished by odors, but in fact Galen never made that claim.

32. *Secretum secretorum,* 1:4, 362, 538, 570.

33. On the use of perfumes to preserve the flesh see also Camporesi, *Incorruptible Flesh.* References to spices as food preservatives are rare in medieval and Renaissance cookbooks and related technical materials. *Le Ménagier de Paris,* an anonymous book of household management written at the end of the fourteenth century, noted that "blood keeps well for two days, even three, when spices are added." Yet the case is so specific that it can be taken to mean that spices were not generally thought of as preservatives of food. When the text goes on to say that "some employ as spices a great deal of pennyroyal, savory, hyssop, marjolaine," it seems to be saying that herbs may be substituted for spices to preserve blood (p. 192). A recipe for keeping mutton over the winter specifies the need for salt only (p. 195). Salt, vinegar, drying, and storing in fat were the main means of keeping food for long periods of time: Scappi, *Opera,* p. 6v. Giambattista della Porta wrote in his *Natural Magick* that salt is the universal preservative and offered the suggestion that honey may be used if one is seeking an alternative (p. 323); spices are not mentioned in connection with preservation of food. In a 1549 Italian cookbook one even finds the idea that pepper can cause spoilage: Messisbugo, *Banchetti,* p. 219. Early in the seventeenth century, when spices were still very much in vogue in England, Hugh Plat, whose *Delightes for Ladies* contains many uses for spices, does not mention them in connection with preserving meat. Plat simply says that freshly killed meat can be kept for nine or ten days in "an high and windy room" (p. 75). I am not saying that spices and herbs have no prophylactic qualities, for some do, although others promote bacterial growth. See Dyson, "Physiological Aspects of the Essential Oils," p. 296.

Similarly, spices were not added to cover the bad taste of rotting food. If the food was tainted, one threw it away if one could afford to do so, or ran the risk of illness if one could not. Platina, for example, advised that a knife be plunged into a ham. Cooking and preparation might proceed only if the smell were good; if the smell proved bad, the meat was to be discarded: *De honesta voluptate*, bk. 6.

Given the availability of alternatives such as salt and lard for preserving meat, and acknowledging that spices were generally more difficult and expensive to obtain than fresh or preserved meat, we can recognize that the misconception is a later, dismissive interpretation to explain why spices had been used in such quantities before the seventeenth century.

34. "Syrup, *shurba* as generally known to the Arabic writers, was known as a juice concentrated to a certain viscosity so that when two fingers were dipped into it, it behaved as a semi-solid when the digits were opened." The julep "was, in actuality, a light syrup. For example, in a prescription of ibn Sīnā [Avicenna], the proportions given are: . . . 794g of sugar, 132g of water, and 66g of rosewater. In Mesuë junior's work, there are 5 parts of rosewater to 4 parts of sugar to yield a fluid which is not very viscous": Levey, *Early Arabic Pharmacology*, pp. 75, 77.

35. Quoted in Sigergist, "Laudanum," p. 543.

36. Bacon, *Opus majus*, 2:619, 621, 623–24, 627.

37. Multhauf, *Origins of Chemistry*, pp. 196, 210–13. See also Pagel, *Paracelsus*, pp. 263–65. For the antecedents of Rupescissa's fifth element see Pagel, p. 100, n. 264. Aristotle adumbrated what was later known as the ether by noting that celestial bodies were informed with a principle beyond the four elements. Later this principle was brought into the sublunar realm. "Already in Stoicism and increasingly so in Neo-Platonic Philosophy the Aristotelian idea that it [the fifth principle] was purely celestial had been modified . . . : [this fifth principle] had been identified with the 'Pneuma' and later the 'Logoi Spermatikoi', the 'seeds' and 'souls' in terrestial objects, notably metals. The 'celestial' had thus been brought down to earth." Taylor, "Idea of the Quintessence," points out (p. 258) that the term "quintessence" does not appear in Greek alchemy. He postulates (pp. 251–52) that the idea of a quintessence in terrestrial matter came to the alchemists of fourteenth-century Europe not from the writings of antiquity but from an Arabic source. *A Book of the Fifth Nature*, attributed to Jabir (eighth century), for example, contains an idea similar to that of the quintessence.

38. Without Ficino, Walter Pagel remarked, Paracelsus would be unthinkable: *Paracelsus*, pp. 218–23, 264. What Pagel had in mind was Paracelsus's *general* dependence on Ficino's Neoplatonic cosmological framework. Yet it is very difficult to believe that Paracelsus would not have denigrated Ficino, as he did almost everyone else, had not Ficino

somewhere in his writings insisted on the efficacy of uncorrupted medicines, as he was doing here.

39. Ficino discussed the concepts of alchemical medicine but avoided the term "alchemy," presumably because of church disapproval of this suspect art. For some thoughts on Ficino and alchemy see the Introduction to Ficino, *Three Books on Life*, pp. 53–54.

40. Pagel, *Joan Baptista Van Helmont*, p. 78. See also pp. 71–78. Piero Camporesi also notes the belief in sixteenth-century Italy of a revitalizing quality in perfumes. See his *Incorruptible Flesh*, chap. 11.

41. Paracelsus, *Bücher und Schriften*, 3:73–75. For Paracelsus's instructions on how to take the essence of Avicenna's cordial, meat juice, see 3:27, 40.

42. Ulstad, *Coelum philosophorum*, pp. 71r, 75r, 79v, 80r.

43. Ruscelli, *Secretes*, pp. 1r–5r; Eamon, "Books of Secrets," p. 28; Eamon and Paheau, "Documents and Translations," pp. 328, 330.

44. Venner, *Via recta*, pp. 138, 143.

45. Hester, *Secrets*, "To the reader."

46. Sydenham, *Dr. Thomas Sydenham*, p. 109.

47. Sheppard, "Egg Symbolism in Alchemy," p. 147; Holmyard, *Alchemy*, p. 122; Thorndike, *History of Magic*, 3:366.

48. Paracelsus, *Hermetic and Alchemical Writings*, 1:87. The translator notes (1:72n) that the treatise "Concerning the Spirits of the Planets," which contains this passage, is not in the 1658 folio, which he mainly followed, but from the Basel edition of 1570.

49. Josten, "Truth's Golden Harrow," pp. 97–98.

50. *Testament of Alchemy*, pp. 23, 25, 51–52, 61. (The story of Khalid and Morienus is first recorded by Arabic historians. See Holmyard, *Alchemy*, pp. 62–63. It was later reproduced in, e.g., Ashmole, *Theatrum Chemicum Britannicum* [1652], p. 53.)

51. Quoted in Montgomery, "Cross, Constellation, and Crucible," p. 79.

52. Pagel, *Paracelsus*, pp. 222–23, 253. Ficino, Paracelsus, Van Helmont, and other medical workers of this persuasion knew that their labor was for God and that their medicine was a revealed one.

53. Ruscelli, *Secretes*, "Epistle."

54. *Traducción española*, pp. 85, 40; Granado, *Libro del arte de cocina*, p. 42; *Two Fifteenth-Century Cookery-Books*, pp. 30, 33, 35. I first suggested an alchemical motive in the ingestion of gold-colored food in my "Arab Influence on Western European Cooking," *Journal of Medieval History* 6 (1980): 328.

55. Ficino, *De vita libri tres*, p. 133, bk. I, chap. 10; Taillevent, *Viandier de Guillaume Tirel*, pp. 33–34, 96, 126; *Ménagier de Paris*, p. 260. Alcabicius is quoted in Klibansky et al., *Saturn and melancholy*, p. 132. "Traité de cuisine" (c. 1300), included with Taillevent's *Viandier*, mentions *poivre aigret*

(sourish pepper) four times and defines it as ginger and cinnamon. In *Viandier*, both *poivre egret* (sourish pepper) and *poivre jaunet* (yellow pepper) contain ginger and saffron. Some cooks, Taillevent tells us, add other ingredients as well, including grains of paradise and cloves.

The substitution of ginger for pepper is a European variation. "A Baghdad Cookery Book" uses nearly twice as much pepper as ginger (but close to twice as much cinnamon as pepper). The Hispanic-Moorish text is much less concerned with the yellowish-red color of the spice mixture; ginger has an incidence of 17% of pepper and cinnamon an incidence of 66% of pepper. Further, in the "Baghdad Cookery Book" the occurrence of saffron is 96% of pepper, whereas in the Hispanic-Moorish text the incidence of saffron is 52% of pepper. Europe must have derived from the Middle East the notion that the color of the spice mixture was very important. Moreover, even in the Spanish cookery texts of the sixteenth century, those of Ruperto de Nola and Diego Granado, ginger and cinnamon are more important than pepper. The overall picture of the European dishes was of spice mixtures with a yellow-red cast, which is still the case in India and the Middle East today.

56. *Traducción española*, pp. 181, 158, and cf. pp. 151, 199, 201; *Libro de cucina*, p. 23, and cf. p. 61. Cf. *Ménagier de Paris*, pp. 230, 238, 219; *Two Fifteenth-Century Cookery-Books*, pp. 38, 52; Messisbugo, *Banchetti*, p. 158.

57. Messisbugo, *Banchetti*, pp. 203, 204. Gelatins may be found in, e.g., *Viandier de Guillaume Tirel*, p. 124. Unclarified liquid is poured over the fish. In the fifteenth-century edition clarified liquid is poured over fish (p. 58) and the liquid from the flesh is clarified and poured over meat (p. 92). The gelatin made from meat and poultry, once clarified, is served plain with the meat: *Libro di cucina*, pp. 16–19. The liquid is poured over meat, fowl, or fish and not clarified: *Two Fifteenth-Century Cookery-Books*, pp. 26, 95. The liquid is clarified only through skimming and then poured over fish or meat: Messisbugo, *Banchetti*, pp. 203–5. Clarified and cloudy liquids are poured over meat and fish and also served as plain dishes of gelatin.

58. Nostredame, *Excellent et moult utile opuscule*, pp. 151, 165–66.

3. The Search for a Greco-Roman Food Tradition

1. Cassirer, Kristeller, and Randall, *Renaissance Philosophy of Man*, pp. 140–43. Note, however, his interest in imagery from *Picatrix* and the magical tradition to portray his Palace of Truth. See Garin, *Astrology in the Renaissance*, p. 27.

2. Garin, *Astrology in the Renaissance*, p. 57; Sarton, *Appreciation of Ancient and Medieval Science*, p. 44. For the importance of Avicenna well into the seventeenth century see Siraisi, *Avicenna in Renaissance Italy*, pp. 175ff., 353.

3. See, e.g., Findlen, "Humanism, Politics, and Pornography."

4. Plutarch, *Plutarch's Lives*, pp. 601–5, "Lucullus," sects. XLI–XLII.

5. Plato, *Republic*, 2:391; Macrobius, *Saturnalia*, p. 187. For a discussion of various points of view on bodily pleasures see Gosling and Whiston Taylor, *Greeks on Pleasure*.

6. Seneca, "On the Happy Life," in *Moral Essays*, 2:127.

7. Seneca, "To Helvia on Consolation," in *Moral Essays*, 2:449.

8. Suetonius, "Vitellius," in *Lives of the Caesars*, p. 267, bk. VII, sect. 13.

9. "Antonius Elagabulus," in *Scriptores historiae Augustae*, 2:147, 153, 159, 165.

10. Montaigne, *Complete Works*, pp. 222–23. Cf. Horace, *Satires*, pp. 187–89, satire II.iv.

11. Coffin, *Villa*, p. 108; Bruyerin, *De re cibaria*, p. 665; Stone, *Crisis of the Aristocracy*, pp. 559–61.

12. Manuel and Manuel, *Utopian Thought*, p. 78; Campana, "Contributi alla biblioteca," p. 199. Cf. Milham, "Apicius," 2:323–30.

13. Rabelais, *Gargantua and Pantagruel*, p. 88.

14. Artus, *Description de l'isle des hermaphrodites*, p. 71.

15. Muret, *Traité des festins*, "Avertissement," n.p.; *Nouveau dictionnaire*, s.v. "Cuisine," p. 664; Pegge, *Forme of Cury*, p. ii.

16. Michel Jeanneret is mistaken when he writes in *A Feast of Words* that the Renaissance humanists were not really interested in what people ate. "One can therefore deduce that cultivated people did not take an active interest in culinary art; gastronomy as such was not, for Humanists, something to be studied" (pp. 70, 79).

17. Koch, "Flower Symbolism," pp. 74, 76; Crosland, *Historical Studies*, p. 17; Bergström, "Medicina," p. 12.

18. Craig, "Pieter Aertsen," p. 6; Ferguson, *Signs and Symbols*, pp. 53, 73–74, 180, 273–74; *Secretum secretorum*, 1:66, 175. Ripley is quoted in Ashmole, *Theatrum chemicum Britannicum*, p. 110.

19. Bergström, *Dutch Still-Life Painting*, p. 154. See also de Jongh, *Still-Life*, pp. 102–3, for the iconography of smoking. I am indebted to William Bassett for his identification of the minerals mentioned in this section. The same ash bowl, this time with only realgar, appears in plate 37 in Sterling, *Still Life Painting*.

20. *Turba philosophorum*, p. 58; Greindl, *Peintres flamands*, pp. 25, 29; Levey, *Substitute Drugs*, p. 56. See also Segal, *Prosperous Past*, p. 65.

21. Bergström, *Dutch Still-Life Painting*, p. 154.

22. Hartman, *Choice Collection*, p. 195.

23. Segal, *Prosperous Past*, pp. 55, 228; Bergström, *Natura in posa*, plate 37 and accompanying text.

24. Virgil, *Eclogues*, p. 43.

## 4. Fungi

1. Platina, *De honesta voluptate*, bk. IX; Bruyerin, *De re cibaria*, pp. 545, 547–49, 551. Bruyerin borrowed the epithet "fungal" from Plautus. Cf. Suetonius, "Tiberius," in *Lives of the Caesars*, 1:353; Nonnius, *Diaeteticon*, p. 84; Pliny, *Natural History*, 4:409, bk. XVI, chap. XI; 6:363, bk. XXII, chap. XLVII; Plautus, *Three Bob Day*, 5:180, IV.ii. "Boletus" is commonly translated as "mushroom" or "champignon." I have chosen the Latin form to avoid confusing it with the cultivated variety known as the mushroom, a bred fungus that does not appear in the wild. Pliny divides his discussion between boleti and fungi, the latter being all fungal matter exlusive of boleti and truffles. *Fungi* here is the Latin as found in Pliny and his modern followers. I use "fungi" to refer to all fungal material.

2. Juvenal, *Juvenal and Persius*, p. 265; Porta, *Villae*, p. 764. Cf. Pliny, *Natural History*, 6:363, bk. XXII, chap. XLVII; Nonnius, *Diaeteticon*, p. 86; Evelyn, *Acetaria*, p. 28; Apicius, *Apicii coelii*, p. 58n.

3. Manelfi, *Mensa romana*, p. 219; Bicais, *Manière de regler la santé*, pp. 182, 187; Royal Society of London, *Philosophical Transactions* 17–18, no. 202 (1693): 825–26; Evelyn, *Acetaria*, pp. 27, 146.

4. *Encyclopédie*, s.v. "Champignon."

5. Farley, *London Art of Cookery*, p. 436.

6. Bruyerin, *De re cibaria*, p. 551. Cf. Galen, *Opera omnia*, 6:656.

7. Bruyerin, *De re cibaria*, pp. 547–49.

8. Bonnefons, *Délices de la campagne*, p. 113; *Encyclopédie*, s.v. "Champignon"; Paulet, *Traité des champignons*, pp. iv–v. Cf. Dioscorides, *Greek Herbal*, p. 481; Pliny, *Natural History*, 6:359, bk. XXII, chap. XLVI: ". . . those taken too much doe hert, being hard of digestion, choking or breeding choler."

9. Dioscorides, *Greek Herbal*, p. 59; Porta, *Natural Magick*, p. 60, and *Villae*, p. 768; Bacon, *Works*, 4:408.

10. Evelyn, *Acetaria*, p. 29; Gassendi, *Mirrour of True Nobility*, p. 45; Nonnius, *Diaeteticon*, pp. 87–88. Cf. Dioscorides, *Dioscoride*, p. 609; Barbaro, *In Dioscoridem corollariorum*, p. 59v; Romoli, *Singolare dottrina*, p. 31v; Bonnefons, *French Gardiner*, 3d ed., p. 260.

11. Evelyn, *Acetaria*, pp. 29–30; Serres, *Théâtre d'agriculture*, 2:279; Lister, *Journey to Paris*, p. 156; Bradley, *Appendix*, p. 568 (cf. Miller, *Gardeners Dictionary*); *Encyclopédie*, s.v. "Champignon."

12. Ray, *Observations*, pp. 403–4; Delamare, *Traité de la police*, 3:351; Lister, *Journey to Paris*, p. 157.

13. Bradley, *Appendix*, p. 583; Evelyn, *Acetaria*, pp. 27–28.

14. Rodinson, "Recherches," p. 148.

15. Scappi, *Opera*, p. 187r.

16. *Dictionnaire portatif de cuisine*, p. 147; R. Bradley, *Country Housewife*, pp. 146, 173.


## 5. FISH

1. Seneca, *Ad Lucilium epistulae morales*, 6:75, epistle XCV; Macrobius, *Saturnalia*, p. 238.

2. Jones, *History of Western Philosophy*, p. 261; Horace, *Satires*, p. 147, satire II.ii.

3. Plutarch, *Moralia*, 8:341, "Table Talk" IV.4. Cf. Athenaeus, *Deipnosophistes*, 3:243–45, bk. VII.

4. Moffett, *Healths Improvement*, p. 141; Castellano, *Kreophagia*, p. 51. Cf. Plato, *Republic*, 1:267–69, bk. III; Plutarch, *Moralia*, 8:345, "Table Talk" IV.4.

5. Macrobius, *Saturnalia*, p. 239, bk. III, chap. XVI.

6. Seneca, *Seneca*, 7:243–45, "Natural Questions," bk. III, chap. xviii.

7. Cian, "Gioviana," pp. 108, 283–85; Coffin, *Villa in the Life of Renaissance Rome*, p. 131.

8. Montaigne, *Complete Works*, p. 218.

9. Thomson, *Life in a Noble Household*, pp. 140–41.

10. *Connoisseur* 4 (1757): 16.

11. Pliny, *Natural History*, 3:235, bk. IX, chap. liv; Seneca, *Ad Lucilium*, 6:239, epistle CVIII. Cf. Cicero, *Letters to His Friends*, 2:79, bk. VII, letter XXVI.

12. Le Roy Ladurie, *Paysans de Languedoc*, 1:61; Aretino, *Lettere*, p. 146; Gesner, *Historiae animalium*, p. 760; Pisanelli, *Traité de la nature des viandes*, p. 177; Moffett, *Healths Improvement*, pp. 160, 162; Delamare, *Traité de la police*, 3:29.

13. Bruyerin, *De re cibaria*, p. 1081; Saint-Evremond, *Letters*, p. 328; *Encyclopédie*, s.v. "Huitre."

14. Bruyerin, *De re cibaria*, p. 1080 (cf. Galen, *Opera omnia*, 6:734; Gesner, *Historiae animalium*, p. 757; Athenaeus, *Deipnosophistes*, 1:395–96, bk. III); Platina, *De l'honneste volupté*, p. 240v, bk. X; Husson, *Etude sur les épices*, p. 78; Moffett, *Healths Improvement*, pp. 47, 161 (cf. Athenaeus, *Deipnosophistes*, 2:5, 109, bks. III, IV); *Thrésor de santé*, p. 284; Menon, *Cuisinière bourgeoise*, p. 180; Delamare, *Traité de la police*, 3:29.

15. Platina, *De honesta voluptate*, bk. X; Delamare, *Traité de la police*, 3:29. Cf. Pliny, *Natural history*, 3:277–79, bk. IX, chap. LXXIX; Varro, *On Agriculture*, p. 525, bk. III, chap. XVII; Columella, *On Agriculture*, 2:405, bk. VIII, chap. xvi, and 3:69, bk. XI, chap. I; Martial, *Epigrams*, 2:42, bk. XIII, epigram LXXXII.

16. Delamare, *Traité de la police*, 3:29 (cf. *Deipnosophistes*, 1:395, bk. III; Nonnius, *Diaeteticon*, p. 390; Belon, *Nature et diversité des poissons*, p. 417); Hentzner, *Journey into England*, p. 97; Scappi, *Opera*, p. 142n.

## 6. FLESH

1. Platina, *De honesta voluptate*, bk. II; Bruyerin, *De re cibaria*, p. 683. Cf. Cicero, *De natura deorum academica*, p. 277, bk. II, chap. lxiv; Pliny, *Natural History*, 3:145, bk. VIII, chap. LXXVII.

2. Bruyerin, *De re cibaria*, pp. 688, 689 (cf. Martial, *Epigrams*, 2:405, bk. XIII, epigram XLI); Pliny, *Natural History*, 3:147, bk. VIII, chap. LXXVIII; Moffett, *Healths Improvement*, p. 65; Nonnius, *Diaeteticon*, p. 202; Delamare, *Traité de la police*, 2:1305.

3. Bruyerin, *De re cibaria*, p. 684. Cf. Plutarch, *Moralia*, 3:171, "Sayings of the Romans."

4. Bruyerin, *De re cibaria*, pp. 683, 685; Moffett, *Healths Improvement*, p. 69; Evitascandalo, *Dialogo del maestro di casa*, p. 891; Moryson, *Itinerary*, 4:139.

5. Marsilio Ficino advised: "If you want your food to take the form of your brain above all, or of your liver, or of your stomach, eat as much as you can of like food, that is, of the brain, liver, and stomach of animals which are not far removed from the nature of man": *Three Books on Life*, p. 247, bk. III, chap. 1. The table at Trimalchio's bears "a round plate with the twelve signs of the zodiac set in a circle and on each one . . . some food fit and proper to the symbol . . . testicles and kidneys over the Twins . . . a barren sow's paunch over Virgo . . . ": Petronius Arbiter, *Satyricon*, p. 53. These ideas could also certainly have influenced the serving of these organs.

6. Athenaeus, *Deipnosophistes*, 1:405–15. See also p. 433, bk. III; 2:94–96, 100, bk. III.

7. Plautus, *Captives*, 1:553, IV.iv. Cf. Plautus, *Stichus*, p. 45, II.ii; *Curculio*, 2:224–25; II.iii.

8. Pliny, *Natural History*, 3:327, bk. X, chap. XXVIII, and 147, bk. VIII, chap. LXXVII; Suetonius, *Lives of the Caesars*, 1:61, bk. I, chap. XLIII.

9. Plutarch, *Moralia*, 9:199, "Table Talk" VIII.9 (Moffett drew on this passage in his section on brains in *Healths Improvement*, p. 111); Suetonius, *Lives of the Caesars*, 2:267, bk. VII, chap. 13.

10. Galen, *Opera omnia*, 6:674–75.

11. Platina, *De honesta voluptate*, bk. V; Bruyerin, *De re cibaria*, pp. 684, 666, 689, 669, 673, 670, 666ff. (quadrupeds), 767ff. (birds). For other coverage of this kind, though not nearly so detailed, see Petronio, *De victu romanorum*, pp. 149ff.; Pisanelli, *Trattato della natura de' cibi*, pp. 15ff.; Moffett, *Healths Improvement*, pp. 110ff.

12. Estienne and Palissy are quoted in Le Grand d'Aussy, *Histoire de la vie privée*, 1:267.

13. Artus, *Description de l'isle des hermaphrodites*, p. 60; Harrison, *Description of England*, p. 313; Moryson, *Itinerary*, 4:98; Nonnius, *Diaeteticon*, p. 199; *Encyclopédie*, s.v. "Abatis"; Delamare, *Traité de la police*, 2:1301.

14. Porta, *Natural Magick*, p. 318; Nonnius, *Diaeteticon*, p. 267 (cf. Horace, *Satires*, II.8; Juvenal, *Juvenal and Persius*, p. 79, satire V; Martial, *Epigrams*, 2:411, bk. XIII, epigram LVIII); Bruyerin, *De re cibaria*, p. 675 (cf. Pliny, *Natural History*, 3:143–47, bk. VIII, chap. LXXVII, and 325, bk. X, chap. XXVII; Scipio Metellus is in fact one person in Pliny); Bacon, *Works*, 4:187; *Thrésor de santé*, pp. 211–12.

15. Scappi, *Opera*, p. 64v; Le Grand d'Aussy, *Histoire de la vie privée*, 1:559.

16. Bruyerin, *De re cibaria*, pp. 664–66.

17. Castellano, *Kreophagia*, p. 57. Cf. Hippocrates, *Opera*, p. 49, *Liber de affectionibus*.

18. Apicius, *Roman Cookery Book*, p. 147; Moryson, *Itinerary*, p. 139; R. Bradley, *Country Housewife*, pt. II, p. 2.

19. *Common Sense* 2 (1739): 11; *Pour et Contre*, 1738.

20. Artus, *Description de l'isle des hermaphrodites*, p. 104.

21. Platina, *De honesta voluptate*, bk. VI; Apicius, *Apicii coelii*, p. 57n.; Alunno, *Fabrica del mondo*, p. 218; Moffett, *Healths Improvement*, p. 69.

22. Gesner, *Historiae animalium*, bk. IV, p. 891 (cf. Platina, *De honesta voluptate*, bk. VI; Apicius, *Roman Cookery Book*, p. 69). In Nonnius, *Diaeteticon*, we see a seventeenth-century example of the kind of philological work that Gesner was engaged in. Nonnius, too, examined Juvenal, Horace, Martial, and their modern commentators; he led the reader through Varro, Athenaeus, and Macrobius, and showed that the categories designated in antiquity were not precise but merged into one another. To make his point he gave a selection of Apicius's recipes.

23. Gesner, *Historiae animalium*, bk. IV, p. 891. Cf. Martial, *Epigrams*, 2:465, bk. XIV, epigram LXXII; Apicius, *Roman Cookery Book*, p. 69.

24. Gesner, *Historiae animalium*, bk. IV, p. 891.

25. Nonnius, *Ichtyophagia*, pp. 153–54, 206. Cf. Petronius Arbiter, *Satyricon*, p. 47.

26. *Two Fifteenth-Century Cookery-Books*, bk. I, p. 38.

27. "A Baghdad Cookery Book," pp. 199, 201; *Traducción española*, pp. 34, 103, 138, 139, 142, 165, 173.

28. Apicius, *Roman Cookery Book*, p. 147: "You give a bird a greater flavor and make it more nourishing, and keep all the fat in, if you wrap it in pastry made of oil and flour and cook it in the oven."

## 7. GARDEN PRODUCE

1. Pliny, *Natural History*, bk. XIX, chap. XLIII.

2. Barbaro, *In Dioscoridem corollariorum*, p. 44v; Calano, *Traicté excellent*, p. 39; L'Aigue, *Singulier traicté*; Ronsard, *Oeuvres*, p. 155, bk. II, ode 18; Artus, *Description de l'isle des hermaphrodites*, p. 106; Gibault, *Histoire des légumes*, 3:418; *Nouvelle Collection des mémoires*, p. 56; Bruyerin, *De re cibaria*, p. 516; Rabelais, *Gargantua and Pantagruel*, p. 518 (see also pp. 576–78, bk. IV, chaps. 32, 59, 60).

3. Barbaro, *In Dioscoridem corollariorum*, p. 44v; Dioscorides, *Dioscoride*, p. 414; Pisanelli, *Trattato della natura de' cibi*, p. 5.

4. L'Aigue, *Singulier traicté*; Le Roy Ladurie, *Paysans de Lanquedoc*, p. 65.

5. Henry VIII, *Privy Purse Expenses*, pp. 77, 117, 142, 163, 167, 218, 220, 224, 232 (1529); Moffett, *Healths Improvement*, p. 215. Cf. Buttes, *Dyets dry dinner*; Evelyn, *Acetaria*, p. 6.

6. Nonnius, *Diaeteticon*, p. 55.

7. *Encyclopédie méthodique*, 1:665.

8. Voltaire, *Correspondance*, 26:216, 53:140.

9. Estienne, *De re hortensi*, pp. 80–81.

10. Dioscorides, *Dioscoride*, p. 414. Cf. Theophrastus, *Enquiry into Plants*, 2:21–31, bk. VI, chap. IV.

11. Dioscorides, *Dioscoride*, p. 414.

12. Dalechamps, *Historia generalis plantarum*, 1:611 (cf. Bruyerin, *De re cibaria*, pp. 511–12; Pisanelli, *Trattato della natura de' cibi*, p. 5); Moffett, *Healths Improvement*, p. 216; Bicais, *Manière de regler la santé*, p. 180; Parkinson, *Paradisi*, p. 503; Thomson, *Life in a Noble Household*, p. 142.

13. Pliny, *Natural History*, 5:515, bk. XIX, chap. XLII; Platina, *De honesta voluptate*, bk. IV; Bruyerin, *De re cibaria*, pp. 512–13 (cf. Nonnius, *Diaeteticon*, p. 52); Gerard, *Herball*, pp. 953–55.

14. Gibault, *Histoire des légumes*, p. 7; Dioscorides, *Dioscoride*, p. 335; Hill, *Proffitable Arte of Gardening*, pp. 62, 147.

15. Gibault, *Histoire des légumes*, p. 11; *Encyclopédie méthodique*, 1:690–95.

16. Parkinson, *Theatrum botanicum*, p. 454; Harvey, *Early Nurserymen*, p. 4; *Cryes of the City of London*, pl. 27; Pope, *Poetical Works*, p. 682.

17. Athenaeus, *Deipnosophistes*, 4:187, bk. IX. Cf. Pliny, *Natural History*, 5:463, bk. XIX, chap. XXIII.

18. La Quintinie, *Compleat Gard'ner*, 1:11; Evelyn, *Acetaria*, p. 87.

19. Bruyerin, *De re cibaria*, p. 482 (cf. Pliny, *Natural History*, 6:67, bk. XX, chap. XLIV); Porta, *Villae*, p. 682.

20. Bruyerin, *De re cibaria*, p. 481; Pisanelli, *Trattato della natura de' cibi*, p. 7; Buttes, *Dyets Dry Dinner*, L. S. R., *L'Art de bien traiter*, p. 54.

21. Platina, *De honesta voluptate*, bk. VI (cf. Celsus, *De medicina*, 1:193, bk. II, chap. XVIII); Estienne, *De re hortensi*, p. 88; Dioscorides, *Dio-*

*scoride*, p. 381 (cf. Theophrastus, *Enquiry into Plants*, 1:337, bk. IV, chap. VII).

22. Pliny, *Natural History*, 5:487, bk. XIX, chap. XXXII; Estienne, *De re hortensi*, p. 86; Bruyerin, *De re cibaria*, p. 536.

23. Athenaeus, *Deipnosophistes*, 2:107, bk. IV; Columella, *On Agriculture*, 3:15, bk. X; Pliny, *Natural History*, 5:493, bk. XIX, chap. XXXIV.

24. Pliny, *Natural History*, 5:493; Horace, *Odes and Epodes*, p. 371, epode III; Plautus, *Little Carthaginian*, p. 133, V.v, and *Haunted House*, pp. 293–95, I.i.

25. Bruyerin, *De re cibaria*, p. 411; Evelyn, *Acetaria*, p. 18.

26. King, *Art of Cookery*, p. 99.

27. *Common Sense* 2 (1739): 10–11; also in *Pour et Contre* 15, no. 211 (1738):78.

28. Le Roy Ladurie, *Paysans de Languedoc*, pp. 63, 68.

29. Pliny, *Natural History*, 5:509, bk. XIX, chap. XLI. Pliny's term *olus caulusque* remains obscure. *Olus* seems to mean garden produce in general and *caulis* means cabbages of various forms. I cannot substantiate the Loeb translation of *olus* as "kale."

30. Bonnefons, *French Gardiner*, p. 167.

31. Horace, *Satires*, p. 33, satires I.iii and II.ii; Martial, *Epigrams*, 2:193, bk. X, epigram XLVIII; Athenaeus, *Deipnosophistes*, 2:127, bk. IV; Pliny, *Natural History*, 4:313, bk. XV, chap. IX.

32. Varro, *On Agriculture*, p. 295, bk. I, chap. LIX.

33. Columella, *On Agriculture*, 3:211, bk. XII, chap. X; Artus, *Description de l'isle des hermaphrodites*, p. 107.

34. Aretino, *Letters*, p. 89, and *Lettere*, p. 146; Le Roy Ladurie, *Paysans de Languedoc*, 1:61; Pliny, *Natural History*, 4:315, bk. XV, chap. XI.

35. Lamb, *Royal Cookery*, p. 8. Cf. Menon, *Science du maître d'hôtel cuisinier*, p. 307.

36. Lamb, *Royal Cookery*, p. 10; *Dictionnaire portatif de cuisine*, p. 55.


## 8. A SPUR TO THE APPETITE

1. Plutarch, *Moralia*, 8:443, "Table Talk" V (cf. Plato, *Timaeus*, p. 153); Pliny, *Natural History*, p. 61, bk. XII, chap. XLI.

2. Plutarch, *Moralia*, 8:345, 443–445, "Table Talk" IV, V.

3. Ibid., p. 347, "Table Talk" IV; Athenaeus, *Deipnosophistes*, 2:131, bk. IV (cf. Plato, *Republic*, 1:159, bk. II, chap. XIII); Pliny, *Natural History*, 8:433, bk. XXXI, chap. XLI.

4. Ficino, *Three Books on Life*, p. 133, bk. I, chap. X; Duchesne, *Pourtraict de la santé*, p. 480; Venner, *Vita recta*, p. 124.

5. Horace, *Satires*, p. 141, satire II.ii; Petronius Arbiter, *Satyricon*, p. 47; Martial, *Epigrams*, 2:411, 403; bk. XIII, epigrams LIV, LV, XXXV; Athenaeus, *Deipnosophistes*, 3:235, bk. VI, and 2:43, 45, 47, 59, bk. III; Columella, *On Agriculture*, 3:281, 283, 297, bk. XII, chap. XLIX.

6. Pliny, *Natural History*, 8:435, 437, bk. XXXI, chaps. XLIII, XLIV; Horace, *Satires*, p. 243, satire II.viii.

7. Rabelais, *Gargantua and Pantagruel*, pp. 83, 121, 575–77, bks. I, chaps. 21, 37; IV, chaps. 59, 60. Cf. Rabelais, *Quart Livre*, pp. 241–42.

8. Platina, *De honesta voluptate*, bk. X; Aretino, *Letters*, p. 265; Calano, *Traicté excellent*, p. 23v.

9. Bruyerin, *De re cibaria*, pp. 567–68; Nonnius, *Diaeteticon*, p. 408. Caviar was actually being imported into Europe by the fourteenth century. See Balducci Pegolotti, *Pratica della mercatura*, pp. 102, 243.

10. Delamare, *Traité de la police*, 3:50.

11. Venner, *Via recta*, p. 142; Pepys, *Diary*, 2:115, 112.

12. Panciroli, *Rerum memorabilium*, pp. 508–9.

13. Bruyerin, *De re cibaria*, pp. 572–73.

14. *Thrésor de santé*, p. 278; Cotgrave, *Dictionarie*, s.v. "garum."

15. Gontier, *Exercitationes hygiasticae*; Apicius, *Apicii coelii*, p. 126; Houghton, *Husbandry and Trade Improv'd*, 3:309.

16. Galen, *Opera omnia*, 6:661; Pisanelli, *Tratado della natura de' cibi*, p. 11; Bruyerin, *De re cibaria*, p. 687; Nonnius, *Diaeteticon*, pp. 172–73; Pope, *Poetical Works*, p. 579.

17. Delamare, *Traité de la police*, 2:1310.

18. Bruyerin, *De re cibaria*, pp. 696–97; Nonnius, *Diaeteticon*, pp. 172–73.

19. Bruyerin, *De re cibaria*, pp. 513, 516, 518–19; Pliny, *Natural History*, 5:463, bk. XIX, chap. XXIII; Nonnius, *Diaeteticon*, pp. 134, 136.

20. Massonio, *Archidipno*, p. 1. A salad appears only once in all of the fourteenth- and fifteenth-century cookbooks I have examined; see *Form of Cury*, p. 41. The terms *insalata* (Italian), *salade* (French), and "salat" (English) do, however, crop up in various other genres of literature during these centuries. The Italians also used other terms to indicate a mixture of greens dressed with salt, oil, and vinegar, such as Bocaccio's *insalatuzze d'herbuccie*. It is possible that this type of food lingered from antiquity, but Apicius uses no special name for preparations of endive, lettuce, horse parsley, or wild herbs. The switch from *garum* to salt in these mixtures may also have been stimulated by Middle Eastern customs.

21. Pliny, *Natural History*, 6:453, bk. XXIII, chap. XXVII; Athenaeus, *Deipnosophistes*, 1:293, bk. II.

22. Estienne, *De re hortensi libellus*, p. 58; Barbaro, *Castigationes Plinianse*, 2:809.

23. Massonio, *Archidipno*, p. 85.

24. Evelyn, *Acetaria*, pp. 3, 65, 1.

25. Jonson, *Works*, 6:262; Markham, "English Housewife," p. 41 (cf. Venner, *Via recta*, p. 135; Holme, *Academy of Armory*, p. 84); Chomel, *Dictionnaire oeconomique*, 3:344; Kettilby, *Collection of Above Three Hundred Receipts*, p. 204. Cf. Smith, *Compleat Housewife*, unnumbered plates at end of book; Farley, *London Art of Cookery*, p. 101.

26. Artus, *Description de l'isle des hermaphrodites*, p. 106.

27. Richelet, *Dictionnaire françois; Dictionnaire portatif de cuisine*, p. 9 (2d pagination); Nott, *Cook's and Confectioner's Dictionary*, s.v. "Marinade."

28. Porta, *Villae*, bk. VI; Bruyerin, *De re cibaria*, bk. IX; Le Roy Ladurie, *Peasants of Languedoc*, pp. 57, 59–60; L. S. R., *L'Art de bien traiter*, p. 123.

29. *Lisle Letters*, 4:121; Evelyn, *Acetaria*, p. 63; R. Bradley, *Country Housewife*, p. 96.

30. Serres, *Théâtre d'agriculture*, 2:626–27; L. S. R., *L'Art de bien traiter*, p. 125 (cf. *Maistre d'hôtel*, p. 5); Moffett, *Healths Improvement*, p. 208; M. Bradley, *British Housewife*, 2:112; Beveridge, *Prices and Wages*, p. 383.

31. Platina, *De honesta voluptate*, bk. IV; *Thrésor de santé*, p. 484; Huetz de Lemps, *Géographie du commerce*, pp. 308–9; M. Bradley, *British Housewife*, 1:8; Beveridge, *Prices and Wages*, p. 389 (cf. Emmison, *Tudor Food and Pastimes*, p. 95; *Lisle Letters*, 5:744); Bonnefons, *French Gardiner*, p. 261; Voltaire, *Correspondance*, 42:5, 56.

32. Lassels, *Voyage of Italy*, p. 152; Nonnius, *Diaeteticon*, p. 169; *Maistre d'hôtel*, p. 5 (cf. *Cuisine et office de santé propre*, p. 206); Thomson, *Life in a Noble Household*, p. 170 (cf. Beveridge, *Prices and Wages*, 1:167; Allen, *Farmer's Wife*); Fielding, *Tom Jones*, p. 52; La Chapelle, *Modern Cook*, 2d ed., 1:iv.

33. Platina, *De honesta voluptate*, bk. X, "Caviare." Scappi, *Opera*, pp. 146r–48r; Moryson, *Itinerary*, p. 97.

34. Gesner, *Historiae animalium*, p. 1147; Delamare, *Traité de la police*, 3:50; *Cuisine et office de santé propre*, p. 206; Smollett, *Travels through France and Italy*, p. 161. Cf. Lémery, *Treatise of Foods*, p. 262.

35. Serres, *Théâtre d'agriculture*, 2:626–27; Collins, *Salt and Fishery*, p. 101; Houghton, *Husbandry and Trade Improv'd*, 3:309 (cf. Delamare, *Traité de la police*, 3:50); Smollett, *Travels through France and Italy*, p. 161 (cf. Lamb, *Royal Cookery*, p. 1; Massialot, *Nouveau cuisinier royal et bourgeois*, 1:88–89); R. Bradley, *Country Housewife*, p. 38.

36. Nonnius, *Diaeteticon*, p. 423. Cf. Evelyn, *Diary*, 2:426; Houghton, *Husbandry and Trade Improv'd*, 3:294; M. Bradley, *British Housewife*, 1:8–9.

37. Nonnius, *Diaeteticon*, p. 412; Moffett, *Healths Improvement*, p. 153. There is confusion over Latin names for common fish. Nonnius used *halec* for herring, but *halec* is really another form of *allex* or *garum*. Alessandro Petronio, in *De victu romanorum*, used *halec* for anchovies.

38. Parry, "Transport and Trade Routes," pp. 171–72; Strabo, *Geography*, 6:291, IV.ii.21; Plutarch, *Moralia*, 8:341, "Table Talk" IV.4.

39. Bruyerin, *De re cibaria*, p. 556.

## 9. Salads in the Cookbooks

1. Apicius, *Roman Cookery Book*, pp. 81, 93, 99, 103.

2. In a discussion of *almorí*, the author of the Hispanic-Moorish

text mentions only fermented grape juice and fermented bread. In the recipes themselves, however, an ingredient called fish *almorí* sometimes appears. In a note to "A Baghdad Cookery Book" the translator gives a recipe for a black *almorí*—a ferment of bread and salt, to which cinnamon and saffron are sometimes added. A 1572 French edition of Mattioli's notes to Dioscorides equated "the Arabic *Muri* or *Almuri*" with *garum* (Dioscorides, *Commentaires*, chap. 31). Salt-fish brine was an ingredient in the Middle East long before it was used in Rome. Jean Bottéro reports its use from at least 1700 B.C. ("Cuisine of Ancient Mesopotamia," p. 39), but of course this does not mean that it was in continual use through the ancient period. The Greeks could have reintroduced it to the Middle East after a hiatus in its use.

3. *Traducción española*, pp. 203, 207, 211, 213; Rodinson, "Recherches," p. 141; "Baghdad Cookery Book," p. 22.

4. *Libro di cucina*, pp. 42, 50, 52, 58, 25, 43; *Ménagier de Paris*, pp. 210, 232, 237, 200. Cf. Holmes, *Daily Living*, p. 93.

5. *Libro de arte coquinaria*, pp. 65ff.; Platina, *De honesta voluptate*, bks. IV, VI, X. Messisbugo, *Banchetti*, pp. 16, 219; Scappi, *Opera*, pp. 6v, 7r, 17v, 29v, 46v, 108r–9v, 146r–v, 327r.

6. Scappi, *Opera*, pp. 23v, 39r, 59v, 175r, 178v, 179v, 199v, 239v, 137v, 153v, 207r, 19v, 70v, 19v, 23v; Messisbugo, *Banchetti*, pp. 215, 168, 189, 190. Scappi calls for ham on practically every page of his recipes for meat dishes (pp. 19r–55v), and it is a constant ingredient in the vegetable dishes beginning on p. 74r.

7. Scappi, *Opera*, pp. 17v, 112v, 113v, 135r. See Messisbugo, *Banchetti*, p. 211, for a rare exception.

8. A. W., *Booke of Cookrye*, p. 14v (cf. Markham, "English House-wife," pp. 39–41); *Grand cuisinier*, menus at end of text.

9. La Varenne, *Cuisinier françois*; e.g., pp. 179, 182, 199, 200, 202, 203 (fish), 97 (chicken), 268 (vegetables), 97 (ham), 75 (ham omelette), 105 (anchovy), 36, 37, 39–42, 44–46 (capers).

10. Massialot, *Cuisinier roial et bourgeois*, pp. 6, 14, 17, 22, 24, 52.

11. Ibid., pp. 65, 69, 104, 454, 52, 68, 70, 71, 86.

12. Glasse, *Art of Cookery*, chap. XIV, pp. 15, 22, 138; Lamb, *Royal Cookery*, p. 80; Raper, *Receipt Book*, p. 15; R. Bradley, *Country Housewife*, pt. I, p. 162; M. Bradley, *British Housewife*, 1:111–12, 457; Nutt, *Complete Confectioner*, p. 476; May, *Accomplisht Cook*, p. 328; Howard, *England's Newest Way*, p. 32; Peckham, *Complete English Cook*, p. 27; Farley, *London Art of Cookery*, p. 274. Cf. Woodforde, *Diary of a Country Parson*, 3:362, 5:184 ("a rost Chicken with pickled mushrooms" and a fish sauce with "Walnut Pickle").

13. Harrison, *House-keeper's Pocket Book*, p. 64; "Britannia languens," p. 491. Cf. Ayres, *Little Book of Recipes*; *Collection of Confections*, pp. 62, 164ff.; Grimston, *Lawyer's Fortune*, p. 26; *Complete Family Piece*, p. 106.

Occasionally a sauce such as a remoulade containing anchovies is found in an English cookbook.

14. May, *Accomplisht Cook*, p. 116; Bailey, *Dictionarium domesticum*; Johnson, *Madam Johnson's Present*, pp. 172, 173. Cf. Glasse, *Art of Cookery*, p. 102 and chap. XIII; La Chapelle, *Modern Cook*, 1:102; *Complete Family Piece*, p. 104.

15. Scappi, *Opera*, p. 287r; Massonio, *Archidipno*, pp. 389, 393; Bonnefons, *Délices de la campagne*, p. 375; May, *Accomplisht Cook*, unpaginated "Bills of Fare."

16. Holme, *Academy of Armory*, bk. III, p. 82. The origin of the word "salmagundi" remains obscure. To Holme, "salmugundi [is] an Italian dish-meat made of cold Turkey and other ingredients" (p. 85), but I have seen it in neither Messisbugo (1549), Scappi (1570), nor Massonio (1627). We have no idea what Rabelais meant by the term when he used it in his list of foods in *Le Quart Livre*. The word appears in Bonnefons's *Délices* in 1654 (p. 317). Into the cavity of a rabbit one puts "salt and water, which is what one calls *Salmigondis*, by a corruption of a Latin term, *Sal mixtum undis* (salt mixed with water)." Perhaps it originally meant ingredients marinated in salt water.

17. Menon, *Nouvelle Cuisine*, p. 92, and *French Family Cook*, p. 167.

## 10. INVENTING THE MODERN WORLD

1. Bethell, *Handlist of Italian Cookery Books*, p. xii. Bethell (Baron Westbury) believed that La Varenne's work was first published in Italy in 1680 but conceded that there might have been earlier editions of which he was unaware. In Italy in the first half of the eighteenth century, he continued, almost nothing was in print on cookery that was not translated from a French work; "even the 'Cuoco Piemontese' had to be 'Perfezianato a Parigi'!"

2. Trevor-Roper, "Paracelsian Movement," pp. 165–67.

3. Ibid., pp. 168, 171ff.

4. Ibid., p. 176; Solomon, *Public Welfare*, pp. 39, 46, 81, 93; Pagel, *Paracelsus*, p. 17.

5. Solomon, *Public Welfare*, pp. 179, 181–82.

6. Taylor, "Idea of the Quintessence," p. 248; Aristotle, *Meteorologica*, p. 287, bk. III, chap. VI; Paracelsus, *Selected Writings*, p. 220.

7. On the irenic vision see Walker, "Prisca Theologica in France," p. 258. The interchange of symbols makes this tapestry more than simply a decorative reference to the Persian miniatures that circulated in the seventeenth century. These paintings and their influence are discussed in Martin, *Baroque*, p. 184.

8. Hill, *World Turned Upside Down*, pp. 290–91, 115; Thomas, *Religion and the Decline of Magic*, p. 270. Cf. Hill, *Milton and the English Revolution*,

p. 76; Schuler, "Some Spiritual Alchemies"; Webster, "English Medical Reformers," p. 29.

9. Hannaway, *Chemists and the Word*, pp. 106–7; Hill, *World Turned Upside Down*, p. 348. On Boyle and the radicals see Rattansi, "Paracelsus and the Puritan Revolution" and "Intellectual Origins of the Royal Society"; Jacob, *Robert Boyle and the English Revolution.*

10. Trevor-Roper, "Paracelsian Movement," p. 150; Debus, *Chemistry*, p. 236; Westfall, "Newton and Alchemy," pp. 315, 317.

11. Jackson, *Melancholia and Depression*, p. 116; Darnton, *Mesmerism*, p. 14.

12. Rattansi, "Intellectual Origins of the Royal Society," p. 137. Hill, *World Turned Upside Down*, p. 294.

13. *Common Sense* 2 (1739): 10–11. Cf. *Pour et Contre* 15, no. 211 (1738): 77–78.

14. *Connoisseur* 4 (1757): 244.

15. Pope, *Poetical Works*, p. 389 ("How good this is! Just taste this!").

16. Blake, "Compleat Housewife," p. 36; Pliny, *Natural History*, 7:5, bk. XXIV, chap. I. Early in the seventeenth century Robert Burton began his discussion of medicaments for melancholy by citing Pliny's invective against these mysterious medicines from India and Arabia, though he did not share Pliny's scorn for them. To Burton they were useful resources in efforts to deal with melancholia: *Anatomy of Melancholy*, pp. 304–5.

17. Porter, "Before the Fringe," pp. 5, 10; Debus, "Alchemy in an Age of Reason," p. 241.

18. Saint-Simon, *Mémoires*, 4:880–81.

19. Mornet, *Histoire de la litérature et de la pensée françaises*, p. 63, and *Histoire de la litérature française classique*, pp. 7–8; Burton, *Anatomy of Melancholy*, p. 80. Cf. Walker, *Spiritual and Demonic Magic*, p. 159. See also Klibansky, Panofsky, and Saxl, *Saturn and Melancholy*, pp. 337–38.

20. Kristeller, "Modern System of the Arts," pp. 164, 194–95n; L. S. R., *L'Art de bien traiter*, pp. 4–5. For discussions of rules, see, e.g., Carter, *Complete Practical Cook*, Preface; La Chapelle, *Modern Cook*, 1:i; Menon, *Professed Cook.*

21. Horace, *Satires*, pp. 187, 189, satires II.iv (cf. Aristotle, *Parva naturalia*, pp. 239ff. "On Sense and Sensible Objects," IV); Athenaeus, *Deipnosophistes*, 1:437–43, bk. III.

22. MacDougall, "Garden Iconography," p. 40.

23. Platina, *De honesta voluptate*, bk. I; Erasmus, *Opera omnia*, pp. 562–63.

24. Scappi, *Opera*, Preface; Bonnefons, *Délices de la campagne*, p. 206.

25. Aretino, *Letters*, p. 88.

26. Scappi, *Opera*, p. 358r; Buttes, *Dyets Dry Dinner*, n.p.; Moryson, *Itinerary*, 4:140; Boileau-Despreaux, *Oeuvres complètes*, p. 187. "Reason" and "judgment": see, e.g., Bonnefons, *Délices de la campagne*, pp. 103, 107, 137, 144, 146, 164, 172, 173, 176, 225.

27. May, *Accomplisht Cook*, Preface.

28. Evelyn, *Acetaria*, pp. 59–61. A century later cookbook writers expressed the same theory. "Let all your ingredients be properly proportioned, that they may not taste of one thing more than another; let the taste be equal, and the whole of an agreeable relish": Briggs, *English Art of Cookery*, p. 22.

29. Menon, *Science du maître d'hôtel cuisinier*, p. iv. Cf. Kristeller, "Modern System of the Arts."

30. King, *Art of Cookery*, pp. 21, 123.

31. *Common Sense* 2 (1739): 10–11. Cf. *Pour et Contre* 15, no. 211 (1738): 77–78.

32. *Hermeticall Banquet*, pp. 10, 17ff., 58, 43. Though *A Hermeticall Banquet* attacks the whole alchemical-magical world, the anonymous author may have been targeting especially Thomas Vaughan (1622–66), who published under the pseudonym Eugenius Philalethes. In his *Anthroposophia theomagica* (1650) Vaughan notes that the body is the darkness that shackles the soul, but "spirits (say the *Platonicks*)" are most at home "in a Spicy odorous aire" (p. 81). *A Hermeticall Banquet* begins with a chapter called "An anthropogeographicall Grace before meat, wherein the Microcosme is Hermetically Analogiz'd to the Sublunary and Elementary Globes."

33. *Hermeticall Banquet*, p. 109.

34. Ibid., p. 111.

35. Ibid., pp. 42–43, 11. Robert Burton, too, brought together passages on problematic foods from antiquity to his own time in his *Anatomy of Melancholy*, pp. 56–63. He noted that a sixteenth-century German physician advised people who suffered from "hot and head melancholy" to avoid spices.

## 11. In the French Style

1. Athenaeus, *Deipnosophistes*, 2:47, bk. II; Montaigne, *Complete Works*, pp. 222–23.

2. Platina, *De honesta voluptate*, bks. IX–X; Bruyerin, *De re cibaria*, pp. 410, 546; Moffett, *Healths Improvement*, p. 247. Moffett has conflated two terms, *salacitas* (lust) and *salarius* (salt) to arrive at the idea that salt provokes lust. See also Plutarch, *Moralia*, 5:352, *Isis and Osiris*. Plutarch actually wrote that the priests ate no salt "during their periods of holy living." The most important reason for this custom is that salt, "by sharpening the appetite, makes them more inclined to drinking and eating." Renaissance scholars, relying on the old linkage of the craving for food and the craving for sex, extended this notion to mean that salt provokes sexual desire.

3. Plutarch, *Moralia*, 8:347, 9:201, "Table Talk" IV, VIII; Martial,

*Epigrams*, 2:397, bk. XIII, epigram XIV; Athenaeus, *Deipnosophistes*, 1:435–37, bk. III.

4. Horace, *Satires*, pp. 239, 191, satire II.viii, iv. See, e.g., Nonnius, *Diaeteticon*, p. 168.

5. Harrison, *Description of England*, p. 144; Nonnius, *Diaeteticon*, p. 168.

6. Massonio, *Archidipno*, pp. 9–11.

7. Bonnefons, *Délices de la campagne*, pp. 229, 242.

8. Voltaire, *Correspondance*, 59:59.

9. Plutarch, *Moralia*, 8:347, "Table Talk" iv. Apicius, *Roman Cookery Book*, p. 107; Platina, *L'Honneste Volupté*, chap. XL; Bruyerin, *De re cibaria*, p. 562; Panciroli, *History of Many Memorable Things Lost*, p. 299; Evelyn, *Acetaria*, pp. 23–24.

10. Massonio, *Archidipno*, p. 129; Evelyn, *Acetaria*, pp. 23–24.

11. Nonnius, *Diaeteticon*, p. 127.

12. La Varenne, *Cuisinier françois*, pp. 104, 140 (see also 37, 136, 143, 182); L. S. R., *L'Art de bien traiter*, p. 58; Menon, *Traité historique*, 1:8.

13. King, *Art of Cookery*, pp. 99, 111, 3–4.

14. Kettilby, *Collection of Above Three Hundred Receipts*, pp. xvii, 201. Some English cookbooks were slow to give up sugar. A 1726 edition of Henry Howard's *England's Newest Way in All Sorts of Cookery* shows the same schism between a savory chicken pie with revivals and sugared chicken pie (pp. 17–18) that we saw in La Varenne in 1651. Hannah Glasse insisted in 1747 that venison must always have a sweet sauce (*Art of Cookery*, p. 10). John Farley wrote in *London Art of Cookery* (p. 149) that caramel syrup was a useful substitute for *jus*, and the cook should never be without it.

15. R. Bradley, *Country Housewife*, p. x.

16. Massialot, *Cuisinier roial et bourgeois*, p. 40.

17. L. S. R., *L'Art de bien traiter*, p. 58; Orléans, *Correspondance complète*, 2:37; Raffald, *Experienced English Housekeeper*, p. 362; Woodforde, *Diary of a Country Parson*, 3:362, 4:110.

18. Pliny, *Natural History*, 4:21, bk. XII, chap. 14.

19. Martial, *Epigrams*, 1:441, bk. VII, epigram XXVII; 22:397, bk. XIII, epigram XIII; 2:393, bk. XIII, epigram V; Petronius Arbiter, *Satyricon*, p. 51.

20. Massonio, *Archidipno*, p. 111.

21. Menon, *Cuisinière bourgeoise*, p. 284.

22. Saint-Evremond, *Letters*, p. 155; *Dictionnaire portatif de cuisine*, p. 253.

23. Bonnefons, *Délices de la campagne*, p. 109, and *French Gardiner* (1669), p. 199.

24. Gesner, *Libellus*, p. 23v; Dioscorides, *Dioscoride*, p. 277, and *Greek Herbal*, p. 277; Bruyerin, *De re cibaria*, p. 754.

25. Flandrin, Hyman, and Hyman, Introduction to La Varenne, *Cuisinier françois*, p. 25.

26. Marin, *Dons de Comus*, Preface.

27. Walpole, *Correspondence*, 20:71.

28. *Connoisseur* 4, no. 137 (1757): 248–49.

29. *London Journal*, February 25, 1738, and *Fog's Journal*, May 22, 1736, both reprinted in *Gentleman's Magazine*, 1738, p. 92, and 1736, p. 277; *Connoisseur* 4, no. 137 (1757): 248–49.

30. Flandrin et al., Introduction to La Varenne, *Cuisinier françois*, p. 27; Lune, *Cuisinier*, "Au lecteur"; Liger, *Ménage des champs*, p. 300; La Chapelle, *Modern Cook*, 2d ed., 1:236; Menon, *Cuisinière bourgeoise*, p. 31.

31. L. S. R., *L'Art de bien traiter*, p. 90; Liger, *Ménage des champs*, p. 300; Menon, *Nouvelle Cuisine*, p. 104; Mercier, *Tableau de Paris*, 12:315; *Nouveau Dictionnaire*, p. 664. When cookery was brought into the battle of the ancients and moderns, the food served at the time of Louis XIV was called *l'ancienne cuisine*, and the food that followed was known as *la nouvelle cuisine*, or modern cooking. Marin's preface to his *Dons de Comus* in 1739 characterized it in a way that was copied through the remainder of the eighteenth century: "Modern cooking, established on the basis of the old with less fuss and as much variety, is simpler, more correct, and perhaps more masterly." In the 1750 edition he observed that the new cooking had proscribed "the burning *jus* and caustic ragouts of the old cooking."

32. La Varenne, *Cuisinier françois*, pp. 45, 173, 253, 304; L. S. R., *L'Art de bien traiter*, p. 72; Massialot, *Cuisinier roial et bourgeois*, p. 97; Menon, *Cuisinière bourgeoise*, p. 251; *Dictionnaire portatif de cuisine*, p. 352.

33. Richelet, *Dictionnaire françois*; Evelyn, *Acetaria*, pp. 52, 77.

34. May, *Accomplisht Cook*, pp. 3, 27, 45; La Chapelle, *Modern Cook*, 2d ed., 1:131, 238; Smith, *Compleat Housewife*, p. 4; Glasse, *Art of Cookery*, p. 27.

35. Flandrin et al., Introduction to La Varenne, *Cuisinier françois*, pp. 14–15.

36. Platina, *De honesta voluptate*, bk. III; cf. Voltaire, *Oeuvres complètes*, 9:277.

37. La Varenne, *Patissier françois*, p. 333.

38. *General Dictionary of Husbandry*, vol. 1, s.v. "allspice."

39. Bonnefons, *Délices de la campagne*, p. 156; *Dictionnaire portatif de cuisine*, p. 297 (2d pagination).

40. Harrison, *Description of England*, p. 354; Evelyn, *Acetaria*, p. 68; R. Bradley, *Country Housewife*, pt. I, p. 158.

41. *Nouveau Dictionnaire*, vol. 2, s.v. "cuisine."

42. Crosland, *Historical Studies*, p. 42.

## SOME POSTPRANDIAL REMARKS ON ACQUIRING TASTE

1. La Varenne, *Cuisinier françois*, "Librarie au lecteur."

2. Summerson, *Georgian London*, p. 36; Shapin and Schaffer, *Leviathan and the Air-Pump*, p. 68.

3. Quoted in Guinness and Sadler, *Palladio*, p. 12.

4. Yates, *Giordano Bruno*, pp. 361, 367, 369, 374, 389–90; Wolf, *Louis XIV*, p. 59; Scullard, *From the Gracchi to Nero*, pp. 213, 241, 244; Cumont, *Astrology and Religion*, p. 94. Under the probable influence of Posidonius, Plotinus saw the physical world "as a web of hidden affinities originating in a world soul and other cosmic souls": Kristeller, *Renaissance Thought*, p. 53.

5. Girard, "Triomphe de la cuisinière bourgeoise," p. 501.

6. Menon, *Manuel des officiers de bouche*, p. 3.

7. Oxford, *English Cookery Books.*

8. I am indebted to Keith Maslen for this information.

9. *Connoisseur*, 1761, 1:146.

10. *Critical Review*, 1759, 8:288–89.

# Bibliography

A. W. *A Booke of Cookrye.* 1591. Amsterdam: Theatrum Orbis Terrarum, 1976.

Aelianus, Claudius. *On the Characteristics of Animals.* 3 vols. London: Heinemann, 1958–59.

Agrippa von Nettesheim, Heinrich Cornelius. *De occulta philosophia.* Ed. Karl Anton Nowotny. Graz: Druck-und Verlagsanstalt, 1967.

Alderotti, Taddeo. *I "Consilia."* Ed. Giuseppe Nardi. Turin: Minerva Medica, 1937.

"Alimentation." In *La France et les français.* Paris: Gallimard, 1972.

Allen, W⸺. *The Farmer's Wife.* London: Hogg, n.d.

Alunno, Francesco. *La Fabrica del mondo.* Venice: Bascarini, 1548.

Apicius. *Apicii coelii de opsoniis et condimentis, sive arte coquinaria, libri decem.* Ed. Martin Lister. Amsterdam: Waesbergios, 1709.

⸻. *Apicii decem libri cui dicuntur de re coquinaria et excerpta a vinidario conscirpta.* Ed. Mary Ella Milham. Leipzig: Teubner, 1969.

⸻. *L'Art culinaire.* Paris: Belles Lettres, 1974.

⸻. *The Roman Cookery Book: A Critical Translation of "The Art of Cooking" by Apicius.* London: Harrap 1958.

Aretino, Pietro. *Lettere.* Paris: Matteo, 1609. Published in English as *The Letters.* Ed. and trans. Thomas Caldecott Chubb. New Haven: Yale University Library, 1967.

Aristotle. *Meteorologica.* London: Heinemann, 1978.

⸻. *Parva naturalia.* . . . London: Heinemann, 1975.

Artus, Thomas. *Description de l'isle des hermaphrodites.* Cologne: Demen, 1724.

Ashmole, Elias. *Theatrum chemicum Britannicum.* [1652.] New York: Johnson, 1967.

Ashtor, Eliyahu. "An Essay on the Diet of the Various Classes in the Medieval Levant." In *Biology of Man in History*, ed. Robert Forster, trans. Elborg Forster and Patricia M. Ranum. Baltimore: Johns Hopkins University Press, 1975.

Asín-Palacios, Miguel. *Islam and the Divine Comedy.* Trans. Harold Sunderland. London: Murray, 1926.

Atchley, Edward Godfrey Cuthbert Frederic. *A History of the Use of Incense in Divine Worship.* London: Longmans, Green, 1909.

Athenaeus. *The Deipnosophistes.* Trans. C. Gulick. 7 vols. London: Heinemann, 1927–41.

Augustine, Saint. *Concerning the City of God against the Pagans.* Trans. Henry Bettenson. Harmondsworth: Penguin, 1986.

———. *Confessions.* Trans. R. S. Pine-Coffin. Harmondsworth: Penguin, 1985.

Avicenna (Abū 'Ali al-Ḥusain Ibn Sīna). *Avicennae Liber canonis, De medicinis cordialibus, et Cantica.* Venice: Iuntas, 1555.

———. *A Treatise on the Canon of Medicine of Avicenna, Incorporating a Translation of the First Book by O. Cameron Gruner.* London: Luzac, 1930.

[Ayres, Ralph]. *A Little Book of Recipes.* Oxford: privately printed, 1922.

Bacon, Francis. *Works.* Ed. J. Spedding, Robert L. Ellis, and Douglas D. Heath. Boston: Brown, 1862.

Bacon, Roger. *The Opus Majus.* Trans. Robert Belle Burke. Philadelphia: University of Pennsylvania Press, 1928.

"A Baghdad Cookery Book." Trans. Arthur J. Arberry. *Islamic Culture* 13 (1939): 21–47 (pt. I), 189–214 (pt II).

Bailey, Nathan. *Dictionarium domesticum.* London: Hitch, 1736.

Balducci Pegolotti, Francesco. *La Pratica della mercatura.* Ed. Allan Evans. Cambridge: Medieval Academy of America, 1936.

Barb, A. A. "The Survival of Magic Arts." In *The Conflict between Paganism and Christianity in the Fourth Century*, ed. Arnaldo Momigliano. Oxford: Clarendon, 1963.

Barbaro, Ermolao. *Castigationes Plinianse et in pomponium melam.* 4 vols. Padua: In aedibus Antenoreis, 1973–79.

———. *In Dioscoridem corollariorum libri quinque.* Cologne: Soterem, 1530.

Bardenhewer, Louise. *Der Safranhandel in Mittelalter.* Bonn: Hauptmann, 1914.

Belon, Pierre. *La Nature et diversité des poissons. . . .* Paris: Estienne, 1555.

Bennett, H. S. *The Pastons and Their England.* Cambridge: Cambridge University Press, 1970.

Bergström, Ingvar. "*Disguised Symbolism in 'Madonna' Pictures and Still Life.*" *Burlington Magazine* 97, no. 631 (October 1955).

———. *Dutch Still Life Painting in the Seventeenth Century.* Trans. Christina Hedström and Gerald Taylor. London: Faber & Faber, [1956].

———. "Medicina, fons et scrinium." *Konsthistorisk tidskrift* 26 (1957).

———. *La Natura in posa.* Bergamo: Lorenzelli, 1971.

Bethell, Richard Morland Tollemache, Baron Westbury. *Handlist of Italian Cookery Books.* Florence: Olschki, 1963.

Beveridge, William. *Prices and Wages in England from the Twelfth to the Nineteenth Century.* London: Longman, 1939.

Bicais [or Bicaise], Michel. *La Manière de regler la santé.* Aix: David, 1669.

Blake, John B. "The Compleat Housewife." *Bulletin of the History of Medicine* 49, no. 1 (1975).

Boileau-Despreaux, Nicolas. *Oeuvres complètes.* Paris: Didot, 1840.

Bonnefons, Nicolas de. *Les Délices de la campagne.* Paris: Des Hayes, 1654; Amsterdam: Smith, 1655.

———. *The French Gardiner. . . .* Trans. John Evelyn. London: Crooke, 1669; 3d ed., 1675.

*Book of the Dead: The Papyrus of Ani . . . A Reproduction in Facsimile. . . .* London: Warner for the Medici Society, 1913.

Boswell, James. *The Life of Samuel Johnson, L.L.D.* London: Murray, 1835.

Bottéro, Jean. "The Cuisine of Ancient Mesopotamia." *Biblical Archaeologist* 48 (March 1985).

Bradley, Martha. *British Housewife.* 2 vols. London: Crowder, [c. 1770].

Bradley, Richard. *An Appendix to the New Improvements of Planting and Gardening.* Bound with Richard Bradley, *New Improvements of Planting and Gardening.* London: Bettesworth, 1739.

———. *The Country Housewife and Lady's Director.* London: Prospect, 1980. First published in two parts, London, 1727, 1732.

Briggs, Richard. *The English Art of Cookery.* Dublin: Byrne, 1798.

"Britannia languens, or A Discourse of Trade (1680)." In *Early English Tracts on Commerce.* Cambridge: Economic History Society, 1952.

Brown, Peter. *The Body and Society: Men, Women, and Sexual Renunciation in Early Christianity.* New York: Columbia University Press, 1988.

———. *The World of Late Antiquity: A.D. 150–750.* New York: Norton, 1989.

Bruyerin, Jean Baptiste. *De re cibaria. . . .* [Lyon], 1560.

Brykczynski, A. "Jesus-Christ représente comme apothicaire." *Revue de l'Art Chrétien,* ser. 5, 3, no. 1 (1907).

*Ein Buch von guter Speise.* Literarischer Verain (Stuttgart) 9, no. 2 (1844).

Budge, Ernest Alfred Wallis. *The Book of the Opening of the Mouth.* London: Kegan Paul, Trench, Trubner, 1909.

———. *Egyptian Magic.* New York: Dover, 1971.

Burton, Robert. *The Anatomy of Melancholy.* [1621.] Ed. Floyd Dell and Paul Jordan Smith. New York: Tudor, 1955.

Butler, Carolina. *The New London and Country Cook.* London: Cooke, 1770.

Buttes, Henry. *Dyets Dry Dinner. . . .* London: Wood, 1599.

Calano, Prospero. *Traicté excellent de l'entretènement de santé.* Translation from the Latin attributed to Jean Goevrot. Paris: Sertenas, 1550.

Campana, A. "Contributi alla biblioteca del Poliziano e il suo tempo." In *Convegno internazionale di studi sui rinascimento* (Florence, 1954), . . . *Il Poliziano e il suo tempo.* . . . Florence: Sansoni, 1957.

Campanella, Tommaso. *The City of the Sun: A Poetical Dialogue.* Trans. Daniel J. Dunno. Berkeley: University of California Press, 1981.

Camporesi, Piero. *The Incorruptible Flesh: Bodily Mutation and Mortification in Religion and Folklore.* Trans. Tania Crofts Murray. Latin text trans. Helen Elsom. Cambridge: Cambridge University Press, 1988. First published as *La carne impassible.* Milan: Saggiatore, 1983.

Carter, Charles. *The Complete Practical Cook.* London: Meadows, 1730.

Cassirer, Ernst, Paul Oskar Kristeller, and John Hermann Randall Jr., eds. *Renaissance Philosophy of Man.* Chicago: University of Chicago Press, 1971.

Castellano, Petro [Pierre Duchâtel]. *Kreophagia: Sive de esu carnium libri IV.* Antwerp, 1626.

Cato, Marcus Porcius. *On Agriculture.* Trans. William Davis Hooper. Rev. Harrison B. Ash. London: Heinemann, 1934.

Celsus, Aulus Cornelius. *De medicina.* Trans. W. G. Spencer. 3 vols. London: Heinemann, 1935–38.

Chaucer, Geoffrey. *The Complete Works.* ed. F. N. Robinson. 2d ed. Boston: Houghton Mifflin, [1957].

Chomel, Noël. *Dictionnaire oeconomique.* 3 vols. Paris: Ganeau, 1765.

Christiansen, Keith, Laurance B. Kanter, and Carl Brandon Strehlke. *Painting in Renaissance Siena, 1420–1500.* New York: Metropolitan Museum of Art, 1988.

Cian, V. "Gioviana." *Giornale Storico della Letteratura Italiana* 5, no. 17 (1891).

Cicero, Marcus Tullius. *De natura deorum academica.* Trans. H. Rackham. London: Heinemann, 1956.

———. *The Letters to His Friends.* Trans. W. Glynn Williams: London: Heinemann, 1952–1954.

Clark, John. "Marsilio Ficino among the Alchemists." *Classical Bulletin* 59 (1983).

Coffin, David. *The Villa in the Life of Renaissance Rome.* Princeton: Princeton University Press, 1979.

Cohn, Norman Rufus Colin. *The Pursuit of the Millennium: Revolutionary Millenarians and Mystical Anarchists of the Middle Ages.* Rev. ed. New York: Oxford Unviersity Press, 1970.

*Collection des anciens alchimistes grecs.* Ed. Marcelin Pierre Eugène Bertelot. Paris: Steinheil, 1888.

*A Collection of Confections and Other Recipes from an English Manor House of the Eighteenth Century.* Northridge, Calif.: Santa Susana Press, 1977.

Collingwood, John. *The Universal Cook.* London: Noble, 1792.

Collins, John. *Salt and Fishery.* London: Godbid & Playford, 1682.

Bibliography

Columella, Lucius Junius Moderatus. *On Agriculture.* Trans. H. B. Ash. 3 vols. London: Heinemann, 1941–55.

*The Complete Family Piece, and Country Gentleman, and Farmer's Best Guide.* 3d ed. London: Rivington, 1741.

*The Connoisseur.* 3d ed. London: Baldwin, 1757; 4th ed., 1761.

Copenhaver, Brian. "Hermes Trismegistus, Proclus, and the Question of Magic in the Renaissance." In *Hermeticism and the Renaissance: Intellectual History and the Occult in Early Modern Europe,* ed. Ingrid Merkel and Allen G. Debus. Washington, D.C.: Folger Shakespeare Library, 1988.

———. "Scholastic Philosophy and Renaissance Magic in the *De vita* of Marsilio Ficino." *Renaissance Quarterly* 37 (Winter 1984).

Cotgrave, Randle. *A Dictionarie of the French and English Tongues.* [1611.] Columbia: University of South Carolina Press, 1950.

Craig, Kenneth M. "Pieter Aertsen and the *Meat Stall.*" *Oud Holland* 96, no. 1 (1982).

*Critical Review; or, Annals of Literature.* London: Hamilton, 1759.

Crosland, Maurice P. *Historical Studies in the Language of Chemistry.* Cambridge: Harvard University Press, 1962.

*Cuisine et office de santé propre.* Paris: Le Clerc, 1758.

Cumont, Franz Valéry Marie. *Astrology and Religion among the Greeks and Romans.* New York: Putnam, 1912.

Dalechamps, Jacques. *Historia generalis plantarum in libros XVIII. . . .* Lyon, 1587.

Darmstaedter, Ernst. "Per la storia dell' aurum potabile." *Archeion* 5 (1924).

Darnton, Robert. *Mesmerism and the End of the Enlightenment Position.* Cambridge: Harvard University Press, 1968.

Debus, Allen G. "Alchemy in an Age of Reason." In *Hermeticism and the Renaissance: Intellectual History and the Occult in Early Modern Europe,* ed. Ingrid Merkel and Allen G. Debus. Washington, D.C.: Folger Shakespeare Library, 1988.

———. *The Chemical Philosophy: Paracelsian Science and Medicine in the Sixteenth and Seventeenth Centuries.* New York: Science History Publications, 1977.

———. *Chemistry, Alchemy, and the New Philosophy, 1500–1700.* London: Variorum Reprints, 1987.

———. "The Paracelsians in Eighteenth-Century France: A Renaissance Tradition in the Age of the Enlightenment." *Ambix* 28, no. 1 (1981).

Deerr, Noel. *The History of Sugar. . . .* 2 vols. London: Chapman & Hall, 1949–50.

Delamare, Nicolas. *Traité de la police. . . .* 4 vols. Paris: Cot, 1705–38.

Díaz García, Amador. "Three Medical Recipes in Codex Biblioteca

Medicea—Laurenziana Or. 215." *Journal for the History of Arabic Science* 4, no. 2 (1980).

Dickie, James. "The Islamic Garden in Spain." In *The Islamic Garden*, ed. Elizabeth B. MacDougall and Richard Ettinghausen. Washington, D.C.: Dumbarton Oaks, 1976.

*Dictionnaire portatif de cuisine.* . . . Paris: Vincent, 1767.

Dionysius the Areopagite. *The Works of Dionysius the Areopagite.* Trans. John Parker. Merrick, N.Y.: Richwood, 1976. First published in two parts, London, 1897, 1899.

Dioscorides, Pedanius, of Anazarbos. *Commentaires de M. Pierre André Matthiole, médecin, senior, sur les six livres de Ped. Dioscoride.* . . . Lyon: Cotier, 1572. Published in Italian as *Il Dioscoride, dell' eccellente dottor medico M. P. Andrea Matthioli.* . . . Venice: Bottega d'Erasmo, 1550. Published in English as *The Greek Herbal of Dioscorides.* Oxford, 1934.

Donne, John. *The Divine Poems.* Ed. Helen Gardner. 2d ed. Oxford: Clarendon, 1978.

——. *The Epithealamions, Anniversaries and Epicedes.* Ed. W. Milgate. Oxford: Oxford University Press, 1978.

Duchesne, Joseph. *Le Pourtraict de la santé.* Paris: Morel, 1606.

——. *The Practice of Chymicall, and Hermeticall Physicke, for the Preservation of Health.* London: Thomas Creede, 1605.

Dyson, G. Malcolm. "Physiological Aspects of the Essential Oils." *Perfumery Essential Oil Record* 21 (1930). Special issue.

Eamon, William. "Books of Secrets in Medieval and Early Modern Science." *Sudhoffs Archiv für Geschichte der Medizin und der Naturwissenschaften* 69, no. 1 (1985).

Eamon, William, and Françoise Paheau. "Documents and Translations: The Accademia Segreta of Girolamo Ruscelli, a Sixteenth-Century Italian Scientific Society." *Isis* 75 (1984).

Emmison, Frederick George. *Tudor Food and Pastimes.* London: Benn, [1964].

*Encyclopédie, ou Dictionnaire raisonné des sciences, des arts, et des métiers.* 17 vols. Paris: Briasson, 1751–65.

*Encyclopédie méthodique.* Vol. 1. Paris: Panckoucke, 1787.

Erasmus, Desiderius. *Opera omnia.* . . . 9 vols. Amsterdam: North-Holland, 1969–93.

*La Escala de Mahoma: Traducción del arabe al castellano, latín y francés, ordenada por Alfonso X el Sabio.* Ed. José Muñoz Sendino. Madrid: Ministerio de Asuntos Exteriores, Dirección General de Relaciones Culturales, 1949.

[Estienne, Charles]. *De re hortensi libellus, vulgaria herbarum, florum, ac fruticum, qui in hortis conseri solent nomina Latinis vocibis efferre docens ex probatis autoribus.* . . . Lyon, 1536[?].

Evelyn, John. *Acetaria: A Discourse of Sallets*. [1699.] Brooklyn: Brooklyn Botanical Garden, 1937.

———. *The Diary of John Evelyn*. Ed. E. S. De Beer. 6 vols. Oxford: Clarendon, 1955.

Evitascandalo, Cesare. *Dialogo del maestro di casa*. Rome: Vullietti, 1606.

Faré, Michel. *Le Grand Siècle de la nature morte en France: Le 17ᵉ Siècle*. Fribourg: Office du Louvre, 1974.

———. *La Nature morte en France: Son histoire et son évolution du XVIIᵉ au XXᵉ siècle*. Geneva: Caillere, [1962–63].

Farley, John. *The London Art of Cookery*. London: Scatcherd, 1792.

Ferguson, George Wells. *Signs and Symbols in Christian Art*. New York: Oxford University Press, [1954].

Ferguson, John. *The Religions of the Roman Empire*. Ithaca: Cornell University Press, 1985.

Ficino, Marsilio. *Three Books on Life: A Critical Edition*. Ed. John R. Clark. Trans. Carol V. Kaske. Binghamton, N.Y.: Medieval and Renaissance Texts and Studies, 1989.

Field, Arthur. *The Origin of the Platonic Academy*. Princeton: Princeton University Press, 1988.

Fielding, Henry. *The History of Tom Jones*. Harmondsworth: Penguin, 1978.

Findlen, Paula. "Humanism, Politics, and Pornography in Renaissance Italy." In *The Invention of Pornography: Obscenity and the Origins of Modernity, 1500–1800*, ed. Lynn Hunt. New York: Zone Books, 1993.

Flandrin, Jean-Louis, Philip Hyman, and Mary Hyman. Introduction to François Pierre de La Varenne, *Le Cuisinier françois et Le Patissier françois* (1690). Paris: Montalba, 1983.

Flückiger, Friedrich A. "Note on Costus." *Pharmaceutical Journal and Transactions*, 3d ser., 8 (1878).

*The Forme of Cury, a Roll of Ancient English Cookery, Compiled, about A.D. 1390, by the Master-Cooks of King Richard II*. Ed. Samuel Pegge. London: Nichols, 1780.

Foxon, David Fairweather. *Libertine Literature in England, 1600–1745*. New Hyde Park, N.Y.: University Books, [1966].

Franklin, Alfred Louis Auguste. *La Vie privée d'autrefois: Arts et métiers, modes, moeurs, usages des Parisiens du XIIᵉ au XVIIIᵉ siècle. . . .* 27 vols. Paris: Plon, Nourrit, 1887–1902.

Galen, Claudius. *On the Affected Parts*. Trans. Rudolph E. Siegel. Basel: Karger, 1976.

———. *Opera omnia*. Ed. C. G. Kühn. 20 vols. in 22. Leipzig, 1821–33.

Garin, Eugenio. *Astrology in the Renaissance: The Zodiac of Life*. Trans. Carol Jackson and June Allen. London: Routledge & Kegan Paul, 1983.

Gassendi, Pierre. *The Mirrour of True Nobility and Gentility, Being the Life of the Renowned Nicolaus Claudius Fabricus, Lord of Peiresk.* Trans. W. Rand. London: Streater, 1657.

*A General Dictionary of Husbandry, Planting, Gardening, and the Vegetable Part of the Materia Medica.* . . . Bath: Cruttwell, 1779.

*Geoponica: Constantini Caesaris selectarum praeceptionum de agricultura libri viginti.* Lyon, 1536.

Gerard, John. *The Herball, or Generall Historie of Plantes.* . . . London: Norton, 1597.

Gersh, Stephen E. *From Iamblichus to Eriugena: An Investigation of the Prehistory and Evolution of the Pseudo-Dionysian Tradition.* Leiden: Brill, 1978.

Gesner, Konrad. *Historiae animalium.* . . . 5 vols. Tigur, 1551–87.

———. *Libellus de lacte.* . . . Tigur, [1543].

Gibault, Georges. *Histoire des légumes.* Paris: Librarie Horticole, 1912.

Girard, Alain. "Le Triomphe de la cuisinière bourgeoise: Livres culinaires, cuisine et société en France aux XVII et XVIII siècles." *Revue d'Histoire Moderne et Contemporaine* 24 (1977).

Glasse, Hannah. *The Art of Cookery Made Plain and Easy.* [1747, 3d ed. 1748.] Hamden, Conn.: Archon Books, 1971.

*Gnosticism: A Source Book of Heretical Writings from the Early Christian Period.* Ed. Robert M. Grant. New York: Harper & Row, 1961.

Gombrich, Ernst H. "Renaissance Artistic Theory and the Development of Landscape Painting." *Gazette des Beaux-Arts* 41 (May 1953).

———. "Tradition and Expression in Western Still Life." In *Meditations on a Hobby Horse and Other Essays on the Theory of Art.* London: Phaidon, [1963].

Gontier, Pierre. *Exercitationes hygiasticae: Sive, de sanitate tuenda et vita producenda, libri XVIII.* . . . Lyon, 1668.

Gosling, Justin Cyril Bertrand, and Christopher Charles Whiston Taylor. *The Greeks on Pleasure.* Oxford: Clarendon, 1982.

Granado, Diego. *Libro del arte de cocina.* [1599.] Madrid: Sociedad de Bibliófilos Españoles, 1971.

*Le Grand Cuisinier de toute cuisine.* Paris: Bonfons, [c. 1560].

Grataroli, Guglielmo. *Turba philosophorum: Ein Beitrag zur Geschichte der Alchemie.* Berlin: Springer, 1931.

Greindl, Edith. *Les Peintres flamands de nature morte au XVIIe siècle.* Steerebeek: Lefebvre, 1983.

Grey, Elizabeth, Countess of Kent. *A Choice Manual, or Rare and Select Secrets in Physick and Chirurgery.* 2d ed. London, 1653.

Grimston, William Luckyn, Viscount Grimston. *The Lawyer's Fortune, or Love in a Hollow Tree.* A comedy. London: Lintott, [1705].

Gruman, Gerald J. *A History of Ideas about the Prolongation of Life: The Evolution of Prolongevity Hypotheses to 1800.* Transactions of the American Philosophical Society, n.s. 56, pt. IX. Philadelphia, 1966.

Guinness, Desmond, and Julius Trousdale Sadler, Jr. *Palladio: A Western Progress*. New York: Viking, 1976.

Hamarneh, Sami Khalaf, and G. Sonnendecker. *A Pharmaceutical View of Albucasis al-Zahrāwī Moorish Spain*. . . . Leiden: Brill, 1963.

Hannaway, Owen. *The Chemists and the Word: The Didactic Origins of Chemistry*. Baltimore: Johns Hopkins University Press, [1975].

Harrison, Sarah. *House-keeper's Pocket Book*. London: Ware, 1743.

Harrison, William. *The Description of England*. Ed. G. Edelen. Ithaca: Cornell University Press, 1968.

Hartman, George. *A Choice Collection of Rare Secrets and Experiments in Philosophy as Also Rare and Unheard of Medicines. Collected by Sir Kenelm Digby*. London: Cooper, 1682.

Harvey, John Hooper. *Early Nurserymen*. London: Phillimore, 1974.

———. *Medieval Gardens*. London: Batsford, 1981.

[Hecquet, Philippe]. *Traité des dispenses du Carême*. Paris: Fournier, 1709.

Henderson, William Augustus. *The Housekeeper's Instructor, or Universal Family Cook . . . to Which is Added, the Complete Art of Carving*. . . . 5th ed. London: W. and J. Stratford, 1795.

Henry VIII, king of England. *The Privy Purse Expenses of King Henry VIII*. . . . London: Pickering, 1827.

Hentzner, Paul. *Journey into England by Paul Hentzer in the Year M.D.XC.VIII*. Strawberry Hill, 1757.

Hermes Trismegistus. *Corpus hermeticum*. . . . Ed. A. D. Nock. Trans. A. J. Festugière. 4 vols. Paris: Belles Lettres, 1945–54.

*A Hermeticall Banquet, Drest by a Spagyricall Cook: For the Better Preservation of the Microcosme*. London: Crooke, 1652.

Hester, John. *The Secrets of Physick and Philosophy, Divided into Two Bookes*. London: Lugger, 1633.

Hill, John Edward Christopher. *Milton and the English Revolution*. London: Faber & Faber, 1977.

———. *The World Turned Upside Down: Radical Ideas During the English Revolution*. London: Temple Smith, [1972].

Hill, Thomas. *The Proffitable Arte of Gardening*. . . . London: Marshe, 1568.

Hippocrates. *Opera quae extant graece et latine*. Venice, 1588.

Hippolytus, Saint. *Philosophumena; or, The Refutation of All Heresies*. London: Society for Promoting Christian Knowledge, 1921.

Hitti, Philip Kkûri. *History of the Arabs from the Earliest Times to the Present*. 6th ed. London: Macmillan, 1956.

Holinshed, Raphael. *The . . . Chronicles of England, Scotlande, and Irelande*. . . . London: Harrison, [1577].

Holme, Randle. *Academy of Armory*. [1688.] Menston: Scolar Press, 1972.

Holmes, Urban Tigner. *Daily Living in the Twelfth Century*. Madison: University of Wisconsin Press, 1952.

Holmyard, Eric John. *Alchemy*. Harmondsworth: Penguin, 1957.

Homer. *The Odyssey.* London: Heinemann, 1953.

Hopkins, Arthur John. *Alchemy, Child of Greek Philosophy.* New York: Columbia University Press, 1934.

Horace. *The Odes and Epodes.* Trans. C. E. Bennett. London: Heinemann, 1978.

———. *Satires, Epistles, and Ars poetica.* Trans. H. Rushton Fairclough. London: Heinemann, 1955.

Houghton, John. *Husbandry and Trade Improv'd. . . .* 4 vols. London: Wooman, 1727–28.

Howard, Henry. *England's Newest Way in All Sorts of Cookery, Pastry, and All Pickles That Are Fit to Be Used. . . .* 4th ed. London: Coningsby, 1717; 5th ed., London: Knapton, 1726.

Huetz de Lemps, Christian. *Géographie du commerce de Bordeaux à la fin du règne de Louis XIV.* Paris: Mouton, 1975.

Husson, Camille, fils. *Etude sur les épices, aromates, condiments, sauces et assaisonnements, leur histoire, leur utilité, leur danger.* Paris: Dunod, 1883.

Jackson, Stanley W. *Melancholia and Depression: From Hippocratic Times to Modern Times.* New Haven: Yale University Press, 1986.

Jacob, J. R. *Robert Boyle and the English Revolution: A Study in Social and Intellectual Change.* New York: Burt Franklin, 1977.

Jeanneret, Michel. *A Feast of Words: Banquets and Table Talk in the Renaissance.* Chicago: University of Chicago Press, 1987.

Johnson, Mary. *Madam Johnson's Present. . . .* London: Cooper, 1754.

Jones, William T. *A History of Western Philosophy.* New York: Harcourt, Brace, 1952.

Jongh, E. de. *Still-Life in the Age of Rembrandt.* Auckland: Auckland City Art Gallery, 1982.

Jonson, Ben. *Works.* London: Midwinter, 1756.

Josten, C. H. "Truth's Golden Harrow: An Unpublished Alchemical Treatise of Robert Fludd in the Bodleian Library." *Ambix* 3, nos. 3 and 4 (April 1949).

Jung, Carl Gustav. *Psychology and Alchemy.* Princeton: Princeton University Press, 1980.

Juvenal. *Juvenal and Persius.* Trans. G. G. Ramsay. London: Heinemann, 1940.

Kettilby, Mary. *A Collection of Above Three Hundred Receipts in Cookery, Physick, and Surgery. . . .* London, 1728.

Kindī, Yaʿqūb ibn Ishāq al-. *Kitāb kīmiyāʾ al- ʿiṭr wat-taṣ īdāt: Buch über die Chemie des Parfüms und die Destillationen.* Ed. and trans. Karl Garbers. Leipzig: Brockhaus, 1948.

———. *The Medical Formulary of Aqrābādhīn.* Trans. Martin Levey. Madison: University of Wisconsin Press, 1966.

King, William. *The Art of Cookery, in Imitation of Horace's Art of Poetry, with Some Letters to Dr. Lister and Others.* London: Lintott, [1709?].

Bibliography

Klibansky, Raymond, Erwin Panofsky, and Fritz Saxl. *Saturn and Melancholy: Studies in the History of Natural Philosophy, Religion, and Art.* London: Nelson, 1964.

Koch, Robert. "Flower Symbolism in the Portinari Altar." *Art Bulletin* 46, no. 1 (March 1964).

Kristeller, Paul Oskar. "The Modern System of the Arts." In *Renaissance Thought and the Arts: Collected Essays.* Princeton: Princeton University Press, 1980.

———. *Renaissance Thought and Its Sources.* New York: Columbia University Press, 1979.

Kritzeck, James. *Peter the Venerable and Islam.* Princeton: Princeton University Press, 1964.

L. S. R. *L'Art de bien traiter.* Paris: Du Puis, 1674.

La Chapelle, Vincent. *The Modern Cook.* 3 vols. London, 1733; 2d ed., 1736.

L'Aigue, Etienne de, sieur de Beauvais. *Singulier traicté contenant la propriété des tortues, escargotz, grenouilles, et artichaultz.* [Paris]: Galliot Du Pré, [1530].

Lamb, Patrick. *Royal Cookery.* London: Nutt, 1731.

"The Land of Cokaygne." In *Early Middle English Verse and Prose,* ed. J. A. W. Bennett and G. V. Smithers. Oxford: Clarendon, 1966.

La Quintinie, Jean de. *The Compleat Gard'ner.* London: Gillyflower, 1693.

Lassels, Richard. *The Voyage of Italy.* . . . Paris, 1670.

La Varenne, François Pierre de. *Le Cuisinier françois.* [1651.] Troyes, 1690. Reprinted with La Varenne, *Le Patissier françois* [1690?], with introduction by Jean-Louis Flandrin, Philip Hyman, and Mary Hyman. Paris: Montalba, 1983.

Le Grand d'Aussy, Pierre Jean Baptiste. *Histoire de la vie privée des français, depuis l'origine de la nation jusqu'à nos jours.* 3 vols. Paris: Pierres, 1782.

Lémery, Louis. *A Treatise of Foods, in General.* . . . London: Bell, 1706.

Le Roy Ladurie, Emmanuel. *Les Paysans de Languedoc.* 2d ed. 2 vols. Paris: Mouton, 1966. Published in English as *The Peasants of Languedoc.* Trans. John Day. Urbana: University of Illinois Press, 1974.

Levey, Martin. *Early Arabic Pharmacology: An Introduction Based on Ancient and Medieval Sources.* Leiden: Brill, 1973.

———. *Substitute Drugs in Early Arabic Medicine, with Special Reference to the Texts of Māsarjawaih, al-Rāzī, and Pythagoras.* Stuttgart: Wissenschaftliche Verlagsgesellschaft, 1971.

Lewy, Hans. *Chaldean Oracles and Theurgy: Mysticism, Magic, and Platonism in the Later Roman Empire.* . . . Cairo: Imprimerie de l'Institut Français d'Archéologie Orientale, 1956.

"Libro de arte coquinaria composto per lo egregio maestro Martino coquo olim del Reverendiss. Monsignor el Patriarcha de Aquileia." [c. 1450.] Manuscript, Library of Congress; copy in library of School of Hotel Administration, Cornell University.

Il "Libro della scalo" e la questione delle fonti arabo-spagnole della Divina commedia. Ed. Enrico Cerulli. Vatican City: Biblioteca Apostolica Vaticana, 1949.

Libro di cucina del secolo XIV. Ed. Ludovico Frati. Bologna: Forni, 1899.

Liger, Louis. Ménage des champs. Paris: David, 1711.

Linden, Stanton J. "Alchemy and Eschatology in Seventeenth-Century Poetry." Ambix 31, no. 3 (1984).

The Lisle Letters. Ed. Muriel St. Clare Byrne. Chicago: University of Chicago Press, 1981.

Lister, Martin. A Journey to Paris in the Year 1698. [1699.] Urbana: University of Illinois Press, 1967.

Lune, Pierre de. Le Cuisinier. Paris: David, 1656.

MacDougall, Elisabeth. "Garden Iconography." In The Italian Garden, ed. David R. Coffin. Washington, D.C.: Dumbarton Oaks, 1972.

Macrobius, Ambrosius Aurelius Theodosius. The Saturnalia. Trans. Percival V. Davies. New York: Columbia University Press, 1969.

Le Maistre d'hôtel qui apprend l'ordre de bien servir sur table. Paris: David, 1659.

Majrīṭī, Maslamah ibn Aḥmad al- [Pseudo]. "Picatrix": Das Ziel des Weisen von Pseudo-Magriti. Trans. Hellmut Ritter and Martin Plessner. London: Warburg Institute, University of London, 1962.

———. Picatrix: The Latin Version of the Ghāyat al-Ḥakīm. Ed. David Pingree. London: Warburg Institute: University of London, 1986.

Mallet, H. "Les Ivoires de François Duquesnoy (1594–1643)." Gazette des Beaux Arts 11 (1875).

Manelfi, Giovanni. Mensa romana: Sive, Urbana victus ratio. Rome: Philippi de Rubeis, 1650.

Manuel, Frank E., and Fritzie P. Manuel. Utopian Thought in the Western World. Cambridge: Belknap Press of Harvard University Press, 1979.

Marin, François. Les Dons de Comus, ou Les Délices de la table. Paris: Prault, 1739.

———. Les Dons de Comus, ou L'Art de la cuisine. 2d ed. Paris: Pissot, 1750.

Markham, Gervase. Countrey Contentments. . . . [1615.] Amsterdam: Da Capo Press, 1973.

Marle, Raimond van. Iconographie de l'art profane au Moyen-âge et à la Renaissance. . . . La Haye: Martinus Nijhoff, 1932.

Martial. Epigrams. Trans. Walter C. A. Ker. 2 vols. London: Heinemann, 1919–1920.

Martianus Capella. Martianus Capella and the Seven Liberal Arts. Vol. 2. Trans. W. H. Stahl and R. Johnson, with E. L. Burge. New York: Columbia University Press, 1971.

Martin, John Rupert. Baroque. New York: Harper & Row, 1977.

Massialot, François. *The Court and Country Cook: Giving New and Plain Directions How to Order All Manner of Entertainments, and the Best Sort of the Most Exquisite à-la-Mode Ragoos's.* London: Churchill, 1702.

——. *Le Cuisinier roial et bourgeois.* Paris: Sercy, 1691.

——. *Le Nouveau Cuisinier royal et bourgeois.* 2 vols. Paris: Prudhomme, 1712.

Massonio, Salvatore. *Archidipno, overo dell' insalata, e dell' uso di essa.* Venice: Brogiollo, 1627.

May, Robert. *The Accomplisht Cook; or, The Art and Mystery of Cookery.* London: Brooke, 1660; 5th ed., London: Blagrave, 1685.

*Le Ménagier de Paris.* Ed. Georgine E. Brereton and Janet M. Ferrier. Oxford: Clarendon, 1981. Translated also as *The Goodman of Paris.* London: Routledge, 1928.

[Menon, ——]. *Cuisine et office de santé propre.* Paris: Le Clerc, 1758.

——. *La Cuisinière bourgeoise. . . .* Paris: Guillyn, 1746. Published in English as *The French Family Cook.* London: Bell, 1793.

——. *Le Manuel des officiers de bouche.* Paris: Le Clerc, 1759.

——. *Nouveau Traité de la cuisine. . . .* Paris: David, 1739.

——. *La Nouvelle Cuisine.* Paris: David, 1742.

——. *The Professed Cook.* Trans. of *Les Soupers de la cour.* London: Davis, 1769.

——. *La Science du maître d'hôtel cuisinier.* Paris: Paulus-Du-Mesnil, 1749.

——. *Traité historique et pratique de la cuisine.* 2 vols. Paris: Bauche, 1758.

Mercier, Louis Sebastien. *Tableau de Paris.* 12 vols. in 4. Amsterdam, 1783–89.

Messisbugo, Cristoforo di. *Banchetti: Composizioni di vivande e apparecchio generale.* [1549.] Ed. F. Bandini. Venice: Pozza, 1960.

Metlitzki, Dorothee. *The Matter of Araby in Medieval England.* New Haven: Yale University Press, 1977.

Milham, Mary Ella. "Apicius." In *Catalogus Translationum et Commentariorum: Medieval and Renaissance Latin Translations and Commentaries. . . .* Washington, D.C.: Catholic University of America Press, 1971.

Miller, James Innes. *The Spice Trade of the Roman Empire, 29 B.C. to A.D. 641.* Oxford: Clarendon, 1969.

Miller, Philip. *The Gardeners Dictionary. . . .* 3d ed. London, 1737.

Moffett, Thomas. *Healths Improvement; or, Rules Comprizing and Discovering the Nature, Method, and Manner of Preparing All Sorts of Food Used in This Nation.* Enlarged by Christopher Bennett. London: Thomson, 1655.

Montaigne, Michel Eyquem de. *The Complete Works.* Trans. Donald M. Frame. Stanford: Stanford University Press, 1958.

Montgomery, John Warwick. "Cross, Constellation, and Crucible: Lutheran Astrology and Alchemy in the Age of Reformation." *Transactions of the Royal Society of Canada,* ser. 4, 1 (June 1963).

Mornet, Daniel. *Histoire de la littérature et de la pensée françaises*. Paris: Larousse, 1924.

———. *Histoire de la littérature française classique, 1660–1700*. Paris: Colin, 1947.

Moryson, Fynes. *An Itinerary. . . .* 4 vols. Glasgow: MacLehose, 1907–8.

Mulon, Marianne. "Recettes Médiévales." *Annales E.S.C.* 19, no. 5 (1964).

Multhauf, Robert P. *The Origins of Chemistry*. New York: Franklin Watts, 1967.

Muret, Jean. *Traité des festins*. Paris: Desprez, 1682.

Nasr, Seyyed Hassein. *An Introduction to Islamic Cosmological Doctrines*. London: Thames & Hudson, 1978.

———. "Islamic Alchemy and the Birth of Chemistry." *Journal for the History of Arabic Science* 3, no. 1 (1979).

———. *Science and Civilization in Islam*. Cambridge: Harvard University Press, 1968.

———. *Sufi Essays*. Albany: State University of New York Press, 1972.

Nauert, Charles G. "Caius Plinius Secundus." In *Catalogus translationum et commentariorum*. Washington, D.C.: Catholic University of America Press, 1980.

Needham, Joseph. *Science and Civilisation*. 6 vols. to date. Cambridge: Cambridge University Press, 1954–.

Nonnius, Louis. *Diaeteticon, sive, de re cibaria*. Antwerp, 1645.

———. *Ichtyophagia, sive, de piscium esu commentarius*. Antwerp, 1616.

Nostredame, Michel de. *Excellent et moult utile opuscule à touts nécessaire*. Paris: Oliver de Harsy, 1556.

Nott, John. *The Cook's and Confectioner's Dictionary; or, The Accomplish'd Housewives Companion*. London: Rivington, 1723.

*Nouveau Dictionnaire, pour servir de supplement aux dictionnaires des sciences, des arts, et des métiers*. 4 vols. Paris: Panckoucke, 1776–77.

*Nouvelle Biographie générale*. Paris: Firmin Didot Frères, 1859.

*Nouvelle Collection des mémoires pour servir à l'histoire de France*. Vol. 1, pt. 1. Paris: Editeur du Commentaire Analytique du Code Civil, 1837.

Nutt, Frederic. *The Complete Confectioner. . . .* London, 1789.

*Eenen Nyeuwen coock boeck*. [Antwerp, 1560.] Wiesbaden: Pressler, 1971.

Orléans, Elisabeth Charlotte, duchesse d'. *Correspondence complète de Mme la Duchesse d'Orléans née Princesse Palatine, mère du régent*. Trans. G. Brunet. 2 vols. Paris: Charpentier, 1863.

Oxford, Arnold Whitaker. *English Cookery Books to the Year 1850*. London: Oxford University Press, 1913.

Pagel, Walter. *Joan Baptista van Helmont: Reformer of Science and Medicine*. Cambridge: Cambridge University Press, 1982.

———. *Paracelsus: An Introduction to Philosophical Medicine in the Era of the Renaissance*. 2d ed. Basel: Karger, 1982.

Panciroli, Guido. *History of Many Memorable Things Lost, Which Were in Use among the Ancients; and an Account of Many Things Found Now in Use among the Moderns. . . .* London: Nicholson, 1715.

———. *Rerum memorabilium jam olim deperditarum: et contra recens atque ingeniose inventarum: libri duo. . . .* Amberg, 1599.

Paracelsus. *Bücher und Schrifften.* [Basel, 1589–90.] Ed. by Johannes Huser. Hildesheim: Olms, 1971.

———. *The Hermetic and Alchemical Writings. . . .* Trans. A. E. Waite. London: Elliott, 1894.

———. *Selected Writings.* Ed. Jolande Jacobi. Trans. Norbert Guterman. Princeton: Princeton University Press, 1973.

Parkinson, John. *Paradisi in sole paradisus terrestris; or, A Garden of All Sorts of Pleasant Flowers Which Our English Ayre Will Permitt to be Noursed Up; with a Kitchen Garden of All Manner of Herbes, Rootes, and Fruites . . . and an Orchard. . . .* London: Lownes & Young, 1629.

———. *Theatrum Botanicum; or, An Herball. . . .* London: Cotes, 1640.

Parry, J. H. "Transport and Trade Routes." In *The Cambridge Economic History of Europe.* Cambridge: Cambridge University Press, 1975.

Partington, James Riddick. *A History of Chemistry.* 4 vols. London: Macmillan, 1961–70.

Paulet, [Jean Jacques]. *Traité des champignons. . . .* Paris: Imprimerie Nationale Executive du Louvre, 1793.

Peckham, Ann. *Complete English Cook, or Prudent Housewife.* Leeds, 1767.

Pepys, Samuel. *The Diary of Samuel Pepys.* Ed. Robert Latham and William Matthews. 11 vols. Berkeley: University of California Press, 1970–83.

Persius Flaccus, Aulus. *Juvenal and Persius.* Trans. G. G. Ramsay. London: Heinemann, 1941.

Peterson, Toby. "The Arab Influence on Western European Cooking." *Journal of Medieval History* 6 (September 1980).

Petronio, Alessandro Trajano. *De victu romanorum et de sanitate tuenda libri quinque. . . .* Rome, 1581.

Petronius Arbiter. *The Satyricon.* Trans. Michael Heseltine. London: Heinemann, 1956.

Petrus Alfonsi. *The "Disciplina Clericalis" of Petrus Alfonsi.* Trans. and ed. Eberhard Hermes. Trans. into English by P. R. Quarrie. Berkeley: University of California Press, 1977.

Pisanelli, Baldassare. *Traité de la nature des viandes. . . .* Arras: Bauduyn, 1596.

———. *Trattato della natura de' cibi et del bere.* Rome: Bonfadino, 1583.

Plat, Hugh. *Delightes for Ladies. . . .* [1627.] Ed. Violet Trovillion and Hal W. Trovillion. Herrin, Ill., 1942.

Platina, Bartolomeo. *De honesta voluptate.* [Venice, 1475.] St. Louis: Mallinkrodt, 1967. Published in French as *De l'honneste volupté.* Paris: Sergent, 1539.

Plato. *The Republic.* Trans. Paul Shorey. 2 vols. London: Heinemann, 1930–35.

———. *Timaeus, Critias, Cleitophon, Menexenus, Epistles.* Trans. R. G. Bury. London: Heinemann, 1952.

Plautus, Titus Maccius. *Amphitryon, The Comedy of Asses, The Pot of Gold, The Two Bacchises, The Captives.* Trans. Paul Nixon. London: Heinemann, 1916.

———. *Casina, The Casket Comedy, Curculio, Epidicus, The Two Menaechmuses.* Trans. Paul Nixon. London: Heinemann, 1951.

———. *The Merchant, The Braggart Warrior, The Haunted House, The Persian.* Trans. Paul Nixon. London: Heinemann, 1950.

———. *[Poenulus, or] The Little Carthaginian, Pseudolus, The Rope.* Trans. Paul Nixon. London: Heinemann, 1951.

———. *Stichus, Three Bob Day, Truculentus, The Tale of a Travelling Bag, Fragments.* Trans. Paul Nixon. London: Heinemann, 1952.

Pliny. *Natural History.* Trans. H. Rackham and W. H. S. Jones. 10 vols. London: Heinemann, 1938–63.

Plutarch. *Moralia.* Trans. F. C. Babbitt, W. C. Helmbold, and H. N. Fowler. 15 vols. Loeb Classical Library. Cambridge: Harvard University Press, 1927–.

———. *Plutarch's Lives.* Trans. B. Perrin. 11 vols. London: Heinemann, 1914–26.

Pope, Alexander. *Poetical Works.* Ed. Herbert Davis. Oxford: Oxford University Press, 1978.

Popkin, Richard Henry. *The History of Scepticism from Erasmus to Spinoza.* Rev. ed. Berkeley: University of California Press, 1979.

Porta, Giambattista della. *Natural Magick.* [1658.] New York: Basic Books, 1957.

———. *Villae . . . Libri XII.* Frankfurt, 1592.

Porter, Roy. "Before the Fringe: 'Quackery' and the Eighteenth-Century Medical Market." In *Studies in the History of Alternative Medicine,* ed. Roger Cooter. London: Macmillan, 1988.

Rabb, Theodore K. *The Struggle for Stability in Early Modern Europe.* New York: Oxford University Press, 1975.

Rabelais, François. *The Histories of Gargantua and Pantagruel.* Trans. J. M. Cohen. Harmondsworth: Penguin, 1955.

———. *Le Quart Livre.* Lille: Giard, 1947.

Raffald, Elizabeth. *The Experienced English Housekeeper, for the Use and Ease of Ladies, Housekeepers, Cooks. . . .* Manchester, 1769.

Raper, Elizabeth. *The Receipt Book of Elizabeth Raper and a Portion of Her Cipher Journal . . . Written 1756–1770.* Ed. Bartle Grant. Soho: Nonesuch Press, 1924.

Rattansi, P. M. "The Intellectual Origins of the Royal Society of London." *Notes and Records of the Royal Society of London,* 1968, no. 3.

———. "Paracelsus and the Puritan Revolution." *Ambix* 11, no. 1 (1963).

Ray, John. *Observations Topographical, Moral, & Physiological Made in a Journey through Part of the Low-Countries, Germany, Italy and France.* London: Martyn, 1673.

Ray, Priyadaranjan. *A History of Chemistry in Ancient and Medieval India: Incorporating the History of Hindu Chemistry by Acharya Prafulla Chandra Ray.* Calcutta: Indian Chemical Society, 1956.

Richelet, Pierre. *Dictionnaire françois.* . . . Geneva: Widerhold, 1679.

Riddle, John M. "The Introduction and Use of Eastern Drugs in the Early Middle Ages." *Sudhoffs Archiv für Geschichte der Medizin und der Naturwissenschaften* 49, no. 2 (June 1965).

Rodinson, Maxim. "Recherches sur les documents arabes relatifs à la cuisine." *Revue des Etudes Islamiques,* 1949 [1950].

———. "Romania et autres mots arabes en italien." *Romania* 71 (1950).

Romoli, Domenico. *La singolare dottrina.* . . . Venice: Tramezzino, 1570.

Ronsard, Pierre de. *Les Oeuvres.* Chicago: University of Chicago Press, 1967.

Royal Society of London. *Philosophical Transactions.* [1693.] New York: Johnson, 1963.

Rudolph, Kurt. *Gnosis: The Nature and History of Gnosticism.* San Francisco: Harper & Row, 1987.

Runciman, Steven. *A History of the Crusades.* 3 vols. Cambridge: Cambridge University Press, 1951–54.

———. *The Sicilian Vespers: A History of the Mediterranean World in the Later Thirteenth Century.* . . . Cambridge: Cambridge University Press, 1958.

Ruscelli, Girolamo [supposed author]. *The Secretes of the Reverende Maister Alexis of Piemount, Containing Excellente Remedies against Divers Diseases, Woundes, and Other Accidents, with the Manner to Make Distillations, Perfumes, Confitures, Dyings, Colours, Fusions, and Meltynges. A Worke Well Approved, Verye Profytable and Necessary for Every Man.* Trans. William Warde. London: Inglande, 1558.

Saint-Evremond, Charles de Marguetel de Saint-Denis, seigneur de. *The Letters of Saint-Evremond.* . . . Ed. John Hayward. London: Routledge, 1930.

Saint-Simon, Louis de Rouvroy, duc de. *Mémoires du duc de Saint-Simon.* Ed. Gonzague Truc. 7 vols. Paris: Gallimard, 1949–61.

Sarton, George. *The Appreciation of Ancient and Medieval Science during the Renaissance, 1450–1600.* Philadelphia: University of Pennsylvania Press, 1955.

———. *Introduction to the History of Science.* 3 vols. Baltimore: Williams & Wilkins, 1927–48.

Scappi, Bartolomeo. *Opera.* Venice: Tramezzino, 1570; Vecchi, 1610.

Schackleford, Ann. *The Modern Art of Cookery Improved.* London: Newberry, 1767.

Schuler, Robert M. "Some Spiritual Alchemies of Seventeenth-Century England." *Journal of the History of Ideas* 41 (1980).

*Scriptores historiae Augustae.* Trans. David Magie. 3 vols. London: Heinemann, 1922–32.

Scullard, Howard Hayes. *From the Gracchi to Nero.* New York: Praeger, 1957.

*Secretum secretorum: Nine English Versions.* Ed. M. A. Manzalaoui. Oxford: Oxford University Press, 1977.

Segal, Sam. *A Prosperous Past: The Sumptuous Still Life in the Netherlands, 1600–1700.* Ed. William B. Jordan. Trans. P. M. van Tongeren. The Hague: SDU, 1988.

Seneca, Lucius Annaeus. *Ad Lucilium epistulae morales.* Trans. Richard M. Gummere. 3 vols. London: Heinemann, 1917–25.

——. *Moral Essays.* Trans. John W. Basore. London: Heinemann, 1958.

——. *Seneca.* Vol. 7. London: Heinemann, 1971.

Serres, Olivier de, seigneur Du Pradel. *Le Théâtre d'agriculture et mesnage des champs.* 2 vols. Paris: Madame Huzard, 1804–5.

Seznec, Jean. *The Survival of the Pagan Gods.* Trans. Barbara F. Sessions. Princeton: Princeton University Press, 1972.

Shapin, Steven, and Simon Schaffer. *Leviathan and the Air-Pump: Hobbes, Boyle, and the Experimental Life.* . . . Princeton: Princeton University Press, 1985.

Sheppard, H. J. "Alchemy: Origin or Origins?" *Ambix* 17, no. 2 (July 1970).

——. "Egg Symbolism in Alchemy." *Ambix* 6, no. 3 (1958).

Sigergist, Henry. "Laudanum in the Works of Paracelsus." *Bulletin of the History of Medicine* 9, no. 5 (1941).

Siraisi, Nancy G. *Avicenna in Renaissance Italy.* Princeton: Princeton University Press, 1987.

——. *Taddeo Alderotti and His Pupils: Two Generations of Italian Medical Learning.* Princeton: Princeton University Press, 1981.

Sivin, Nathan. *Chinese Alchemy: Preliminary Studies.* Cambridge: Harvard University Press, 1968.

Smith, Andrew. *Porphyry's Place in the Neoplatonic Tradition: A Study in Post-Plotinian Neoplatonism.* The Hague: Martinus Nijhoff, 1974.

Smith, E. *The Compleat Housewife, or Accomplish'd Gentlewoman's Companion.* . . . 4th ed. London: Pemberton, 1730; 9th ed., 1739.

Smollett, Tobias George. *Travels through France and Italy.* Ed. Frank Felsenstein. Oxford: Clarendon, 1979.

Solomon, Howard M. *Public Welfare, Science, and Propaganda in Seventeenth-Century France: The Innovations of Théophraste Renaudot.* Princeton: Princeton University Press, 1972.

Sterling, Charles. *Still Life Painting from Antiquity to the Present Time.* Trans. James Emmons. Rev. ed. Paris: Tisne, 1959.

Stone, Lawrence. *The Crisis of the Aristocracy, 1558–1641.* Oxford: Clarendon, 1965.

Strabo. *The Geography of Strabo.* Trans. H. L. Jones. 8 vols. London: Heinemann, 1917.

Suetonius. *Lives of the Caesars.* Trans. J. C. Rolfe. 2 vols. London: Heinemann, 1920–51.

Summerson, John Newenham. *Georgian London.* 3d ed. Cambridge: MIT Press, 1978.

Sydenham, Thomas. *Dr. Thomas Syndenham (1624–1689): His Life and Writings.* Berkeley: University of California Press, 1966.

Taillevent, Guillaume. *Le Viandier de Guillaume Tirel dit Taillevent. . . . On y a joint . . . la réimpression de la plus ancienne édition connue de son livre, une édition nouvelle du plus ancien "Traité de cuisine" écrit en françois. . . .* Paris: Techener, 1892.

*I Tarocchi: Le carte di corte i tarocchi: Gioco e magia alla corte degli Estensi.* Ed. Giordano Berti and Andrea Vitali. Bologna: Nuova Alfa, 1987.

Taylor, Frank Sherwood. *The Alchemists.* New York: Collier, 1962.

———. "The Idea of the Quintessence." In *Science, Medicine, and History: Essays on the Evolution of Scientific Thought and Medical Practice Written in Honour of Charles Singer,* ed. Edgar Ashworth Underwood. Oxford: Oxford University Press, 1953.

Temkin, Owsei. *Galenism: Rise and Decline of a Medical Philosophy.* Ithaca: Cornell University Press, 1973.

———. "On Galen's Pneumatology." *Gesnerus* 8 (1951).

Tempest, Pierce. *The Cryes of the City of London Drawne after the Life.* London: Overton, 1711.

Tertullian. *Apology. De spectaculis.* Trans. T. R. Glover. London: Heinemann, 1931.

*A Testament of Alchemy, Being the Revelations of Morienus, Ancient Adept and Hermit of Jerusalem to Khalid Ibn Yazid Ibn Mu'awiyya, King of the Arabs, of the Magisterium and Accomplishment of the Alchemical Art.* Ed. and trans. Lee Stavenhagen. Hanover, N.H.: University Press of New England, 1974.

Theophrastus. *Enquiry into Plants, and Minor Works on Odours, and Weather Signs.* Trans. Arthur Hort. 2 vols. London: Heinemann, 1916.

Thomas, Keith V. *Religion and the Decline of Magic.* New York: Scribner, 1971.

Thompson, Reginald Campbell. *The Devils and Evil Spirits of Babylonia. . . .* London: Luzac, 1904.

Thomson, Gladys Scott. *Life in a Noble Household, 1641–1700.* New York: Knopf, 1937.

Thorndike, Lynn. *A History of Magic and Experimental Science.* 8 vols. New York: Macmillan and Columbia University Press, 1923–58.

*Le Thrésor de santé; ou, Mesnage de la vie humaine.* Lyon: Huguetan, 1607.

Tolkowski, Samuel. *Hesperides: A History of the Culture and Use of Citrus Fruits*. London: Staples, 1939.

*Traducción española de un manuscrito anónimo del siglo XIII sobre la cocina hispano-magribi*. Trans. Ambrosio Huici Miranda. Madrid: Ayuntamiento de Valencia, 1966.

Trevor-Roper, Hugh R. "The Paracelsian Movement." In Trevor-Roper, *Renaissance Essays*. Chicago: University of Chicago Press, 1985.

Tryon, Thomas. *The Way to Health, Long Life and Happiness*. London: Sowle, 1683.

*The Turba Philosophorum, or Assembly of the Sages*. Ed. and trans. Arthur Edward Waite. London: George Redway, 1896.

*Two Fifteenth-Century Cookery-Books*. Ed. Thomas Austin. Early English Text Society 91. London: Trübner, 1888. Book I is printed from Harleian ms. 279, c. 1430, Book II from Harleian ms. 4016, c. 1450.

Ulstad, Philipp. *Coelum philosophorum*. . . . Paris, 1544.

Vaanen, V. "Le 'Fabliau' de Cocagne." *Neuphilologische Mitteilungen* 48 (1947).

Varro, Marcus Terentius. *On Agriculture*. Trans. William Davis Hooper. Rev. Harrison Boyd Ash. London: Heinemann, 1936.

Vaughan, Thomas. *Works*. Ed. Alan Rudrum. Oxford: Clarendon, 1984.

Venner, Tobias. *Via recta ad vitam longam*. London: Hood, 1650.

Verral, William. *The Cook's Paradise, being William Verral's "Complete System of Cookery," published in 1759 with Thomas Gray's Cookery Notes in Holograph*. London: Sylvan Press, 1948.

Vickers, Brian. "On the Writing of History." *Journal of Modern History* 51, no. 2 (June 1979).

Villon, François. *The Works of François Villon*. Ed. and Trans. Geoffroy Atkinson. London: Partridge, 1930.

Virgil. *Eclogues*. London: Heinemann, 1986.

Voltaire [François Marie Arouet]. *Correspondence*. 107 vols. Geneva: Institut et Musée Voltaire, 1953–65.

——. *Oeuvres complètes de Voltaire*. 54 vols. Paris: Garnier, 1877–85.

Walker, Daniel Pickering. "The Prisca Theologica in France." *Journal of the Warburg and Courtauld Institutes* 17 (1954).

——. *Spiritual and Demonic Magic: From Ficino to Campanella*. London: Warburg Institute, University of London, 1958.

Wallis, R. T. *Neoplatonism*. London: Duckworth, 1972.

Walpole, Horace. *Correspondence with Sir Horace Mann*. Ed. W. S. Lewis, Warren Hunting Smith, and George L. Lam. 2 vols. New Haven: Yale University Press, 1954–71.

Webster, Charles. "Alchemical and Paracelsian Medicine." In *Health*,

*Medicine, and Mortality in the Sixteenth Century,* ed. Charles Webster. Cambridge: Cambridge Universtiy Press, 1979.

——. "English Medical Reformers of the Puritan Revolution: A Background to the "Society of Chymical Physitians." *Ambix* 14 (1967).

Webster, John. *Metallographia; or, An History of Metals.* London: Walter Kettilby, 1671.

Westfall, Richard. "Newton and Alchemy." In *Occult and Scientific Mentalities in the Renaissance,* ed. Brian Vickers. Cambridge: Cambridge University Press, 1984.

Willich, Jodocus. *Ars magirica, hoc est coquinaria.* Tigur, 1563.

Wolf, John B., ed. *Louis XIV: A Profile.* New York: Norton, 1968.

Woodforde, James. *The Diary of a Country Parson: The Reverend James Woodforde, 1758–1802.* Ed. John Beresford. 5 vols. London: Oxford University Press, 1924–31.

Woolley, Hannah. *The Queen-like Closet, or Rich Cabinet, Stored with All Manner of Rare Receipts for Preserving, Candying and Cookery. . . .* 5th ed. London: Chiswel, 1684.

Yates, Frances Amelia. *The French Academies of the Sixteenth Century.* London: Warburg Institute, University of London, 1947.

——. *Giordano Bruno and the Hermetic Tradition.* Chicago: University of Chicago Press, 1979.

——. *The Rosicrucian Enlightenment.* Boulder, Colo.: Shambhala, 1978.

# Index

*Only anonymous works are cited by title in this index. All other works are found under the author's name.*

Index

Kalk, William, 57
Kettilby, Mary, 143, 188–89, 206
al-Kindi, Ya'qub, 24
King, William, 119, 179, 187

La Chapelle, Vincent, 75, 88, 107, 127,
    145, 196, 198–99
Lamb, Patrick, 128, 154
La Quintinie, Jean de, 115
La Varenne, François Pierre de, 186,
    205; backers of, 205–6; and fungi,
    73–74; on herbs, 118, 196; recipes
    of, 74, 87, 106, 125, 153–54; on sea-
    soning, 139, 198; and sweet foods,
    188; on vegetables, 119, 125, 129, 152;
    as writer of modern French cook-
    books, 163, 173, 176, 179–81, 191–93,
    199–201, 203
lemons, 57–58, 151, 152, 186
Lent. See fast days
Leo X (pope), 79, 91, 98
Le Roy Ladurie, Emmanuel, 111, 119–
    21, 143
Libavius, Andreas, 170
*Libro di cucina*, 40, 72, 86, 104, 129, 150
Liger, Louis, 196
light, 15, 19–24, 45
*liquamen*, 71n, 134, 138, 186. *See also*
    anchovies; *garum*
Lisle, Lady, 144
Lister, Martin, 70, 139, 188
Locke, John, 36, 171, 172
longevity, 26, 29–38
Louis XIV (King of France), 175,
    190, 205, 232n.31
L. S. R., 115, 144, 176, 198
Lucullus, Lucius, 46, 89, 122
Lune, Pierre de, 87, 196
Luther, Martin, 38

mace, 7, 14, 200
Macrobius, 46, 77, 78
magic. *See* Christians: and magic; di-
    vine medicine
Malherbe, François de, 175
Manelfi, Giovanni, 64, 65
Marin, François, 194–95
marinades, 143, 152, 154, 155, 198
Markham, Gervase, 142
Martial: on foods, 109, 121, 135, 139,
    184; humanists' interest in, 49, 51,
    65, 66, 85, 94, 99, 101
Massialot, François, 74, 88, 106, 127,
    154, 198, 204
Massonio, Salvatore, 141, 157–58, 185,
    187, 190
mastic, 7, 8

Mattioli, Andrea, 8, 69, 111–14, 116,
    125, 192–93
May, Robert, 119, 129, 156, 178, 198,
    200; recipes of, 74, 87, 125–26
*Meadows of Gold* (medieval Arabic
    poem), 4, 10, 15–17, 150
meat broth, 40. See also *jus*
meats: chopped, 97–103, 107, 164; fat
    from, 53, 91, 150; foie gras, 94–95,
    101, 105–7; game, 60; high, 52, 96–
    97, 101; organ, 52, 91–94, 101, 104–
    5; rare, 52, 95, 101; salted, 135, 139–
    40, 145, 151, 152, 154, 156, 160;
    sweetened, 188–89, 231n.14. *See also*
    beef; pork; poultry; sausage
mechanical philosophy, 171–73, 181
medicine. *See* divine medicine
melancholy, 53–54, 134, 172, 175;
    treatment of, 17–19, 25–29, 40, 181,
    229n.16, 230n.35
*Ménagier de Paris, Le*, 3, 5, 10, 11, 102,
    150, 214n.33
Menon, 75, 83, 127, 160, 179, 192, 193,
    196, 206
Mercier, Louis Sébastien, 197
Mesmer, Anton, 172
Messisbugo, Cristoforo di: as cook-
    book writer, 7, 49, 138, 151–52, 177,
    185; on fungi, 72; on garden pro-
    duce, 123–25, 128, 129; and herbs,
    196; on meat, 103; recipes of, 9, 57,
    86–87, 123–24; and salty foods, 151
Mesuë the younger, 24, 28
Milton, John, 178
Moffett, Thomas: as humanist
    scholar, 52; on meats, 90, 91, 98;
    on olives, 144; on salt, 184; on sea-
    food, 78, 82, 83, 146; on sugar, 5;
    on vegetables, 111, 113
Montaigne, Michel de, 48–49, 79,
    183
Moryson, Fynes, 91, 94, 96
mother–of–pearl, 56–57
Muhammad II, 45, 46
mushrooms. *See* fungi
Muret, Jean, 50
"myron," 23
myrrh, 28, 29, 31

Neoplatonism, 19, 26, 34, 165, 181, 205
Newton, Isaac, 171, 172
Nomentanus, 47
Nonnius, Louis: on meat, 90, 94, 139,
    140, 145; research of, 52, 69, 100,
    222n.22; on salty foods, 137, 140,
    145, 146, 185, 187; on thistles, 111
Nostredame, Michel de, 41

Nott, John, 143
*Nouveau dictionnaire*, 50–51, 197, 201
nutmeg, 7, 31, 58, 199, 200
nuts, 109, 121–22

olive oil, 136, 143–44, 150. *See also* salt-
    acid-oil sauces
olives, 134, 135, 142, 146, 149, 150, 154,
    185, 190; still lifes of, 62
onions, 115–18, 122
oranges, 11, 58, 151–52, 186
oysters: as aphrodisiac, 184; cultiva-
    tion of, 84–85; humanists' interest
    in, 58, 80–84, 113; as lure to appe-
    tite, 122; mother-of-pearl from, 56;
    raw, 52, 53, 83–85; recipes for, 85–
    88, 153

Pagel, Walter, 34, 215n.38
paintings: of eclectic food, 53–62, 153,
    156, 191; of fungi, 66, 67; of garden
    produce, 120, 124, 126, 128; of
    meats, 96, 97, 105, 116, 155; of
    melancholia, 27; of seafood, 80–
    84, 116, 156
Palissy, Bernard, 94
Palladian architecture, 204–5
Palladius, 69, 94
Panciroli, Guido, 51, 138, 187
Paracelsus, 33, 168; alchemical views
    of, 36–38, 194, 202; medicinal
    views of, 34, 180, 181; opposition
    to ideas of, 165, 170, 171
Parkinson, John, 113, 114
parsley, 109, 115, 119, 122, 183, 192
paté. *See* chopped meats
Patin, Gui, 165
Paulet, Jean Jacques, 68–69
peaches, 122
pearls, 18, 20, 24, 57, 80
Pegalotti, Balducci, 11
Pegge, Samuel, 51, 72
pepper, 3, 6–8, 40, 178, 183, 190–92.
    *See also* salt and pepper
Pepys, Samuel, 137
Pereisc, Claude Fabri de, 69
perfumed food, 1, 5–8, 14–18, 39, 53,
    163. *See also* fragrances
Perrault, Charles, 176
Peter the Venerable (abbot), 13
Petrarch, 45
Petronius, 49, 51
Petrus Alfonsi, 13
philosopher's stone, 19, 26, 36–37, 55
*Picatrix*, 20, 24, 28, 40
pickling, 135, 140, 141–45, 151, 154–57,
    160, 203